# BRITTANY

# *Also in the Series*

*Buenos Aires* by Jason Wilson
*Oxford* by David Horan
*Mexico City* by Nick Caistor
*Rome* by Jonathan Boardman
*Madrid* by Elizabeth Nash
*Venice* by Martin Garrett
*Lisbon* by Paul Buck
*Havana* by Claudia Lightfoot
*New York City* by Eric Homberger
*Brussels* by André de Vries
*Prague* by Richard Burton
*Calcutta* by Krishna Dutta
*Helsinki* by Neil Kent
*Edinburgh* by Donald Campbell
*San Francisco* by Mick Sinclair
*Cambridge* by Martin Garrett
*Kingston* by David Howard
*Athens* by Michael Llewellyn Smith
*Istanbul* by Pater Clark
*Hamburg* by Matthew Jefferies
*Lagos* by Kaye Whiteman
*Miami* by Anthony P. Maingot
*Sicily* by Joseph Farrell
*The Scottish Highlands* by Andrew Beattie
*Bali* by Arthur Cotterell

# BRITTANY

*A Cultural History*

WENDY MEWES

Interlink Books

An imprint of Interlink Publishing Group, Inc.
Northampton, Massachusetts

First published in 2016 by
**INTERLINK BOOKS**
An imprint of Interlink Publishing Group, Inc.
46 Crosby Street, Northampton, Massachusetts 01060
www.interlinkbooks.com

**Library of Congress Cataloging-in-Publication Data**
Mewes, W. (Wendy), 1955-
 Brittany : a cultural history / Wendy Mewes.
    pages cm
 Includes index.
 ISBN 978-1-56656-088-7
 1. Brittany (France)--Social life and customs. 2. Brittany (France)--History. I. Title.
 DC611.B851M4697 2015
 944'.1--dc23
                    2015025234


Cover Images: © Alexandre Croisier, Wendy Mewes

Printed and bound in the United States of America


To request our complete 48-page full-color catalog, please call us toll free at
1-800-238-LINK, visit our website at www.interlinkbooks.com, or write to
Interlink Publishing 46 Crosby Street, Northampton, MA 01060
e-mail: info@interlinkbooks.com

# *Contents*

*Preface*   ix

*Chapter One*
**ON THE EDGE**   1

Starting points (1); Out on a limb or in the swing (3); Four or five *départements*? (3); *Armor* and *Argoat* (5); Haute- and Basse-Bretagne (6); Formative years: the Age of Saints (and sinners) (7); Brittany and France (9); War and peace (12); Anne de Bretagne and union with France (13); Revolution and aftermath (14); The nineteenth century (15); Nationalism and World War II (17); Post-war Brittany (19); Oral tradition (20); Breton language (21); Celticism (22); The past is always with us (23)

*Chapter Two*
**STONE: FROM CHAOS TO CONTROL**   25

Silent stone: megaliths, not the Celts, and Flaubert has fun (26); Carnac (32); Living stone: sleeping with the animals and minding one's manors (37); Stone symphony: parish closes, devilish priests, and men in hairy tights (45); Stone cacophony: Vallée des Saints, art or theme park? (53)

*Chapter Three*
**THE MARCHES: FRONTIER TERRITORY**   55

Border country: conflict, triumph, and disaster (55); Fougères: love, war, and literature (65); Combourg: the invention of boredom, a rambling wooden leg, and scary dead cats (73); Man of the Marches: history, patriotism, and a prophet in his own country (80)

*Chapter Four*
SEA: A WAY OF LIFE AND DEATH   85

Threats from the sea: sea wolves, abduction, a famous sinking, and black tides (85); Legends: a doting father, sirens, and the night boat (89); St-Malo: men at sea, an infernal machine, and high adventure (94); Paimpol: sad women, salt cod, and superheroes (100)

*Chapter Five*
COAST: ON THE THRESHOLD   109

Douarnenez: sardines, communists, and butter cake (110); Around Penmarc'h: dark and dangerous coast, Chaucer, and a beacon of light (116); Art and graft: the working man's artist, sorrow, and seaweed (123); Carantec: the brave boatbuilder and *The Shark* (127)

*Chapter Six*
LAND: THE HEART OF THINGS   131

Poher: Romans, Red Caps, and railways (131); *Blé noir*: a humble foodstuff for eating and drinking (140); *Fest noz*: from farming to fête, or dancing with the Devil (144); One bard after another (151)

*Chapter Seven*
TOWN: WALLS THAT BIND   155

Rennes: serious architecture, beware of fire (and fireworks) (155); Pontivy: what's in a name?: sycophancy, symmetry, and an expensive pisspot (166); Tréguier: religion, secularism, and the goddess Athene (172); Quimper: an English prisoner, the bourgeoisie, a celebration, and a quarrel (176)

*Chapter Eight*
MOOR: STRUGGLE AND STRIFE   185

The Monts d'Arrée: rag-men, nocturnal washerwomen, and wolves (185); *Pilhaouerien*: life on the road, rags to paper, and an independent attitude (192); Legend: Death at large, fatal dancing, and a black dog in the bog (198); Wolves: tamed by saints and hunted by an enthusiastic Welshman (203)

*Chapter Nine*
FOREST: LIFE AND LEGEND IN THE GREENWOOD   209
> Forêt de Fougères: learned oak trees, spilled salt, and nasty insect bites (209); Forêt de Paimpont: Merlin's tomb, the Valley of No Return, and the emperor's new clothes (215); Forêt de Coatloc'h: clogs, miserable Margot, and a nursery rhyme (221); Forêt du Cranou: traveling trees, blood sacrifice, and imbecile tourists (225)

*Chapter Ten*
RIVER: FLUENT LINKS   231
> The Loire: Nantes the siren city and a house in the water (231); The Rance: a Miocene sea, heroic Dinan, and donkeys with twisted heads (239); The Oust: witness of history, a journey on foot upriver (245); The Queffleuth: floods, paper-making, and the associative life (252)

*Chapter Eleven*
ISLAND: ALL AROUND THE EDGE   255
> Ouessant: Island the Terrible, a swimming cow, and 'Bye, bye black sheep (255); Île de Sein: wet, wet, wet and flat, flat, flat (262); Île de Groix: "qui voit Groix, voit sa croix," the Sea Wolf and his land of many colors (267); Belle-Île: Hamlet eaten by a crocodile (273)

*Afterword*   277

*Further Reading*   279

*Index of Literary & Historical Figures*   281

*Index of Places & Landmarks*   285

For Joan Field
with admiration, thanks, and a daughter's love

# *Preface*

Brittany has been a place of discovery for me on many levels, so I am grateful for the opportunity to share some of its compelling complexity with others who either already love the country or who may be inspired to come and see for themselves. This book is the starting point for a journey into the multi-layered entity that is Brittany today. The portrait given here is inevitably selective in terms of area and literature—at least a dozen volumes would be needed to present the full range—but I hope it transmits a worthy sense of this singular landscape and people. I make no apology for an emphasis on the Breton-speaking west, which has left the greatest legacy in terms of the oral tradition and distinctive culture. Brittany has long fascinated travelers with its highly evocative image, arcane customs of sea and land, a misty past of Neolithic monuments and Celtic legends, lace headdresses and decorative costumes, the living legacy of music and dance, but here simple reality is always more interesting than tourist hype, with struggles for freedom, survival, and defense of the Breton language leaving their mark in every corner. The much-vaunted issue of Breton identity is not something I have dwelled on, preferring to give the varied context in which such ideas have been formulated, and believing, as Breton friends tell me, that the genuine article is a quiet thing that lives steadily in the rhythm of the heart.

So many individuals have helped my understanding of history and issues over the years I have lived here that it is impossible to list them all, but I would like to thank Anne Guillou, Loic Quemener, Lionel Pomard, Christophe Déceneux, la Comtesse de La Tour du Pin, Marc Le Dret, Jérôme Lemesle, Philippe Bohuon, Michel Morel, Jean-Pierre Daffniet, Jean and Adrian Brooks, Jeanne le Bourgeois, Lesley Rice, John Hanson and Danièle Gehan. Thanks also to fellow-writers Vicki Trott and Patricia Stoughton, and supportive friends Sylvia Rendall and Sue Gregory.

I owe a special debt to Yves Marhic for his tolerance of questions and exceptional linguistic skills.

Finally, many thanks to James Ferguson at Signal Books. I could ask for no more compatible editor than a fellow-member of the Border Terrier fan club.

*Chapter One*

# ON THE EDGE

## STARTING POINTS

The westernmost point of France is the Pointe de Corsen, northwest of Brest on Brittany's Atlantic coast. This is the notional tipping point between the waters of the Channel and the mighty fronts of the ocean. Until recently a rather tacky signpost on the headland showed that here you are closer to London (580 kilometers) than Paris (630). Now a neat orientation table presents the sweeping view over the Mer d'Iroise: the islands of the Molène archipelago and the silhouette of craggy Ouessant on the horizon. Then there is nothing until America. We are on the edge.

Evidence of geological fragmentation in Brittany's coast is all too visible here in the sharp off-shore rocks and scattered islets which necessitate a chain of signaling against the all too obvious naval hazards. Nearby high points are the inland lighthouse of Trézien and the tallest standing stone in France, and just behind the headland is the CROSS Corsen sea surveillance headquarters, where ex-President Nicolas Sarkozy is said to have made his famous comment, "Je m'en fous des Bretons" (I don't give a damn about the Bretons) during politicking before the 2007 elections.

There is nothing very glamorous about this particular spot. Not surprisingly the tourist industry manages to imply that the dramatic Pointe du Raz, forty kilometers south on the wild tip of Cap Sizun, is the furthest edge of the Breton world. Here are towering cliffs, the thunderous Raz de Sein lashing every rock and lighthouse between the mainland and the tiny Ile de Sein, lying virtually flat against the swell of the Atlantic. Even the huge, hideously sentimental statue of the Virgin of Shipwrecked Sailors on the point cannot spoil the sense of awe at the constructs of nature in this location.

When it was announced in 1978 that a new nuclear plant was to be built on this lonely headland, a furious public reaction centered on the appropriately named *commune* of Plogoff led to mass demonstrations and a standoff with armed police. In March 1980, 50,000 people demonstrated during the public inquiry and two months later many thousands cheered

Tumultuous Raz de Sein (Sonja Pieper/Wikimedia Commons)

the rejection of the proposal with a *fest noz*, a vibrant explosion of celebration in music and dance. Protest songs from this era have entered the oral tradition, and there is even a film: *Pierres contre les fusils* (Stones against Guns).

Beside the Pointe du Raz lies the Baie des Trépassés, the Bay of the Dead. Was this where souls were rowed across to the Île de Sein by Death's henchman Ankou, the Breton Grim Reaper, before going on westward to a mysterious final resting place? Or has there been a linguistic confusion of Breton *An Aon* (the river) and *Anaon* (departed soul)? Currents do wash drowned bodies into this bay, a phenomenon which may also have contributed to the gloomy tales, but the close presence of death is part of the popular tradition in Brittany, where everything contributes to the strata of legends that fizz through Breton culture like veins of quartzite in the peninsula's granite heights.

So much can be glimpsed in miniature in these two edge points, one much vaunted for its natural dominance and wild romanticism, the other more muted and anchored in everyday life. There is the surrounding sea with all its dangers and advantages, the fringe of a land with a hard granite heart, a culture of legend and song rooted in realism and the life and language of ordinary people, a strong role for Death and its best friend the Catholic Church, and a penchant for political and environmental activism. They well present the big and beautiful melting pot of bubbling issues and swirling, often conflicting images that is Brittany, for little here is clear or straightforward.

## OUT ON A LIMB OR IN THE SWING

Brittany's physical position has been a strong factor in its history, the Armorican peninsula jutting out into the ocean on the northwest corner of the continent, just a short Channel hop from Britain. This position on the route between northern and southern Europe may account for the great concentration of Neolithic monuments (see Chapter Two). It is the combination of the Atlantic edge and the intrinsic nature of the landscape itself that contributes to a sense of isolation and remoteness mentioned by many nineteenth-century travelers, although in fact Brittany (*Bretagne* in French/*Breiz* in Breton) has enjoyed the most international of connections in all phases of its development. Internal divisions both geographical and historical do, however, give a plethora of small worlds, from valley to valley and village to village, an idea enshrined in the Breton saying *Kant bro, kant giz*: a hundred neighborhoods, a hundred fashions. Each has its own customs and traditions, from styles of lace-headdress (*coiffes)* and embroidered costumes to dances and legends.

## FOUR OR FIVE *DÉPARTEMENTS*?

Today there is not even agreement about what constitutes the region. Paris and practical administration tells us there are four *départements*: Ille-et-Vilaine (including the capital Rennes), Côtes d'Armor (called Côtes du Nord until the 1990s), Morbihan, and Finistère. But many Bretons routinely regard Nantes and Loire-Atlantique as part of Brittany as indeed they were up until World War II, when they were hived off by the Vichy government, an insult confirmed by post-war organization of new regions in 1957.

The "five departments" issue raises all degrees of reaction from genuine outrage to singular indifference. In opinion polls and consultations it has often been Finistère, farthest of all from Nantes, which shows the highest

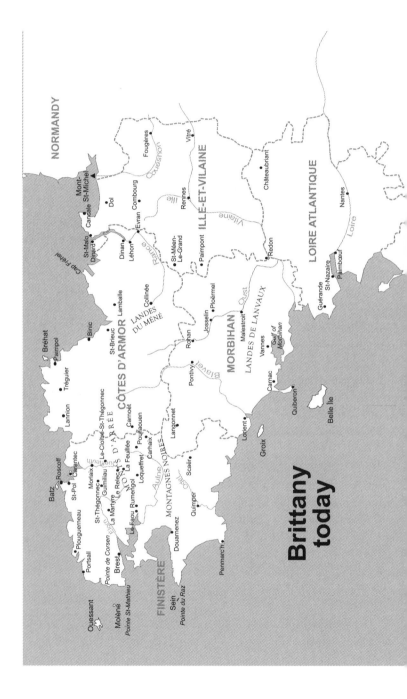

Brittany today

vote in favor of the official reunion of "historic Brittany." The Breton-speaking heart of the region clings fastest to old ways and notions of historical rightness. As always in Brittany the roots of the situation are controversial, buried deep under layers of deprivation, oppression, injustice, injured pride, energetic defense, and lethargic acceptance.

The artificial departmental divisions imposed at the Revolution cut across the medieval divisions of Brittany, based via geography on the old nobility (counts) and bishoprics. Léon, Cornouaille, Trégor, Penthièvre, and the areas (*pays*) of Rennes, Vannes, and Nantes are by no means dead—an association today works for the reunion of the Trégor, now divided between Finistère and Côtes d'Armor—but they have no official recognition. Traditional rivalries remain enshrined in popular sayings like "A funeral in Cornouaille is as cheerful as a wedding in Léon" or "Crows fly on their backs to avoid the miserable sight" (when passing the border from Trégor into Cornouaille).

## *ARMOR* AND *ARGOAT*

People from the coast differ from those in the interior, a contrast enshrined in the words *Armor* (land by the sea) and *Argoat* (land of the forest). Throughout history the former was open to the world by virtue of trade and travel, the other to some extent closed or enclosed by poor soil and even poorer communications.

Brittany has a lot of edge when it comes to coastline, up to 1800 kilometers if you count right to the Loire estuary (see above for whether you do include it or not). Certainly the prime image not only in tourism but in the lyrical nostalgia of many French (and Breton) adults is the lure of the coast and the beaches, happy hours spent sailing or fishing or delving among crevices at low tide for edible plunder. Cliffs, coastal defenses, and lighthouses dominate the photographic iconography: Cap Fréhel with its pink and green sandstone stacks; Fort La Latte, where Kirk Douglas and Tony Curtis did their Viking bit in the 1958 film; the Phare des Perdrix decorated with squares in black and white Breton colors. Apart from the natural beauty of the littoral, easily accessible from the encircling footpath GR34, there is infinite variety in coastal towns and villages, with fishing ports like Douarnenez, Le Guilvinec, and Concarneau, the oyster capital Cancale, former corsair bases St-Malo and Roscoff, and international (and therefore blander) resorts like Erquy and Benodet.

Much less well known is the large interior where tough terrain, lack of investment, and primitive roads have kept life isolated and often at poverty level. Cheap housing has attracted a new wave of British settlers in the last twenty years, but it has always been a space where getting a living is hard. Apart from the Golden Belt in the north across Léon and the Trégor, enriched by seaweed-based fertilizers since time immemorial, and some kinder soils in the south of Morbihan and the east, the granite and schist of the center are resistant to productivity and hard to breach, as builders of the Nantes-Brest Canal discovered in the nineteenth century. The Monts d'Arrée, the highest hills in Brittany, with their sharp schist crags, have long been a byword for poverty and hardship—and radical politics bred of tough daily challenge.

Wooded valleys, hillsides spattered with bulky boulders, and stretches of open moor characterize the hinterland, but nowhere is far from the water of streams and rivers, the often overlooked beauties of Brittany's landscape. The Rance, Vilaine, Oust, Odet, Elorn, and Aulne are all magnificent waterways.

## HAUTE- AND BASSE-BRETAGNE

But we are not at the end of the road of distinctions and divisions. The east/west divide of Haute-Bretagne (high = nearer to Paris) and Basse-Bretagne (low = farthest from Paris) is not simply one of geography. The origins lie much earlier and stem from the truly formative period of Breton history in the Dark Ages, then later reflecting the boundary of Breton-speaking which shifted back westwards after the Viking incursions stemmed the expanding Breton state. The constant intrusion of the French language also took its toll in the east, with Alain Fergent, who ruled from 1084 to 1112, the last duke to speak Breton at court.

The "language line" today runs roughly north-south from St-Brieuc to the east of Vannes.

English travelers in the nineteenth century give the most graphic descriptions of the stark contrast between Haute- and Basse-Bretagne, thrusting British modernism evident in their every expression of amazement. Adolphus Trollope (brother of novelist Anthony) arrived from Normandy, which he had found considerably more advanced.

But although the differences in the people, and the general appearance of the country on crossing the frontier are quite sufficiently remarkable to make it evident to the traveller that he is no longer among the same race, or surrounded by the same manners and habits of life, yet it is not here that he must seek for those striking peculiarities, which make the inhabitants of the lower province [i.e. Basse-Bretagne] objects of so much curiosity and interest.

On staying in the central hill town of Collinée he gets his first sight of the fabled peasants from the west as they arrive to attend the large cattle fair taking place near Trollope's hotel.

Anything so strange, so wild, so picturesque, so unlike all that English eyes are accustomed to look upon, can hardly be conceived… with their immense black hats, their long streaming hair and quaint square cut coats, they looked more like men belonging to some forgotten century than aught that could be living in the present age.

He goes on to note that in Cornwall such things have only recently disappeared "before the rapid advances of English civilisation and our highly perfect system of internal commerce and communication." Passing over the controversial perception of what constitutes civilization, it is hard to argue with his latter point that lack of roads, transport, and well-organized business practices were contributory factors to the undeveloped center and west of Brittany, where history and lack of resources have hampered progress and prosperity.

## FORMATIVE YEARS: THE AGE OF SAINTS (AND SINNERS)

The settlement of Celtic tribes in the Iron Age gave some political organization to the peninsula with the Osismes in the west, the Vénètes in what is now Morbihan, the Coriosolites to the north with a capital at Corseul, the Riedones to the north and east of Rennes, and the Namnetes from the Loire northward with Condevicnum (Nantes) their main town. The extent to which subsequent Roman control of the peninsula meant actual occupation is uncertain, but, as in Britain, the material advantages of this new civilization appealed to the upper echelons of Celtic society as the excavation of villas and bathhouses indicates. Corseul in

Côtes d'Armor has many remains on show, including the huge Temple of Mars.

After the Romans left Armorica, individual rulers lined up to fill the vacuum. Conan Meriadec, said to have been established as king by imperial pretender Maximianus, is the subject of foundation legends galore. The great Rohan family claimed their descent from this man who may have been nothing more than the figment of Geoffrey of Monmouth's vivid imagination. It is certainly anachronistic to see him as a first "king of Brittany" when no such entity existed nor was practically possible then, but he remains a significant figure for later Bretons searching for forebears who preceded the Franks.

We are on safer, although still semi-legendary ground, with the Breton saints. The period from c. 400-700 CE is often referred to as the Age of Saints, as across the Channel mainly from Wales and Ireland came the holy men and their followers who were to mark the peninsula so profoundly. They arrived not as a single wave of migration, but in groups large and small over a long period of time. The monasteries of Wales must have been practically denuded by these hordes of migrants full of zeal to convert the pagans of Armorica, although on reaching the wild shores many were equally attracted by a contemplative life in wild surroundings. They were often alleged to have arrived miraculously in stone boats, although this may derive from a scribe's linguistic confusion of Latin *cumba* (a small boat) and old Breton *koum* (valley or stone trough). Some were welcomed and found easy acceptance; others were confronted by hostility from the word go. St Ké was beaten with gorse twigs, St Herbot pelted with stones by the women of Berrien, St Ronan chased away for spoiling the coastal wreckers' fun in the Bay of Douarnenez. Some moved on altogether and some returned to Great Britain, but many stayed to labor at the foundations of the future Brittany—"little Britain."

Traditionally there were seven "founding saints," each associated as bishops with a later cathedral (Rennes and Nantes were not part of Breton territory at this time). This gives the route of an important medieval pilgrimage, the Tro Breiz, between St-Pol-de-Léon (St Pol), Tréguier (St Tugdual), St-Brieuc (St Brieuc), St-Malo (St Malo), Dol-de-Bretagne (St Samson), Vannes (St Patern), and Quimper (St Corentin). The first five saints all came from Wales, whereas Corentin and Patern were second-generation natives of the peninsula. These founding saints are only a few out of hundreds whose legacy may now be nothing more than a local story or a toponym.

Place-names give away the patterns of settlement at this time: the spread of names in *Plou* (parish), *Loc,* and *Lan* (holy place) reveal a preponderance of missionary works in the west of Brittany, and reflect the spread of Breton as the incomers brought their Brittonic languages to take on its new form in their new land. The great majority of Breton legends spring from this time of genesis, and the religious traditions of Pardons (procession with statues and relics, mass, and a fête), pilgrimages, sacred healing springs, and chapels speak of roots set at this time.

The turbulent Dark Ages also give us one colorful secular figure, the Breton Bluebeard Conomor, a sixth-century character truly of his time, historically attested but given a legendary garnish. He probably came from Cornwall before establishing control of strategic sites in Brittany, and possibly acted on behalf of the king of the Franks in this crucial corner of Europe, a good reflection of the multifaceted political reality of the time, when individual rulers vied for power, territory, and resources. Conomor's aggressive expansionism led to his downfall, brought to book for tyrannical behavior by assorted saints and political opponents.

## BRITTANY AND FRANCE

The eastern border of Brittany proved vulnerable to both military attack and cultural influence from the start. The Franks were knocking at the door of the peninsula as early as the fifth century, and although a deal was struck during the reign of Clovis, the first leader of the Franks to convert to Christianity, the Marches of Brittany, including the territories of Nantes and Rennes, were to become hot spots of disputed ownership during the next few hundred years. Brittany's history has been dominated—usually in a negative sense—by its relationship with France. Resistance to invasion by the Franks and the subsequent development of a Breton state was to be followed by constant French interference and finally determined acquisition in the late fifteenth century (see Chapter Three).

The greatest strides towards an energetic independent Breton state came in the ninth century with the initiatives of Nominoë (see pp.59–61 and pp.80–81) who first maintained peace with the Franks under Louis the Pious and then drove Louis' son Charles the Bald out of the Marches of Brittany. If not a time of unity, this period was a time of consensus, a

Normandy in Brittany: William besieges Dinan
(Bayeux Tapestry/Wikimedia Commons)

willingness to fight together for something with a meaningful identity that could for the first time be called Breton-ness.

Nominoë died in the course of this achievement, and it was his son Erispoë who became the first King of Brittany, acknowledged as such by the beleaguered Charles. During his rule, Breton territory reached roughly to the limits of "historic Brittany" mentioned above. But the kingdom of Brittany was shortlived, petering out under inter-family feuds and the lack of a character capable of commanding the respect and fealty of other nobles.

In the end it was the Viking threat that came along and spoiled everything. As raids proliferated, the Breton tide of energy turned westward. Many nobles left their homes and estates to seek safety in France, and many religious institutions shipped their valuables in the same direction. These actions may have preserved the property of certain individuals and institutions, but it did nothing for the Breton state. On return these influential aristocrats were speaking French and adopting French customs. The Breton language was soon in retreat, creeping back towards its heartland in the west.

Alain the Great achieved an impressive victory over the Vikings in 888 but he was the last king. His grandson Alain Barbetorte, brought up in the Saxon court of Athelstan in England, eventually ruled an independent Brittany as duke. He was count of Cornouaille and Nantes, providing a wide power base, but to what extent the other nobles accepted his supremacy is debatable.

The cracks in Breton political unity were soon wide enough to drive a large military force through. Opponents of Duke Conan II called in William of Normandy, and although his campaign (shown on the Bayeux tapestry) floundered in the marshes, there was an important consequence of this collaboration: many eminent Breton nobles were in William's forces in England for the 1066 campaign. Later good service done by these knights resulted in many English and (later) Scottish lands falling into Breton hands. Alain le Roux, son of the count of Penthièvre, was rewarded with Richmond in Yorkshire in 1071.

Shifting alliances and competition among Breton nobles for the dukedom of Brittany made it only a matter of time until more outsiders would be invited in as strong-arm partners. Some did not wait for an invitation: the Conqueror's great-grandson, Henry II, keen to bolster his

French holdings with a foothold in Brittany "helped" Duke Conan IV, who was struggling to assert his authority. Henry managed to put his son Geoffrey in control via a marriage with Conan's daughter.

France could not ignore this backdoor English move. Plantagenet squabbles over the throne after Henry's death allowed the French King Philippe Auguste to intervene and he was finally able to place one of his own relatives, Pierre de Dreux, later known as Mauclerc, as Duke of Brittany in 1213. This rather muddies the waters for claims that Brittany was an independent state right up to union with France in 1532, despite the duke's attempts to weave a precarious path between English and French interests.

## WAR AND PEACE

These rivals clashed as Brittany became an arena in the Hundred Years' War. Duke Jean III died without heir in 1341, and two claimants, his half-brother Jean de Montfort and his niece Jeanne de Penthièvre, the latter a member of one of the most powerful families of Breton nobility, were soon at war over the succession. Jeanne's husband, Charles de Blois was a nephew of the French king Philippe VI, while Jean de Montfort had grown up in the English court of Edward III, so a polarization of support for the two factions saw English and French troops pouring onto Breton soil between 1341 and 1364. A famous set-piece engagement now called the Battle of the Thirty took place halfway between Josselin and Ploërmel in 1351. This supposedly pitted thirty Bretons against thirty English knights and so has evolved as a symbol of foreign interference and native triumph. Things are never so simple in Brittany. A few Bretons and German mercenaries were to be found in the English team that lost the day.

The victory of Jean de Montfort's son, who became Duke Jean IV, staved off French control of the peninsula for two hundred years, during which a period of peace and stability nourished economic growth, and the Montfort dynasty saw a flourishing of Breton architecture—the beloved Flamboyant Gothic—and culture. But the last duke, François II, who was brought up in France and relied heavily on French (and low-born) advisers, became unpopular with the Breton high nobility. François did all he could to secure his daughter Anne's succession, floundering among France's rival powers in Europe—England and Austria—for support. His attempts further enraged the many Breton nobles who were not averse to a deal with the French to secure their own future prosperity. In 1488 François was decisively defeated at the battle of St-Aubin-du-Cormier, which has become a symbolic spot for Breton nationalists, the beginning of the end (see p.64).

## ANNE DE BRETAGNE AND UNION WITH FRANCE

Anne was forced to marry the young French king, Charles VIII, which at least allowed her to remain the duchess of Brittany as well as queen of France. An indication of the French determination to hang on to Brittany was a clause in the marriage settlement: if Charles died, Anne had to marry his successor. So when he succumbed to an accident, she became the wife of Louis XII. Anne has become—rather unrealistically—something of a symbol of the last throw of independent dice for Brittany, but despite a firm attachment to her paternal inheritance she was part of the French establishment. Her court became a center of the arts—histories of Brittany were commissioned from Pierre le Baud and Alain Bouchart—and she donated money toward various constructions from the famous *Cordelière* ship built near Morlaix (see p.87) to a chapel at Le Folgoët during her Tro Breiz journey in 1505. This procession around the peninsula must account for her enduring popularity in Brittany and a very positive press, although ultimately she did not have the political clout to keep Brittany independent. Louis insisted that their daughter was married to François d'Angoulême, who would succeed him on the French throne. It was this François I who pushed through the union of France and Brittany in 1532 in Vannes. The Bretons hung grimly to their few remaining privileges, including the agreement that no new taxes would be levied on the province without consent and that Bretons would not be expected to fight outside their own territory. The French lack of faith over the former would ultimately lead to seething resentment and rebellion.

If we look at Breton history as a series of waves crashing hopefully onto the beach of prosperity and peace then the early years as a part of France were good ones, a Golden Age of stability and cultural confidence. The boom of the linen trade brought wealth to many areas, best illustrated today by the architectural glory of the *enclos paroissiaux* or parish closes (see p.45) in the west. This period of growth eventually turned sour with ruthless royal exploitation of resources and incessant demands for "gifts"—to get round the terms of union—to finance French wars and regal ostentation. Economic protectionism brought an end to lucrative exchanges with England from Brittany, and the essentially rural economy's struggle with poverty led inevitably to social and political unrest. The rebellion of the *Bonnet rouges* (Red Caps) against new taxes imposed without consent in 1675 attracted widespread support (see p.135). It heralded a period of frequent clashes between the Parlement de Bretagne and the French king's appointees, and furnished wider signs of social conflict and financial woes, dissatisfactions that rumbled on in the years up to the Revolution.

## REVOLUTION AND AFTERMATH

The Revolution was received enthusiastically in much of Brittany. A deputy from Landivisiau in Léon made a damning verbal attack on the nobility in a speech of 4 August 1789 in Paris. Bretons' special privileges, the key issue of the union with France in 1532, were given up; what need would there be in a new world of equality? The earliest decrees of the Revolution were even published in minority languages, a sign surely of respect for regionalism? It was time for change, with the growth of urbanization and a new power-hungry bourgeoisie.

The turning point for strongly Catholic Brittany arrived when state and Church came into direct conflict. In 1791 priests were required to swear an oath of loyalty to the new Republican constitution: if they refused they could no longer work. Some signed, but wrote a disclaimer in Breton underneath. The vast majority (seventy-five percent) in Brittany refused, with the proportion as high as ninety percent in the far west. Many went into hiding, protected by their parishioners who resented the zeal with which new bourgeois officials pursued them. This attack on the Church was a blow struck at the very life of the rural areas where faith remained strong and loyalty to the old ways was unchanged by Republicanism.

It gave rise to the counter-Revolutionary movement known as Chouannerie, with the rebel Chouans active in groups all over the region and in connection with the huge uprising in the Vendée. Although an attempted landing in Quiberon by a force of English-backed émigrés failed dismally, pockets of resistance continued in many places, especially in Morbihan. Balzac and Victor Hugo both wrote novels about this counter-revolution (see Chapter Three).

After initial respect for minority languages, the second great blow fell with attempts to impose French as the only one acceptable in a Republic. The suppression of Breton continued with the ethos of conformity and unity during Napoleon's supremacy, and active persecution of the language soon followed. The painful irony of believing that a Frenchman would naturally want to speak his language as a mark of identity and that there was no further need of petty regional tongues was lost on Paris. The pain of being made to feel shame for speaking one's own language was a wound that has not surprisingly fueled resentment to this day.

In the west of Brittany a large percentage of the inhabitants had no French at all. The enforced teaching in French only was designed to wipe out the next generation of Breton speakers. Many tales are told, right up to the 1950s, of punishments being meted out to children who dared to speak a word of their home language on school premises. It was a double-edged sword: French was the currency of success. To go on to university, to get a job in administration, to serve in the army would require speaking and understanding French. Parents had to make difficult decisions for their children's futures. It was largely the Church and its priests, mostly local men, who fought to keep the Breton language alive.

## THE NINETEENTH CENTURY

This was a difficult time for Brittany. Industrial decline, agricultural stagnation, poverty, disease and famine in the countryside, a growing sense of oppression, and exploitation all took their toll. The loss of privileges and the subsequent expectations of conformity as a region of France went against the grain of Breton culture and the Breton character. The resistance to change noted as a negative by many foreign visitors (who saw themselves as at the cutting edge of modernity) was more than stubbornness. It was a silent determination to retain a certain way of life not dictated by the lure of money and aggrandizement, those darlings of the Victorian age in England. It produced a degree of self-containment and separateness that both fascinated and repelled outsiders.

Despite the coming of the railway in the 1860s, Brittany was marginalized in terms of investment and industrial development in this most progressive of centuries elsewhere in northern France. Traditional industries like cloth, mines, and forges declined in the face of cheap imports, although the more international ports of Brest and Lorient continued to flourish. There was not enough work or opportunities for a

658. Morlaix — Le Viaduc, vu de l'Hôtel-de-Ville

Collection Villard Quimper

Progress: Morlaix's railway viaduct, early twentieth century (Wikimedia Commons)

growing population, and a huge exodus from country to town and from Brittany to France or abroad began to empty the countryside.

Relations between town and country deteriorated as the century wore on and political parties of White and Blue persuasions developed. The latter represented the entrepreneurial activities of an urban bourgeoisie, a world apart from the largely unchanged conservative rural society of small farms, laboring peasants, and rock-solid Catholic values. Adolphus Trollope observed that "the inhabitants of the larger towns and the *campagnards* are no longer one and the same people. Not only their manners and way of life, but their characters and modes of thinking upon all subjects, are altogether at variance."

Clashes between supporters of the Church and progressive Republicanism were rife, and education became a field of battle as modernizers sought to wrest influence over young minds from the clergy. There was violence and misery as seminaries were forcibly closed and nuns turned out of their homes. Events in Tréguier (see p.175) were typical of the strength of feelings. Church and state were finally formally separated in 1905.

But a reaction against the tide of stagnation and negativity, and the influence of Romanticism, also saw the flowering of inquiry into Brittany's past and traditions, history, and oral culture. Learned societies and amateur archaeologists were at work everywhere, and the publication of collections of folklore and legends which enshrined the vivid stream of oral tradition only whetted the appetite for all things authentically Breton. Interest in Celticism (see below) and the origins of the Breton state burgeoned, and Arthur de La Borderie's historical researches (see p.80) restored a sense of national pride and achievement. They also coincided with the rise of political nationalism and EMSAV (the Breton Awakening), an umbrella term for the general political and cultural Breton movement.

## NATIONALISM AND WORLD WAR II

The cartoon character Becassine, very popular in Paris in the first half of the twentieth century, exemplifies the French attitude of superiority that has so enraged many Bretons. The provincial maid-servant, stupid and naïve, is drawn without a mouth. The portrayal was taken by Bretons as slur on their character and national identity, a typical gesture of contempt by the Parisian bourgeoisie. Such apparent trivia lie beneath an unpalatable reality that has fermented anti-French feeling in Brittany from political moderates to extremists, and stirred up memories harking as far back as the dynamic independent Breton state that repelled the Franks so long ago.

The first Breton nationalist party was founded before World War I, and various others developed in the inter-war years of polarization and extremist politics. The black and white flag, or Gwenn ha Du, so ubiquitous today, was invented in 1923 by the nationalist Morvan Marchal, his design incorporating bands representing the nine "Breton" bishoprics of Basse- and Haute-Bretagne and the ermines of the medieval state. Olivier Mordrel (see p.180) began his rise to prominence at this time, becoming a founder of the PNB (Parti National Breton) in 1931. Other eminent figures of the nationalist movement, like Célestin Lainé (director of active military units) and Roparz Hemon (creator of "modern Breton") worked for cultural and political goals.

The numbers of nationalists have never been great—perhaps a few thousand at their height—nor successful at the ballot box, but their vo-

Gwenn ha Du flags at Carhaix (ludovicmaudit/Wikimedia Commons)

ciferousness and anti-establishment actions have often made for a high profile. The issue of collaboration during German occupation in World War, when certain nationalists fully embraced the Nazi propaganda of Celticism (a plan to subvert the "Celtic fringe" territories of Scotland, Ireland, Wales, and Brittany and undermine English resistance) remains problematic today. Nationalists saw (and see) France as the true enemy and rejoiced at the notion of independence being restored to Brittany by a victorious Germany. Many were "patriotically" motivated by the desire to revitalize the Breton language after French attacks, an aim the Germans appeared to support for their own ends. Some went further: after the assassination of a nationalist priest, Abbé Perrot (see p.191), a militia unit of Bretons in German uniforms set up to destroy Resistance units took his name, the Bezen Perrot. When the tide turned, collaborators escaped before the Allied advance or were condemned to death/exiled by court judgment at the end of the war, only to be free to return under an amnesty later.

The occupation of Brittany took place swiftly in June 1940 as the Germans were eager to seize the strategic site of Brest, which was to be their base for the future Battle of the Atlantic, along with Lorient and St-Nazaire, other important submarine stations. The Resistance, often in conjunction with Allied agents, waged a war of attrition on Breton soil throughout the war years, many losing their lives with summary executions. The contrast between their widespread heroic sacrifices and the collaboration of a few Breton nationalists is another source of bitterness and recrimination that continues to the present day. Allied air raids on ports and the capital Rennes inevitably left urban devastation and displaced populations.

The playwright and poet Saint-Pol-Roux was born in Marseille, but like so many others who have found a release of vital creativity on this soil, became a Breton by adoption. He lived truly on the Atlantic edge, transforming a cottage on the cliff top at Camaret into a turreted manor house, named after his son Coecilian who died fighting in World War I. He is perhaps best known for his romantic evocation of the Celtic lineage of the Bretons in the poem "Bretagne est universe."

The civilized idyll was shattered one summer evening in June 1940. A German soldier burst in, killed the servant Rose, assaulted the poet's daughter Divine, and injured the elderly man himself. While he was in hospital in Brest his house was plundered, manuscripts scattered on the cliff top, and an Allied bomb later caused further destruction. Saint-Pol-Roux died of grief and despair a few months after the attack. The eerie remains of the house, symbol of the barbarity of war, can still be seen above the beach tossed by Atlantic tides driving around the Pointe de Toulinguet.

## POST-WAR BRITTANY

During the war the Vichy government had separated Nantes and its economically powerful region from Brittany. Post-war rearrangements of the region confirmed this separation, yet another French slap in the face of Breton integrity which has remained a running sore ever since. The UDB (Union Démocratique Bretonne), started by students in Rennes in 1964, still works today for reunion and an autonomous Brittany.

The immediate aftermath of occupation and Allied bombing was a time of essential reconstruction and urgent regard for the economic future. Brest and Lorient lay in ruins and had to be hurriedly thrown up in a basic form to meet the needs of a displaced population. In St-Malo, on the other hand, the *ville close* was painstakingly reconstructed stone by stone to its former glory. Thoughts centered on practicalities, the restoration of communications, the revival of resources and the need for industrial investment—

Citroën, Michelin, and Alcatel all set up plants—and development to replace the irreplaceable, the loss of Nantes and Loire-Atlantique.

Following the shock and energy charge of the student riots in Paris in the late 1960s, the world in the West was ready for a new cultural impetus, one that would draw on native traditions but tap into the spirit of the times. Step forward Alan Stivell (see p.152) who almost single-handedly tugged Breton music to the forefront of the international scene and paved the way for many others. The 1970s were suddenly awash with Celtic music and symbols, new links with Ireland, Cornwall, and Wales driving the festival scene that characterizes Brittany today, the great Interceltic event in Lorient being one initiative of that time.

After a second revival in the 1990s, the twenty-first century calendar is currently full of music, dance, and song. While the large-scale festivities grab the headlines, local communities happily celebrate their own traditions—the vibrant costumes once woven with such skill and pride, dances which vary from one *commune* to the next, legends fixed in the landscape, rural crafts, and delicious recipes, all expressions of the continuity and endurance that has made Breton society strong.

## ORAL TRADITION

The greatest achievement of the Breton people must be the creation and transmission of the living organism that is Breton oral culture, characterized by the extraordinary range and extent of tales and songs preserved over centuries via generations of *conteurs* (storytellers) and bards. During the nineteenth century efforts began to research and transcribe these oral traditions in Breton, Gallo (see below), and French. The first notable collection was the *Barzaz Breiz* (1839) by Théodore Hersart de La Villemarqué, who was inspired by his forays into Welsh medieval literature to record the music and words of Breton songs. This book can be described without exaggeration as a treasure-trove of Brittany's cultural heritage.

La Villemarqué's contemporary François-Marie Luzel, a folklorist and poet in his own right, worked extensively in the Trégor region and then further afield to publish *Chants et chansons populaires de la Basse-Bretagne* in 1869. He later encouraged the work of writer Anatole Le Braz (1859–1926), a great observer of all things Breton who devoted many years to painstakingly recording the memories of the older generation. *La légende de la mort* (1893) is a remarkable text of traditions and customs around the subject of death.

It was not only Breton that benefited from the labor of these and many others. The folklore of eastern Brittany, often in the language of Gallo, was studied and recorded by Adolphe Orain, who published *Chansons de la Haute-Bretagne* in 1902. All these works contain the beliefs, values, and sense of identity of the Breton people and emphasize that to speak of culture in Brittany is to refer to the language of ordinary people.

## BRETON LANGUAGE

The language issue, as we have seen, is complex and controversial. Breton is from the Brythonic (or Brittonic) branch of Celtic languages, like Welsh and Cornish. The historical speaking of Breton largely reflects the movements of British incomers from the fourth to the seventh century. You might be confused about this today as political correctness has led to dual-language signage even in places where Breton was never spoken. There are four main dialects, based on the western areas of settlement: Léon, Trégor, Cornouaille, and the Vannes district. Breton is essentially an oral language, but attempts by Roparz Hemon and others were made in the last century to develop a vernacular literature to consolidate its survival and significance. Hemon (originally not a Breton speaker), a prolific writer and militant Bretonist ("we must destroy the French language or it will destroy us"), introduced a unified orthography in 1941 with the intention of adapting the language to embrace modern terms and ideas. He was backed in this by German propagandist Leo Weisburger, who had also placed Hemon in charge of Breton radio broadcasts in Rennes. This collaboration with the Germans has tainted Hemon's Breton for many native speakers, who also not surprisingly prefer their own dialects to an "artificial" amalgam. Diwan (meaning "to germinate") schools have offered teaching in this modern Breton since 1977, although this is inevitably not the language spoken by previous generations. It comes from the principle of survival of the fittest: there is strength in presenting a united front and engaging future generations.

Inevitably "Celtic culture" has become a product of export value and high tourist worth, but it is also a vital conduit for the preservation of the Breton language, an issue of real concern in contemporary society. Estimates put the number of native speakers at about 250,000.

Although the demise of the older generation, the last who habitually spoke Breton at home, will seriously affect these levels, many of those most active in promoting Breton today only learned the language later in life and there is always opportunity for new recruits.

The position of the French government is the greatest bone of contention, given the past history. Ratification of the European Charter for Regional or Minority Languages has been blocked by the Constitutional Council (on the grounds that the Republic can have but one), but an election promise by François Hollande in 2012 to move past this may at last be coming to fruition with constitutional change (at the time of writing). It has been a very long time coming.

In all the publicity rightly surrounding the preservation and promotion of Breton the fact that Haute-Bretagne has its own language in need of support as a vehicle of culture and oral traditions is often overlooked. Gallo is essentially a romance language, a *dialecte d'oïl* ultimately derived from Latin, a reflection of Roman influence in the east of the region, often in appearance like old French. Supporters work to conserve and disseminate its literature and daily speech.

## CELTICISM

Interest in the Celtic roots of Brittany became formalized in the nineteenth century when the search for Breton identity and a history separate from that of France began. The twin peaks of Celticism were the original pre-Roman tribes with their polytheistic, animistic religion and colorful Druidic priests, and the influx of British migrants after the fall of the Roman Empire, resulting in the Celtic language of Breton. The Celts were believed (correctly) to have resisted Roman invasion—the Vénètes tribe of the southern coast were cruelly punished by Julius Caesar for their spirited opposition—so becoming important symbols of the struggle of a small power against a larger aggressor, analogous with Brittany and France. It was also thought (anachronistically) that the Celts were responsible for the megaliths (see Chapter Two). Celtic studies were all the rage in the Romantic era, to the extent that enthusiastic practitioners earned the ephithet "Celtomanes."

The historian Arthur de La Borderie (see p.80), whose *Histoire de Bretagne* was published posthumously in 1914, was one of the most influential in laying emphasis on Brittany's beginnings in the migrations of the fourth to seventh centuries. The holy men and their followers, Britons who arrived from Britain to evangelize and stayed to create settlements, were truly the originators of Breton society, laying foundations on which a national entity was later built.

Use of the term "Celticism" today is rooted in language and culture, the latter a shared notion with other Celtic areas like Wales, Ireland, and Cornwall. There are obvious affinities in music, dance, and the significance of legends (Brittany also has its King Arthur tales) as well as oral tradition. This solid earth of identification has acquired a thick topsoil of more dubious veracity, like the ubiquitous three-legged triskell more relevant to the Isle of Man than of any Breton pedigree before the nationalist use when it was adopted as a symbol. Restored to a positive image by appearing round the neck of massively influential musician Alan Stivell during the 1970s revival of Breton music, the symbol has become a cultural image much exploited in tourism and commercial ventures as designating something authentically Breton, for some almost a badge of non-conformity outside of the strictures of French formal structures.

Celtic connections are ultimately a confirmatory factor linking edge peoples and consolidating an important sense of ancient languages and mutual identity in the aggressive but bland face of globalization. The iconic annual Interceltique festival at Lorient now includes, in addition to the old hands of Wales, Ireland, Scotland, Cornwall, and Brittany, Galicia and Asturia in northern Spain, ancient edge cultures with their (non-Celtic) languages.

## THE PAST IS ALWAYS WITH US

Memory is one of the great strengths of the Bretons—witness an unrivaled oral culture and passionately preserved historical heritage—so it is not surprising that past issues still live vividly on into the present. There is an echo of Adolphus Trollope's nineteenth-century comment: "This sombre land, where every thing seems to belong to and to speak of the past."

If the somberness has largely disappeared—and there is plenty of joy in Breton culture—an element of Trollope's assessment lingers even today in western Brittany, with people speaking in the twenty-first century of the "wounds of the Revolution," a reference to suppression of the Breton language and the reorganization of territories regardless of historical divisions. Jacobinism—narrow Parisian centralism diametrically opposed to regional or departmental powers—continues to be held responsible for disadvantaging Breton economic development, a trend started by the rapacity of the *ancien régime*. Painful defense of the native language against draconian French attempts to destroy it will never be forgotten, even by those who may be politically moderate and essentially Republican at heart. The nationalists go further, looking back to a perceived golden age of proud independence and national distinction to point out the contrast with today's ignominious subservience to French political power.

One does not need to be an extremist, a nationalist, or even a Breton to dwell on the effects of oppression and suppression by the French over centuries. The question is whether the energy this generates can be turned to positive developments in economic and cultural initiatives or if resentment becomes in itself a stifling factor in future evolution. The weight of the past can be millstone or fulcrum.

Breton products, whether foodstuffs and drinks or music, song, and dance are a draw in their own territory as well as valuable export commodities, taking the strong breath of Breton life to a worldwide audience.

Today Brittany has a vigorous, multifaceted cultural scene, drawing on the past, filtering the present, and looking to the future. It still operates best at the level of its popular roots. To an outsider the inclusiveness is striking: a circle of Breton dancers often includes children, young couples, the middle-aged in need of exercise, and old people, who hold themselves so beautifully and gracefully with no need to concentrate on their feet, which have performed these steps time after time since they too were children. We started with an edge and end this introduction with a circle, symbol of infinity and continual flow, a fitting emblem for Breton culture.

## Chapter Two

# STONE

## FROM CHAOS TO CONTROL

"It is one of our staunchest legacies: stone for shaping."

Pierre Jakez Hélias

"[Brittany] has carved a proud domain from granite."

Saint-Pol-Roux

Hundreds of millions of years of folding, settlement, compression, and extrusion have left the Armorican peninsula coursed by high central ridges of granite and slate running from east to west. Here the landscape—with its thin, acidic soil—is littered with boulders of every shape and size, or sharp outcrops of schist protruding from tracts of moor. Edging this mass are lower plateaux of more fertile land, interspersed by a myriad of river valleys connecting the center to what Kenneth White calls the "broken coast."

Stone has entered the very minds of the people in this rough terrain, with many legends not surprisingly attached to the brooding, man-made megaliths, but also to natural landscape features like impressive caves—where a dragon or King Arthur may be lurking—and the granite Chaos. This latter phenomenon, the result of magma movement over millennia, has created truly extraordinary shapes and patterns, most strikingly found at Huelgoat in Finistère, where rocks the size of houses tumble down the Argent Valley. Local tradition attributes the spectacle to the throwing contest of fighting giants or Gargantua pelting the inhabitants for serving him unpalatable gruel.

Brittany is actually a very colorful place geologically, despite a received notion that fifty shades of gray was originally a reference to Breton architecture. The Côte de Granite Rose around Perros-Guirec in Côtes d'Armor is famous for distinctively weird pink granite shapes, tinged by the feldspar crystal content. Even humbler schist, also an important building material, has a remarkable range of hues, including a rich purple to the southwest of Rennes and the bluey-green of Locquirec. Near the Rade de Brest,

Logonna-Daoulas produces a glorious golden stone for construction; and from the same area comes Kersanton, the sculptors choice with its dark grain, often confused with granite. All these have contributed to the varied palette of Brittany's secular and religious architecture.

## SILENT STONE: MEGALITHS, NOT THE CELTS, AND FLAUBERT HAS FUN

> "As to the theories, the interpretations and the calculations, I listen to them attentively, in a stony silence, before moving back to some rock, any old rock on shore or moor on which frost or sea-salt have written the weather of the ages."
>
> Kenneth White

The significance of the edge position of Brittany begins visually with the plethora of Neolithic monuments, more densely concentrated here than elsewhere, for which the region is famous, marking a well-populated place of passage and assembly during the earliest period of settlement in western European history. As man's relationship with the land began in earnest, he started to assert a degree of control by the clearance of forest areas, establishment of pasturage, and the sowing of crops, all powered by a technology based on stone. Hand in hand with a more settled lifestyle and cohesive communities came the urge towards non-essential expression and the first pictorial artwork, so as man began to shape his life he also began to shape and decorate stone. In Brittany this begins after 5000 BCE with the megaliths (large stones), still memorably imprinted on the landscape despite the loss of many to time, weather, and deliberate destruction. Their existence points to an organized and presumably hierarchical society which could raise and support considerable man power during the construction of these great projects.

The rituals of Neolithic life and death were marked by burial sites and (usually later) alignments of standing-stones, often monuments of impressive size and scope, at least some of which may have been associated with foundation legends, the first claims of man to ownership and possession of territory. Large ceremonial locations like Carnac and St-Just must have had a religious, social, and probably economic cohesion of function, places to meet and exchange on the many integrated levels of an evolving society.

The conventional terminology of *menhir* (long stone in Breton) for upright stones and *dolmen* (stone table) for covered burial chambers was invented in the eighteenth century by Théophile-Malo de La Tour d'Auvergne-Corret (1743–1800), a career soldier from Carhaix who found time for enthusiastic Breton language studies, amateur archaeology, and the publication of historical texts. The words are still with us, even if Breton offers *peulven* (upright stone) and the multiple forms of graves are ill-served by a single name. The *dolmen* idea, stemming from two uprights and a horizontal lintel looking like a simple table, is very misleading and has led to unsubstantiated ideas of sacrificial stones. In fact such structures are the stone casings of burial places and they come in very varied shapes and sizes from small single graves to multiple chambers. Most were subsequently covered in earth, sometimes on a grand scale like the large artificial hills of tumuli, or given a vast carapace of small stones in the form known as a cairn.

The design of the chambers themselves has been subject to much (inconclusive) analysis. The inverted boat shape is one possibility, although more popular ideas favor the womb analogy, where the chamber was reached by a tunnel-like passage offering a symbolic ritual journey between life and death. This may have been undertaken by shamans who experienced altered states of consciousness by spending large periods of time in the isolated, dark, and silent chambers, representative of another world. Another proposition suggests simulations of caves (an echo of Paleolithic history), an enclosed world separated from the everyday earth surface (darkness vs. light), and from the structures of the sky. In other words, the megalithic monuments recreated the cosmological consciousness of the people who built them. In this way, dead ancestors could still wield influence in Stone Age societies.

The acidic soil of Brittany has led to the survival of relatively few bones from the megalithic graves, which seem initially to have been for important individuals and their families, and only later for more collective interments. The earliest burial sites dating back to the fifth millennium BCE are simple chambers with a long or short corridor, the whole then covered with earth. Few retain that topsoil today, but the Ty ar Boudiked site at Brennilis near Lac St-Michel in Finistère is as near as it gets, topped by a grassy mound. Later forms developed into a wedge or V-shape and later still (c. 3000 BCE) into the *allée couverte* or covered passage grave, either buttressed or with flat roof-slabs as at Mougau-Bihan near Commana in the Monts d'Arrée. Standing at that exceptional site and looking across the marsh at the rugged line of stark hills is to survey a landscape little changed since the monument was built.

Archaeological studies suggest that the bones of the dead at these burial places may have been routinely moved, perhaps taken outside for ceremonial purposes and then returned, as part of ancestor worship over the centuries in which many sites were in use. This could relate to the influence of the "founding fathers" notion of the first settlements. Certainly some live activity inside the tombs is envisaged, even if restricted to certain individuals thought to have special "religious" powers to communicate with the dead. There is plenty of room for movement inside one of the most remarkable monuments in Brittany, the so-called Roche aux Fées in Ille-et-Vilaine. It is on such an extraordinary scale (19.5 x 4.7 x 4.1 meters with a massive lintel stone weighing more than twenty tons and space for internal subdivisions) that a temple function for the structure itself has been postulated rather than that of a simple burial plot. It is so enormous that local legends naturally assume supernatural powers at work: hence the rather incongruous name Fairies' Rock.

The Neolithic was not a static period of practice and allegiance. Burial sites, whose use may have changed, may also have become politically

Roche aux (muscular) Fées (Wendy Mewes)

significant places as divisions and conflicts arose, providing a demonstration of continuity with ancestral connections and, potentially, a legitimate hold on certain tracts of land. That old locales were continually reused and new designs like *menhirs* were added to existing sites tends to reinforce this idea.

Some of the burial chambers display artwork in the form of raised or incised carvings. Typical motifs include axes and pairs of bumps often interpreted as the breasts of a goddess, spirals, and U-shapes. The monument at Mougau-Bihan has the first two and also strange oar or paddle-shaped designs. Most renowned for heavily decorated work is the cairn on the island of Gavrinis in the Gulf of Morbihan, where a huge mound conceals one fairly small chamber. The passage is lined with large stones absolutely covered in abstract, swirling patterns, stylized axes, and wiggly lines that may be snakes (or not, but skin-shedding snakes have easy relevance to death and rebirth). Some believe that there may be method in these intense lapidary scribblings, a symbolic language deriving from altered state practice such as shamans followed in many primitive societies. Another tomb famous for its decor is the so-called Table des Marchands at the enclosed site of Locmariaquer on the Baie de Quiberon. Here the full-height chamber has a large roof-slab decorated by an axe and part of an animal. Neolithic artisans were keen on recycling—incredibly enough, the other part of this stone is to be found at the tomb on Gavrinis. Places with free access and impressive patterning that give a real sense of the distinct "world" of these graves include the Pierres Plates near Locmariaquer where the passage is low and twisting (and often waterlogged) and a group of three underground *dolmen* at Mane Kerioned north of Carnac.

*Menhirs* or standing-stones generally date from the later Neolithic period and represent a specific intention to create impact on the landscape. They are only apparently randomly situated: many have been lost through farming practices, natural decay, and destruction by the elements, so that what seem to be single columns may well once have been part of an alignment. The tallest *menhir* in France is that of Kerloas to the northwest of Brest (mentioned in the last Chapter), a whopping eleven meters tall despite having lost its top to extreme weather. This imposing stone, known for its fertility properties, attracts couples to this day and on occasion, especially around the summer solstice, the odd pair of underpants flutters hopefully from the surrounding bushes.

The Daddy of them all lies broken into pieces on the ground at Locmariaquer: upright, it was twenty meters high. Size isn't everything: many stand little more than a meter from the ground, but arrangement or location can enhance their impression on the land. Lines are more common than circles in Brittany, although there are a few exceptions, like the circle on the island of Er Lannic in the Gulf of Morbihan. When it was constructed this was attached to the mainland, but now with higher sea levels, the ring is half-in, half-out of the water.

The significance of the *menhirs* is harder to analyze, although there are plenty of possibilities. Some may have marked out territory in the era when the concept of land-ownership was beginning to crystallize with more settled communities, or indicated specific spots of spiritual or natural significance, such as the common siting near springs. (The role of water in connecting and defining megalithic sites is increasingly a topic for research.) Others have the position of directional landmarks, potential shipping aids, or signposts towards a significant site where communities may have met together for celebrations. Long lines of stones grouped together are usually thought to indicate processional usage, and that handy catchall term "ritual." We know from finds at the base of many raised stones that their erection was accompanied by ceremony, as fires were lit at the foot and bones/stone/pottery fragments buried below the base. The theory that the stones represent people—either as specific individuals or in general roles like sentinels or tribal ancestors—is another possibility. *Menhirs* among earlier burial chambers suggest a reenhancement of status which could have political connotations.

Exceptional concentrations of standing-stones can be found at Lagatjar on the Crozon peninsula, Erdeven (the Giants of Kerzerho) on the south coast, Carnac (see below), and Monteneuf in eastern Morbihan where hundreds have been reerected in recent times. This latter site now has a pedagogic section which analyzes Stone Age techniques—such as the raising of *menhirs*, hut-building and the firing of pottery—making it a pragmatic experience rather than the magical and mystical effect so many seek from these stones (which resolutely refuse all answers to the many questions asked of them).

Before the questing archaeologists of most recent centuries, these stone relics were assumed by antiquarians to have been the product of the Celts and in particular the Druids, those repositories of arcane knowledge and sacred ritual. Many megalithic sites have names reflecting local legends of this type: the Cordon des Druides in the forest of Fougères or the Chaire des Druides near Maël-Pestivien, where one of the stones is said to have been used for human sacrifices. The vague resemblance to a body shape in the surface gives rise to this idea, but those early Celts must have been exceptionally tall.

Local traditions of a rural population often attribute the megaliths to the work of giants or see them as houses of fairies and little people, an aspect they have retained in popular imagination, especially in isolated locations. Interest in the mystery of the megaliths grew with the burgeoning of Celtic studies and Romanticism, while the Church was doubtless behind legends of petrification when drunken men or frivolous young girls dancing were punished for their immorality. An Eured Vein, a line of dozens of small stones winding across the plain below Mont-St-Michel-de-Brasparts in a spectacular Monts d'Arrée setting, is said to be a reveling wedding party which failed to make way for a priest carrying the sacrament to a dying parishioner. Many *menhirs* were Christianized with anything from a simple cross added to the top—like the huge stone Men Marz near Brignogan Plage in north Finistère—to elaboration such as the detailed engravings of the instruments of Christ's passion at St-Uzec north of Lannion, the result of seventeenth-century missionary endeavor against paganism and the eroticism of the stones.

The greatest concentration of megaliths lies around the coast, most famously at Carnac on the Gulf of Morbihan and nearby Locmariaquer in southern Brittany, once at Penmarc'h on the southwest tip, now mostly lost, and on the west coast above the Paleolithic site at Menez Dregan, at Lostmarc'h and Lagatjar on the Crozon Peninsula or Barnenez in the north. Their positioning is a mark of well-established Stone Age trade routes from southern Europe to Britain and through the recently opened up channel to Germany and Scandinavian countries. Perhaps the inhabitants of the island of Ouessant out in the Atlantic were already offering their services as pilots to negotiate the treacherous seas on approach to the channel as they were to do later on. There may also be significance in the placing of monuments near the coast in the sense of a threshold between land and sea, two contrasting entities, perhaps analogous to life and death. Water levels have risen as much as ten meters since 5000 BCE, giving wet feet to more than a few of those monuments set near the shoreline, but clear outlines of standing stones and burial mounds visible from boats at sea may have marked sites of ceremonial significance, looming out of the Atlantic mist as party invitations to mark seasonal and astronomical festivities for a people gradually turning to agricultural and more fixed lifestyles.

For construction material, proximity was as crucial as adaptability. Granite and schist are the commonest stones used for both reasons. Some were fashioned with hand tools, but many split naturally from their mass ready-made in a suitable shape for *menhirs*. The oldest sizeable structure in Europe, the great Cairn of Barnenez on the promontory of Kernéléhen overlooking the Bay of Morlaix, was built in two phases. The first was a unit of five covered passage graves in local dolerite some time around 4600 BCE; the second development of six more tombs followed more than a thousand years later, this time in granite from the nearby Ile de Sterec, an islet today connected to the mainland by a curving sweep of rocks at low tide. Some are roofed with capstones, the others in the corbeled *tholos* style, which can be seen clearly in one of the partially revealed tombs. The site was still in use in the Bronze Age, as finds of arrowheads and a dagger showed.

The placing of the monument, described by André Malraux as "the Parthenon of pre-history," is significant, highly visible from the sea, structurally fitted to its landscape context, but also dominating the skyline. It is a construction of extraordinary size and imposition. Recent studies have revealed traces of red and black paint on one of the tomb walls, the first such artistic evidence in Brittany. Carved symbols include a common cup or horn shape, squiggly lines that could be snakes, and a square shape similar to a shield with cartoon-like sprouting hair that has led to interpretation of an idol's head (not unlike Bart Simpson in appearance).

Barnenez also turned into a test case for the protection of historic monuments soon after its rediscovery in 1954. A developer began to use the site as a quarry, bulldozing a burial chamber before protests halted the destruction and the monument could be classified. The first successful prosecution for willful damage of an ancient structure followed.

## CARNAC

"Leaving Brittany now, we enter the world of the Celts… The country district of Vannes has the appearance of a huge skeleton which having lost skin and flesh, still displays its twisted carcase and disjointed limbs." So Émile Souvestre (1806–54) describes the megalithic scene in southern Morbihan, where the best known of all Neolithic sites in Brittany is the World Heritage site of Carnac. Here up to eleven lines of standing-stones run for several kilometers across the plain behind the town near the Gulf of Morbihan. The landscape itself is unremarkable and quite changed since the Neolithic period, as both trees and the water were much further away at the time of original construction. The sheer scale of remains warrants its status, but international fame inevitably beings a volume of visitors that detracts from an atmospheric experience of the site. It is still possible to get a sense of the design in the landscape by entering the Kerlescan alignments from the east and walking up through the rows, which were quite likely processional avenues, toward the enclosure on a slight eminence. A palpable anticipation is both created and then thwarted by the closely set stones here which mar an outsider's view of whatever religious ritual or ceremonial celebration went on inside. To be alone with stones (albeit small ones) at Carnac, Le Petit-Ménec in its woodland setting is a better bet.

Alignement de Kerlescan: lines like snakes? (Myrabella/Wikimedia Commons)

The alignments are interspersed by burial sites of various types. The Tumulus de St-Michel is a huge mound today topped by a chapel to the Christian patron saint of high places, a vantage point for surveying the context of the alignments. For a closer insight into underground burials, the Tumulus de Kercado can be visited, although the addition of electric light detracts from the authenticity and takes away that head-banging thrill that is such a key factor in exploring megaliths.

Adored by the modern visitor and venerated beyond all reason by contemporary tourism (to the detriment of other equally interesting sites), Carnac was a disappointment to nineteenth-century visitors, an interesting indication of how expectations have changed. We seem far more inclined to believe hype and eschew individual judgment today. There is a touch of the Emperor's clothes about Carnac. Fortuné du Boisgobey turned up in 1839 to find a "spectacle more bizarre than great":

> At last I was to discover these famous stones… a little disappointment awaited me.
>
> In my head I had a quite other idea of the Carnac monument; I imagined a vast plateau, battered by the sea under a glowering sky and far from any habitation, eleven lines of enormous menhirs like huge ghosts. Carnac offers nothing like that and yet is not less curious.

Many fanciful and romantic interpretations of the megaliths at Carnac created even then a good deal of excitement and made it a minefield of unscientific speculation. "Here then is the famous plain of Carnac which has had more nonsense written about it than it has stones." This is the opening salvo fired by novelist Gustave Flaubert, who visited in 1847, in his swingeing attack on the "Celtomanes," before he runs through the long list of contemporary theories. The local legend held that St Cornely was chased by Roman soldiers and turned them all to stone when he was cornered here. Or maybe each stone marks where a hero fell in battle. Or was it the remains of an Egyptian colony because, after all, there is a Karnak in Egypt? Another story makes the stones the skeleton of Caesar's army camp or the cemetery of the Vénètes tribe he conquered. What about a Druid temple or even (bizarrely) accommodation prepared by the Druids for visiting dignitaries on festive or political occasions? All quite practical ideas. More outlandish was the postulation of a serpent cult based on obscure links to the works of Pausanias or, failing that, the wavy lines in which the stones are placed. Or lapidary reflections of the signs of the Zodiac, a notion proposed by eminent antiquarian Jacques Cambry, founder of the Académie Celtique. Then there was the phallic cult connection—and here Flaubert gives up. "Carnac is in barren countryside where nothing except the conjectures of these gentlemen has ever grown…"

He was rather more taken by a handsome barefoot peasant girl carrying a sheaf of hay on her head than the stones, although he sympathizes with their plight: "We perfectly understand the irony of these granite stones which, since the Druids, laugh in their mossy green beards at all the imbeciles who come to see them." His main interest is in debunking the speculations of learned pontificators, pointing up their fundamental ignorance when confronted by the silent stones, and the futility of speculative huffing and puffing. With all the confident arrogance of a young man with his wits about him, Flaubert has the last word:

> After reviewing all the learned opinions… if someone asks my opinion about the stones at Carnac—and everyone in the world has an opinion—I will put forward an irrefutable, cast-iron and unarguable view, one which shatters the Zodiac of Cambry and chops the Python cult theory into little pieces, and this is it: the stones at Carnac are large stones.

British travelers were also unimpressed and often found the sites alien and unnerving. Edward William Lewis Davies, author of *Wolf-hunting in Brittany* (see p.206), rated his visit to the "dismal spectacle" of Carnac a sobering experience, walking among the stones, "grim and silent witnesses of unknown rites." He notes that there is not a scrap of history to reveal anything about the people who erected the stones. He also laments the willful destruction by locals: "If time has wiped out the history of these monuments, man is guilty of a worse desecration by carting away the very monuments themselves."

Altogether his party was glad to see the back of Carnac:

> The picture gallery was too sombre, too monotonous, and too long for any man who was neither a philosopher nor an enthusiast in such matters.

Another visitor, Henry Blackburn, together with his artist friend Randolph Caldecott, took in Carnac on their round of Breton sites in 1880. He says the majority of stones were lying pell-mell on the ground, half-buried in the earth or hidden by gorse or long grass. The open setting was "grey and monotonous," not quite what they were expecting, and sand blew into their eyes as the wind "moaned between the stones":

> Is this then the famous field of Carnac with its 'avenues of menhirs,' the object of so many pilgrimages, the origin of so many theories, the birthplace of so many legends? The first impression, we need hardly say, is disappointing.

He acknowledges the received theory that these megaliths are monuments of the dead and marks of burial places, but thinks the bones discovered there lend credence to the Druidic sacrifice notion (Blackburn assumes that the date of the site is Celtic, the commonly held view of his time). He feels that the wild, colorless landscape contributes to an alienation of historical fact and the tendency to weave the sort of imaginative fantasies that are so much part of Breton culture and landscape: "All else seems vague and mysterious, leading men of succeeding ages to surround the scene with legends and traditions."

Greater rigor of research and excavation eventually led to a better perspective on the timescale of the monuments. Scotsman James Miln, who was responsible for the first serious archaeological work on the site, pondered the question: "how is it that the Romans, masters of the world, came and went whilst this race of primitive builders remains?" When he died in 1881 Miln left his extensive collections to the town of Carnac and so began the excellent museum developed by his assistant, Zacharie Le Rouzic, and named after both men. It really is the best starting point before setting foot among the stones to obliterate all those pseudo-cultural images of Druids in long, white robes. What the exhibitions clearly demonstrate are the practical and technical skills of a well-organized and socially developed society, even if their beliefs are a little harder to pin down.

Crowds may flock to Carnac and Locmariaquer, but the comparatively little-visited alignments and unusual burial chambers of St-Just (northeast of Redon in Ille-et-Vilaine) are just as impressive, perhaps more so in that you may well have a solitary experience of their isolated setting.

A terrible fire in 2009 blackened much of the moor and damaged some of the uprights, but it remains an evocative demonstration of why the megaliths are so important in Brittany's history and identity. The strong presence of these silent stones makes a major contribution to the image of mystery and otherness: the sense of an unknown people and strange gods; the wild, harsh landscape settings; legendary associations; and anachronistic Celtic connotations all play their part. These are all things associated with Brittany itself, to which may be added that the prevalence of burial sites is all too easily fitted to notions of the Breton and typically Celtic fascination with death and all its ramifications. Perhaps it is fortunate that we do not actually know exactly what the megaliths were for or exactly who raised them: a case where ignorance is not only imaginative bliss but leaves cultural power in popular oral tradition rather than with the intelligentsia.

LIVING STONE: SLEEPING WITH THE ANIMALS AND MINDING ONE'S MANORS

> "…the quaint old houses, which betray the same unconquerable aversion to a perpendicular line that Nature is said to feel to a vacuum."
>
> Adolphus Trollope

The seeker of fancy châteaux à la Loire Valley will be disappointed in Brittany, which shines more in ruined castles, with one of the finest in Europe at Fougères, but as ever it comes up trumps in economies of scale as far as living accommodation is concerned. From vernacular peasant dwellings to the rural *manoir*, the essentially modest and practical nature of Breton domestic architecture is dominated by the use of local stone, often granite and particularly schist, the latter providing not only walls but also the thick roof tiles indicative of relative means. The countryside is full of austerely beautiful, solid, functional, and individually varied houses that were once home to the *petite noblesse*, the backbone of rural Breton society. It is calculated that there were about 12,000 *manoirs* throughout Brittany in the sixteenth century; slightly less than half remain in some form today.

At the lowest end of the scale is the basic cottage or *penty (*as whitewashed coastal cottages in particular were called). *Ty* means house in Breton, in this context a single space on one level, often with an earth floor and no facilities beyond a fireplace and chimney. These first permanent constructions for living quarters remained little changed for many centuries. Unrendered, it is the archetypal Breton house, epitome of the gray stone picturesque poverty dear to romanticized images of rural Brittany. Building methods naturally varied in the region: in areas where stone was in short supply, like around Rennes, earth or mud walling was common practice, and in the towns timber frames were the norm until the eighteenth century.

Humble houses in the countryside were noted by many foreign travelers, such as Henry Blackburn in 1880: "We pass substantial-looking farmhouses, but the dwellings of the peasants are generally hovels with tumbledown mud walls and immovable windows."

Blackburn was concerned at the lack of progress in the peasant's lot during the nineteenth century, quoting another visitor back in 1818 who had reported with opprobrium that the peasants were rude, uncivilized and simple, living "like pigs" lying on the ground and sharing their rooms with animals, with further evidence from a report in the *Morning Post* from the 1850s also emphasizing the primitive conditions. Adolphus Trollope, visiting Brittany in 1840, made the observation that while a cottage in Normandy generally had good light "a great deficiency of windows… is almost universal in Brittany." He equates this with a "backward state of civilization." Here we see again perhaps the curled lip of a rapidly developing industrial Britain, already out of touch with rural living, but to find the same conditions still prevailing in the 1880s is a shock to Blackburn: "The problem of a life of labour and monotony is yet unsolved." He was surprised that even the modern world of the train had failed to bring benefits to the smallholder in the countryside—in other words, most of the population of Brittany. No wonder that a great exodus from country to town within the region (and to urban centers like Paris outside it) was to characterize the later years of the nineteenth century.

It should be noted, however, that the jibes of outsiders about rude peasant living conditions in tandem with animals were often based on a misunderstanding of what was practical and precious. The presence of large beasts like horses and cows within the domestic environment contributed considerably to internal warmth, and the value of these animals to the family made the safety and security of shared accommodation a sign of worth. Pigs, with their rapacious snouts and love of mud, were kept outside, for all their crucial role in the Breton diet.

Wealthier peasant farmers could afford larger premises. An outstanding example of a house in traditional style built from local stone can be found in St-Rivoal, an isolated Monts d'Arrée village, eulogized by Anataole Le Braz, an indefatigable collector of oral traditions, in the 1890s: "This corner of poor land, lost in a fold of the hills, is a happy place. Wretchedness is unknown, and so there is no begging."

A few years later it struck Frédéric Le Guyader rather differently:

A whole area, sunk into lethargy,
Stagnant, dead, far from any buzz, cut off from gossip...

The Maison Cornec (1702) in St-Rivoal is an interesting example of a type often called—for no very persuasive reason—*maisons anglaises*, English houses. It was opened to the public in 1969, as one of the first eco-museums in France, and can still be visited today at certain times. The style was traditional in the Monts d'Arrée from the seventeenth century until about 1830: a two-story abode of schist blocks with an outside stone

Solid stone: the Maison Cornec (Wendy Mewes)

staircase sheltered by a narrow overhang of roof. It is a solid, comparatively spacious house, with a large fireplace below and a second smaller one on the upper floor, an area which may have provided separate accommodation (with lower headroom) and an attic area.

This was not just a home but a working farming enterprise. Outside is a large courtyard and threshing floor space with outbuildings that served as stables, sheepfold, and storage as well as two bread ovens, the smaller perhaps original to the household, but the large turf-topped one from 1830 presumably used as a communal village resource. Two water sources on the spot served the house and animal needs. The land remains pretty much unchanged from its original appearance: small fields and orchards divided by banks and hedges that provided timber in rotation, the terrain gently sloping down to a small river in the bottom of the valley.

The south-facing exterior of the Maison Cornec—built for Yvon Cornec, his wife Anna, and their children—has changed little since its construction. There were no foundations to level the land so the house follows its line directly and the floors are of beaten earth. The ashlars are mostly rough-cut, with the only very careful craftsmanship applied to the doorway, which bears the owner's name, while the back door has a zigzag frieze, a typical local design. The thick slate slabs of the roof mark the quality of the build at a time when most houses were of smaller dimensions and roofed by turf. The tiles are held by pegs of wood and sealed by clay, and there is a decorated roof ridge featuring figures of animals and symbols, such as a fleur-de-lis.

There was some external extension in the nineteenth century, a barn for farm carts on one end of the house and a stable on the other, next to the pigsty neatly managed under the external stairs (to which a modern wooden handrail has recently been added). Nearby is another local feature: the standing-stone barn, with schist uprights used to support a timber and straw roof. Today it is where they put the press to make apple juice by traditional methods at the annual Fête des Pommes.

The characteristic feature of the house, an *apoteis* or protruding gable on one side, gave an L-shaped extension to the main living area, a place for a table, usually a storage box doubling its function, where the family could eat meals rather than crouched around the fireplace, a not inconsiderable social development. Above the table, a rack holds the wooden spoons that served as cutlery for all.

The rounded main doorway leads into a central passage going straight through to the back door—a means of keeping air circulating. One side of the house is arranged for animals with a rough paved floor, hayracks and troughs, while a chute for food waste leads directly to the pigs' quarters outside. The other side is the family space, with the huge fireplace for heat and food preparation, and wooden box beds from the nineteenth century. These *lits clos* were often marriage gifts inscribed with the couple's initials: a step was needed to clamber in and then the sliding door was pushed to, leaving the couple in confined darkness and a degree of warm privacy. They slept propped up on straw-filled bolsters; lying down, the position of death, was superstitiously avoided. A baby's cradle could be hung on a hook in the narrow space above the bed.

Before this minute "bedroom" was in use, sleeping was considerably more basic, on rough mattresses fashioned from logs and straw or other plant material, with places nearest the fire going to children and the elderly. Trollope comments that he has been in a Breton laborer's cottage which had no furniture at all, just piles of bedding four feet high. Storage chests, wardrobes, and later dressers were the only other commonly found furniture, and these large items were often used as room-dividers. Even for a family who could afford such a house as the Maison Cornec, a step up from the rudest cottage, it was minimalist living.

Moving on up the social scale, Breton *manoir*s were once found in great density in areas of fertile soil, particularly along the northern Golden Belt from Léon to St-Malo, and each parish may have contained several dozen. They generally differ in origin from châteaux, which may have been aristocratic residences but also frequently had a deliberately defensive origin, arising from the turbulent period of Viking attacks, with a military presence and the capacity to harbor a larger population in times of danger. The smaller-scale manor house, on the other hand, was of an essentially residential and economic purpose, with an owner who was fixed in his locality and saw to the exploitation of his land. These properties remain symbols of the Golden Age of Breton prosperity and rural stability.

The often sober and unobtrusive structures were situated in a sheltered position with water close by for the mill and good, arable land for the *metairie* or home farm. The layout was usually self-contained, often with a protective wall to seal four sides of a square around an open courtyard and sometimes even a large *logis*/ (gatehouse), an elaborate entrance containing accommodation. Square or round towers, complete with turning stone staircases, are a common symbol of the status of these houses and an architectural embellishment. At the Manoir de Fornebello in Plouagat, an attractive house now at the center of a *gite* complex, the huge-centrally placed stair-tower dwarfs the house itself and even contains the main entrance door.

The farmhouse, home of a peasant of superior status who managed the farm, may have been in close proximity to the *manoir*, even inside the main complex. It was the hub of the economic activity on which the property relied. Other external signs of the status of manor houses include mills, dovecotes (the number of openings depending on the overall size of the land), fishponds, and bread ovens, not all of which have survived the passage of time. A separate private chapel was also a common feature.

These manor houses were the homes of the *petite noblesse*, often only a small step up from the peasants and rarely affluent themselves after the rural economy began to decline in the eighteenth century, well below the great lords with vast property holdings answerable only to the duke or king. They were the secular heads of the parish as much as priests were religious authorities, and though they may often have had less money than their own tenant farmers, their social status was inviolable. They had fishing and hunting rights, and enjoyed exemption from some of the taxes so burdensome to the peasant population (*fouage* or hearth tax and *foncière* or building tax). These families were traditionally the local *seigneurs* who lived in situ, holding the power of justice over their feudal tenants and collecting annual dues of rent, labor, or produce. Respected and deferred to in their communities, many struggled to maintain appearances in hard times and more than a few families had even died out altogether by the time of the Revolution. This violent upheaval often saw the destruction or desecration of their *manoirs*, which continued as they were turned into farms or upgraded rural retreats for the wealthy urban bourgeoisie.

The philosopher Ernest Renan (see p.173) preserves a memorable picture of the Manoir de Kermelle (probably the actual Manoir du Carpont) near his home town of Tréguier in *Le broyeur de lin* (1876), a semi-legendary story of unrequited love related by Renan's mother.

A manor house like all the others, a well-cared for farm, an ancient appearance, surrounded by a long, high wall of pleasing grey hue. You entered into the courtyard via a great arched gate covered by a slate roof, next to which was a smaller door for everyday use. At the far side of the courtyard was the house with a high-pitched roof and gable covered in ivy. A dovecote, a stair-tower, two or three beautifully made windows, almost like those of a church, indicating a noble abode, one of the old manors which were inhabited before the Revolution by a class of person whose characters and customs are now impossible to imagine.

Renan has never forgotten his mother's characteristically vivid portrayal of one of these *nobles de campagne,* the *seigneur* himself, Kermelle de Trédarzec, a handsome old man—"serious and solemn, a little sad because he was almost the last of his type"—who kept his long hair up with a comb except on Sundays for church. Here he sat in his own pew for Holy Communion, taking off his ceremonial gloves to receive the Host, and no one else stirred to reach the altar-rail until he had sat down again and put his gloves back on.

He was very poor but he concealed this in the way a man of his rank naturally would. These nobles of the countryside once had certain privileges which enabled them to live a bit differently from the peasants, but that's all gone now. Kermelle was in a very embarrassing position. His rank as a nobleman prevented him from working in the fields; he stayed up shut up at home all day, and busied himself indoors with tasks which didn't necessitate going outside.

In fact he was forced to earn money by secret labor, separating the outer husks from retted flax (*lin*) to liberate the textile fiber. "This was the work which poor Kermelle believed he could carry out without demeaning himself. No one could see him, his professional honor was safe, but everyone knew it and he was soon called 'le broyeur de lin.'"

Near Bulat-Pestivien, south of Guingamp, the Manoir de Bodilio—which now houses a museum devoted to the Breton manor house—was built in the mid-sixteenth century. Part of the parish of Pestivien, the current house in Renaissance style with enclosed courtyard, well, and arched doorway, replaced an earlier version referred to in a document of

1481. At the time of the Revolution the manor was partially dismantled, losing those marks of status, the chapel and dovecote, but continuing as a farm. Its permanent exhibition, the devoted work of Michel Morel and his association Arts, Culture & Patrimoine de Bretagne, uses photos, plans, models, and documents to give a vivid sense of the development of the multifaceted Breton manor house over several centuries, drawing on many detailed examples, mostly from Côtes d'Armor. It is also illustrates the complex network of crafts and skills required in the construction of each edifice: not least of the workmen were the *picoteurs* who laboriously shaped the quarried stone before the masons put it to practical use, secured with clay or lime mortar, and the sculptors refined the finished product with decorative detail. The master masons (or later architects) who were responsible for the plans worked equally on churches and fine châteaux, making replication of motifs across these genres an organic process.

One observer in search of fine buildings had clear expectations for the required scale and grandeur, and was sometimes disappointed. In 1839 Fortuné du Boisgobey, on his travels in north Finistère, was encouraged by his guide to make for the Château de Kerlivré, a league from Plouescat and claimed as the finest in the *département*. He soon moaned that it was actually called Kerliviri, was only half a league away and was not at all remarkable...

> This château or rather manor-house is not in my opinion very old. It must date from the end of the sixteenth century and... is more a "maison de plaisance" than a fortified retreat. As it stands today the manor-house presents a particularly wretched appearance: a farm has been established in the logis, which is still habitable. The large courtyard is full of dung, the remaining tower (containing the most beautiful stone staircase I've seen) has been invaded by a flock of sheep. It's hard to distinguish between what's old and what's modern, which bits are abandoned and which still in use, such is the local greed for taking away the poor stones of these fine buildings which suffer the indignity of lending their granite walls and vast rooms to wretched farmers after having housed a noble and powerful lord.

This picture of decline applied to all too many Breton manor houses from the time of the Revolution, and many a block of quality stone was squirreled away to grace humbler constructions. The ultimate insult to a way of life once so important in Brittany would have been the tarting up of surviving *manoirs* for new urban-based masters as power moved firmly away from the countryside to the towns.

## STONE SYMPHONY: PARISH CLOSES, DEVILISH PRIESTS, AND MEN IN HAIRY TIGHTS

> "Altogether the calvaires of St Thegonnec and Guimiliau, whether regarded from a picturesque or antiquarian point of view, are the most interesting monuments we have yet seen; interesting in their very loneliness, the object of so much thought and labour in the middle ages, left thus neglected and in ruin."
>
> Henry Blackburn (1880)

Despite its western edge position, Brittany was no cultural backwater. The glory of stone-working reached a pinnacle in the sixteenth and seventeenth centuries, mostly manifested in religious art and architecture, with Flamboyant Gothic churches gradually adorned with the insignia of the Renaissance. A phenomenon closely tied to this time and one particular district is that of the parish closes (*enclos paroissiaux*) of Léon in northern Finistère (although they exist elsewhere, about seventy in all). These religious precincts share the same essential elements—church, enclosure, triumphal entrance gate, ossuary, and *calvaire*—but they are very individual creations, an orchestrated harmony of stone expressing the living spirit of a people. Skilled craftsmen, well aware of current European styles, were summoned to work on the Château de Kerjean in the 1590s and subsequently also applied their talents in this religious context, including the extravagantly lavish interior church décor beloved by the Bretons. St-Thégonnec, Guimiliau, and Lampaul-Guimiliau just to the west of Morlaix are three (out of many) fine examples of parish closes in easy proximity to each other.

In this area an extraordinary period of economic growth fueled by the cloth trade with England had resulted in small villages awash with cash in the hands of farmers who grew the flax, laundry owners who processed it, weavers who produced the cloth, and those who carried a finished product to the merchants in Morlaix and Landerneau for shipment. The social manifestation of material prosperity in this part of Léon can be seen in

Stone harmony at Guimiliau (Wendy Mewes)

the emergence of an oxymoron, a caste of rich peasants (*juloded*) who formed a veritable aristocracy in their communities. Some were wealthy enough to leave manual labor to others and go to church escorted by a retinue of servants or devote their time to politics. Their local ascendancy was ensured by careful intermarriage to preserve and increase their resources.

These were the men who formed the *fabrique* or church council, which decided on the embellishment of the church, made the orders, and paid the craftsmen for completed work. In typical Breton fashion, money was spent on collective expressions of local pride rather than ostentatious houses and personal possessions. And while thoughts of personal salvation may have figured high on the list of criteria for donations to the Church, a sincere manifestation of the glory of faith marks out the parish closes.

The *enclos* are church precincts within a boundary wall marking off the sacred space, the place where the living and dead come together, a mini-City of God. The *placitre,* or open area within, changed in use over time. It was originally where trees were grown and markets held, to the financial benefit of the church: as a general meeting place it formed the social heart of the community.

People were once buried inside the church, their bones being removed to an ossuary building when there was no more room. This practice was forbidden in 1719 and the *placitre* often became a cemetery. Some parish closes like Commana and Lannédern still retain this feature; others are grassed over with a burial ground established elsewhere outside the wall.

The first impression of the *enclos* is usually of an elaborate entrance gate, often on the lines of the triumphal arches of Roman generals, for it is the victory of Christianity over death that is trumpeted throughout the architectural ensemble. The Renaissance revival of classical styles also suited this convention. A crucifix tops the structure which is sometimes decorated with angels and scenes of the Annunciation, the beginning of the story of Christ. This gate was the Porz ar Maro or Gate of Death, reserved for the funeral cart. Access for the living was via steps at the side which had stone slabs at the top to protect the *placitre* from the intrusion of animals, a reminder that pigs often roamed free through medieval villages. This was something of a social leveler—everyone had to clamber over to get in.

The parish close is a monument of social history, indicating the place of the Church at the center of the community as well as being a reminder of inevitable mortality and the redemption of Christianity. Themes of death and eternal life through the sacrifice of Jesus are depicted by means of coherent architecture and sculptural design. On entering the *enclos* the physical artistic impression is intended to stimulate awareness of human frailty (in contrast with the glory of God), the mystery of crucifixion and resurrection, and a sense of hope for reward in the afterlife—all promoted in the grandeur of concept and construction. Originally the sculpted figures would have been brightly painted, giving a quite different appearance from the dull grays today. Symbolically it is an architecture of triumph expressed in verticals: everything points in an upward direction—finials, columns, crosses, soaring spires—in an echo of the soul's rise to heaven. Entering St-Thégonnec, the most famous and muscular *enclos* of them all, the effect of sheer ostentatious exuberance is overwhelmingly emphasized by this skyward onslaught. It is a highly dramatic expression of Christian aspiration, a kind of religious theater. *Bradshaw's Railway Handbook to Brittany* (1899) advised the contemporary tourist: "St Thegonnec, at which a halt should be made to examine the fine church… the deep cornices and entablatures, and the rich effect produced by buttresses and raised stones, will strike the visitor."

The *enclos* is also a reminder of the universal mortality that precedes eternal life. Ossuary buildings which once contained the bones of the dead (a few like Lanrivain and St-Fiacre in Côtes d'Armor still do) bear the imagery of death in the form of skulls and crossbones or the skeletal figure of Ankou, the Breton Grim Reaper. Some show people from a variety of social backgrounds to illustrate Death the great leveler, a sentiment reflected in the commonly inscribed phrases: *Je tue vous tous* (I kill you all), *hodie mihi, cras tibi* (today me, tomorrow you) and *memento mori*. The fitting subject of a *mise en tombeau* group showing the laying out of Jesus' body by his closest followers was often contained in the ossuary. Once their function was redundant, many of these buildings were converted into chapels and today are small museums or souvenir shops, detached from their original chilling message.

Most conspicuous of all the elements is the *calvaire*, a free standing sculptural *tour de force* usually placed near the south porch. Guimiliau has the best, more than two hundred figures in Kersanton stone, malleable and yet remarkably hard-wearing against the demanding Breton weather. This extravaganza of carving, which attracts visitors from all over the world, is no less impressive in its finer details than the grand themes.

The *calvaire* in principle tells the Christian story in a series of friezes. The lower tier usually shows the birth of Christ, his early life, and events leading up to his arrest, while the upper level concentrates on the Passion, with scenes like Pilate washing his hands, the way of the Cross, and at the very top are the crucifixion and resurrection. It is all a reminder of Redemption—Jesus died for our sins to give the faithful hope of an afterlife. The choice of scenes and their order may vary, but favorites include the Annunciation, Adoration of the Magi, Flight to Egypt, Last Supper, and Jesus washing his disciples' feet. From the Passion, his arrest, flagellation, and abuse by soldiers is often accompanied by Ste Veronique holding up her handkerchief with Christ's face imprinted on it.

There is a split-screen effect to indicate the developing stages of the story. The crucifixion between the robbers—with angels below catching blood in the Holy Grail and Mary holding her son's body at the foot of the cross—is placed above the later tomb scene where one of the sleeping guards wakes in amazement to see Jesus ascending to heaven, symbolized by his finger pointing upwards. (There were some things even these stone-workers of genius could not manage literally.)

If some scenes are formulaic in content, they are distinguished by individual treatment and by tiny details of storytelling or emotional involvement: at Guimiliau the pathos of Mary gently holding the foot of her baby as they flee to Egypt to escape Herod's edict, or the disciple eagerly taking off his sandal in anticipation as Jesus—with carefully rolled sleeve—washes a comrade's feet. At the Last Supper, the traitor Judas keeps a full purse out of sight of the others.

St-Thégonnec's *calvaire* is smaller but the figures—by Roland Doré, a master craftsman from Landerneau—are superbly represented. The dress of Mary Magdalene, mourning at the foot of the cross, is a masterpiece in itself. It is precisely the particular details ("grotesque and often even downright disgusting") that shocked Fortuné du Boisgobey in 1839:

> One doesn't know why: might it be one of the traits of the Breton character to always do things differently to the rest of the world? The scenes of the flagellation above all astonished me by their bizarre and indecent detailing.

He must be talking of the lolling tongue of the idiot and the soldiers who have just slapped Jesus' face, all portrayed in post-medieval dress with crass features and bulging codpieces. And yet it is their ruffed sleeves and wrinkled boots that offer a supreme example of the potential finesse of stoneworking.

The *calvaires* provided visual lessons before the eyes of the community on a daily basis and served as moral guidance during outdoor sermons. There are often added extras in addition to the standard scenes. At Guimiliau the gaping mouth of a vast leviathan contains the entrance to Hell, and little devils are busy dragging a young woman with prominent naked breasts inside. This is Katel Gollet or Lost Kate, a subject of a cautionary tale no doubt promulgated by priests in notoriously prudish Léon. She is supposed to have defied her father's orders and sneaked out for nights of dancing and drinking. One day she went a man too far and supped with the Devil, who danced her literally to death and the punishments of hell for her iniquities. It has to be said that her breasts are lovingly carved.

There is interest well beyond the religious in the *calvaires*. Enormous care has been taken in the depiction of the figures who often wear dress contemporary to the time of their construction. The sporting of large

Old devil at Plougonven (Wendy Mewes)

moustaches is not something one immediately associates with the New Testament. Also at Guimiliau, the figure of Mary Magdalene appears to be modeled on that of Mary Stuart in her distinctive headdress. We can assume that the highly individualized faces are taken to some extent from life and many a villager must figure in the crowd scenes. Some people had fun with it: at Plougonven, southeast of Morlaix, the *calvaire* has an almost life-sized depiction of the Devil—but he is wearing the garb of a seventeenth-century priest and has most distinctive ugly features. Was this payback time for a sculptor who had fallen out with the *curé*?

Much sculptural detail was also lavished on the important south porch entry to the church, although many of the original statues from this vulnerable position are lost. The early seventeenth-century entrance arch at Guimiliau blends Old and New Testament vignettes reading from bottom to top: on the left are Adam, Eve, and the serpent opposite Noah's Ark, and the man himself drunk as a lord after discovering the fruits of the vine. St-Thégonnec's entrance offers an exquisite statue of St John the Evangelist, the softly graceful and tender face characteristic of Roland Doré's work. Inside the porch the *fabrique* once met on stone benches below the statues of the twelve apostles, who carry their gruesome symbols of martyrdom. The community could gather round outside and listen to deliberations, until a decree of 1655 enforced notions of privacy and security, and sacristies were added onto the northeastern exterior of the church, often as at Guimiliau and Pleyben in the new Renaissance style.

The decoration of the closes became competitive as villages vied to have larger towers or finer altarpieces (*retables*). Stories are still told of jealous parishioners from Lampaul-Guimiliau crossing the Monts d'Arrée to steal a bell from the upstart parish of Pleyben in Cornouaille (which does indeed have an exceptional *enclos*). St-Thégonnec was determined at all costs to have a better tower than Pleyben. Bosoms swelled with pride as tiny villages sported vast church edifices and the noise and chaos of building, rebuilding, and decorating went on, for several hundred years in some places.

The English organ-maker Dallam family, refugees from Cromwell's England and Puritanical strictures against music-making, found a warm welcome for their skills in Brittany. Thomas Dallam had three children in the years it took him to finish the organ at Pleyben, and he died at work in the parish of Guimiliau in 1705. The distinguished twentieth-century English organist Robert Woolley has made recordings on the remaining Dallam organs in Brittany, including those at Guimiliau and Ergue-Gaberic near Quimper.

The closes were very much about community, with everyone contributing to a symbol of salvation that physically dominated each village. Even recently in 1998 solidarity was in action when the *enclos* at St-Thégonnec was badly damaged by fire. A human chain tried to save religious objects at the time, and an association was soon formed to organize a complete restoration of charred remains. The *retable* (altarpiece) of Notre-Dame du Vray-Secours, left a heap of cinders by the conflagration, was completely remade and a copy of Nicolas Poussin's painting of the Assumption ordered.

The parish closes are not mere bastions of conventional Catholicism: on the contrary, they are quintessentially Breton in taste and content. The interiors are illuminated by spectacular altarpieces of fulsome detail, brightly colored and copiously gilded; as the twentieth-century artist and poet Max Jacob said, the Bretons love "le doré." The incredible sumptuousness of decoration was a matter of pride to the rich, and comfort to the poor in contrast with their own circumstances. Breton saints, unrecognized by Rome, are patrons of many churches. At Guimiliau Miliau (the parish of Miliau), a legendary sixth-century local ruler, assassinated by his own brother, is honored. Within the church, his beautiful blue and red altarpiece showing biographical scenes—his wife supporting her headless husband—stands next to that of St Joseph, a Vatican favorite whose veneration came to the fore only in the seventeenth century with the fostering of a cult of the Holy Family. At St-Thégonnec, the eponymous saint was the Welsh monk Coneg, famous for forcing a wolf that ate his stag to take its place pulling a cart of building materials. This story is recalled in the saint's iconography outside and inside the church.

There are decidedly pagan and secular details in the artistic decoration, such as men in hairy tights in the porch at Guimiliau and an odd representation of a babyish face next to a cockerel, probably in reference to a traditional cockfighting title. If the idea was that we leave the pagan world at the door and enter a sacred space inside the church, no one told the sculptors, who took advantage of the height of their work on the string-beams to depict some decidedly irreligious scenes in many churches.

One of the most unusual parish closes is at La Martyre, above the Elorn Valley. The eponymous martyr was in fact a man: King Salomon, who ruled from 857 to 874 when the nascent Breton state was at its height, can be seen inside. Dazzled by the splendor of his garb and golden crown, it takes a moment to notice the dagger hilt protruding from his side. Murdered by his son-in-law, Salomon was in fact "the killer killed" as he himself had murdered his cousin Erispoë to seize the throne.

This early *enclos*, dating from the fifteenth century, is a strangely disturbing spectacle with its wonky entrance porch, complete with a sculpted figure of Mary, now shorn of her revealed breast thanks to a prudish priest. The walkway up beneath the crucifix on the triumphal arch gives a good view over the main street of this tiny village, where in medieval times international fairs were staged. A local legend persists that Shakespeare's father came here to ply his trade in gloves—perhaps with young Will in tow? The playwright was certainly aware of Breton products like cloth from Locronan, referring to a kitchen maid's scarf as a "lockram 'bout her reechy neck" in *Coriolanus* (Act II, Scene I).

Most mysterious of all is a caryatid on the corner of the ossuary. Neither siren nor mummy, despite the bandaged body effect, her connection with the context of death is unknown. Nearby is a Breton inscription that sums up the ethos of the *enclos*: "Death, Judgement and cold Hell—man must tremble when he thinks on these. Foolish he who ignores it, knowing he must die."

## STONE CACOPHONY: VALLÉE DES SAINTS, ART OR THEME-PARK?

The Valley of the Saints is on a hill. This is not the only incongruity of the project, designed to put 1,000 lumpen statues on this beautiful natural site over the next twenty-five years. The granite figures merge in unholy blend two of Brittany's strongest draws, the megaliths and religious heritage: good for tourism and the local economy certainly, worthy factors in the current economic climate, but the claims of cultural and artistic significance are more controversial.

A medieval *motte* crowns a hill giving spectacular views over Côtes d'Armor. I have been several times to follow the progress of these monoliths, my most recent visit in spring with flowers and lush grass reinforcing the sense of a bucolic paradise, the lovely old Chapelle St-Gildas, with its *fontaine* in the valley, looking forward to the emergent soft leaves soon to provide a welcome modesty barrier between the church and its crude army of new neighbors.

The project is organized by an association, with support from the *commune* of Carnoët in whose territory the site lies. It is already attracting many visitors to an attractive area little developed for tourism. The plan is this: chosen sculptors use granite from various quarries in Brittany to create towering statues of the Breton saints whose heritage apparently is in need of such hodgepodge perpetuation. More interestingly, a functional area on site allows visitors to watch the honing of stone when work is in progress.

St Anne and St Yves, the two patron saints of Brittany—one from the Apocrypha, the other a well-documented historical figure from the thirteenth century—start the trail and immediately underline the glaring lack of historicity. The seven founding saints have pride of position in a ring around the *motte* on the highest point, and then a strange smattering of ill-matched holy men and women has begun to dot the southern slopes. There is no sense of order or organization to reflect the long time period involved, the differing places of origin, or any sense of individual significance. Is Miliau, a native Breton ruler, no different from Tugdual's Welsh mother Pompaea or St Clair, a Roman Bishop of Nantes?

There is a single impressive moment in breasting the brow of the hill and seeing the stark outlines raised against a huge sky, but that is a back-view, a fleeting anticipation of abstract sculptural forms. Face to face, the emptiness of these stylized Easter Island mimics is a sad disappointment in many cases. They look remote, not from the world in an aesthetically saint-like kind of way, but from life and their own essentials. Their souls are not at home inside these empty mummy cases of blank expression, freestanding statuary miraculously turned two-dimensional.

This is the greatest incongruity of all: the Breton saints were so incredibly human, so intravenously linked to their own communities, and yet here they stand in mass, stripped of all context, all humanity, and *humanitas*, their individuality reduced to unsubtle iconography. To elevate them to the size and shape of idols, impossible to connect with on a level playing field, is to miss the whole point of their original scale, a crucial factor in their influence on the early settlements.

Is this to be a substitute for the incredibly rich local cultural detail of the saints in almost every community in western Brittany? Like a mini-Tro Breiz achieved by walking around Bishop Du Parc's tomb in Quimper cathedral to save the trouble of a 600-kilometer journey between the seven cathedrals of the founding saints: why not come here instead of going to the actual chapels and *fontaines* connected with the individual saints, and retain the visual mass memory of these unlovely giants of widely variable quality in place of the divine and subtle finesse of statuary from Brittany's Golden Age? It is sobering to think that this epitaph for granite may be how early twenty-first-century art in Brittany is remembered by people of the future. Discovering a parish close from the seventeenth century and then comparing this show, they are going to wonder: what on earth happened?

*Chapter Three*

# THE MARCHES
## FRONTIER TERRITORY

The Marches form the eastern edge of Brittany, a much disputed frontier with France from the flatlands of the Couesnon basin, the shifting border between Brittany and Normandy in the north, to the salt marshes of Brière and the Loire in the south. In between lay castle country, a huge area of wooded hills, plains, and river valleys offering entry to the crucial centers of Nantes and Rennes, today split by long, straight roads that minimize distance. Apart from the great fortresses whose remains still stand, the number of place-names containing *motte* attests to the need for defensive structures in a region of uncertainty and changing fortunes. This is the land gateway to Brittany, source of conflict with the Franks and the French for many hundreds of years.

Today it is a prosperous, well-worked agricultural region, famous for cattle-rearing, but in the formative period of Breton history the two-faced area witnessed a seesaw effect of aggression and defense by both sides. It was then enveloped within the expanding boundary of a nascent Breton state after the triumph at Ballon in 845 and Jengland in 851, but geography alone made close ties with France and the French nobility inevitable, ensuring that the Breton language never got a firm hold. In proximity across the border are Tours, the Metropolitan Roman Catholic see governing the Breton Church, and the powerful political territories of Angers and Laval. Not surprisingly the Marches were to be the scene of the final throes of Breton independence and its demise in 1488 at the hands of Charles VIII, King of France, in the Battle of St-Aubin-du-Cormier.

BORDER COUNTRY: CONFLICT, TRIUMPH, AND DISASTER
Once upon a time the legendary Forêt de Scissy covered the Baie de Mont-St-Michel from Avranches to Brittany, a local tradition claiming this to have been engulfed by a huge tide in the year 709. Remains of oak and birch trees found today in the marshes are adduced as physical evidence to

support the stories, but tests reveal that these date much further back to the end of the prehistoric period. Documents about land clearance from the abbey on the Mont may have been misinterpreted to suggest a great disaster. The many remaining fragments of forest were once part of a great sweep of wooded territory, subject to severe cutback in the medieval period. Convincing arguments are made that the "real" Brocéliande of Arthurian fable lay actually in this lost sylvan world around Dol-de-Bretagne (see p.219). The author Chateaubriand says that in the twelfth century an area extending to Bécherel and Dinan was covered by the "forêt de Brécheliant."

The changing course of the Couesnon River has resulted in disputed "ownership" of one of the top landmarks in France: Mont-St-Michel. A nineteenth-century collection of popular sayings includes:

*Coesnon fit une grand'folie/Mettant le Mont en Normandie*
The river made a big mistake/When it placed the Mont in Normandy

Soon to be an island: Mont St-Michel (Terry Cudbird)

The land in the north around the Bay of Mont St-Michel is notoriously unstable, requiring careful drainage and dyke work to reclaim polders for agricultural use. As early as the twelfth century, Henry II's enquiry into the holdings of the bishopric of Dol mentions dykes and farms on drained land, and fragile conquest of this sea land was more widely achieved in the sixteenth century.

Today it produces cereals, fodder, and salad crops and offers grazing for cattle and sheep, lamb fed on saltwater grass being a noted product of the bay. The marshes or *marais* have shrunk from 3,500 hectares to just 500 with these methods. A sea-dyke runs from the Chapelle de Ste-Anne to Mont St-Michel: outside is the *herbus*, a grassy area under water at high tide, and within are large fields enclosed by banks and ditches in an elaborate drainage system. The old "digue de la Duchesse Anne," built to respond to a disastrous breach of the earliest defenses in 1606, is now a Green Way, snaking across the polders from Les Quatre Salines to the chapel. Walkers and cyclists are glad of the lines of trees protecting the raised path from ferocious winds that flash across these flatlands. A few high points—a beautiful belvedere at Roz-sur-Couesnon, rocky Mont Dol, St-Broladre—provide views over this artificial territory and the bay where work is currently underway to destroy the causeway which inhibits the natural movement of the tidal currents and return the Mont to a real island state with only a low *passerelle* (bridge) connection.

William of Normandy arrived here with an army in 1064 at the request of Rivallon, lord of Dol and Combourg, to attack Conan, Duke of Brittany, who was besieging his fortress at Dol. There was trouble, however, in crossing the Couesnon, as the Bayeux tapestry records in graphic illustration with the caption: *Hic Harold dux trahebat eos de arena.* It was Harold of all people, on campaign with William just two years before his own demise at Hastings, who had to drag the beleaguered Normans out of the deadly sands.

William pressed on to Rennes before other matters took over his attention. The most lasting consequence of his brief appearance in the Armorican Peninsula was that many Breton nobles went with him across the Channel on the expedition of 1066 and were rewarded for their prowess and support with lands in England. Richmond in Yorkshire went to the Penthièvres, and Ashby-de-la-Zouche gets it curious name from the La Zouche family. In fact the Stuart dynasty of Scotland owes its ancestry to

Alan Fitzflaad, a noble from Dol-de-Bretagne made official "steward" in the north, who went over to Britain soon after William's successful bid for the crown.

It was the Marches farther south that saw the main movements of struggle between Bretons and Franks. From the moment the Merovingian kings showed an interest in western expansion, this zone became a bone of territorial contention, especially in the rough triangle between Nantes, Rennes, and Vannes. At this time different parts of the Armorican Peninsula were ruled by separate leaders, the main territories being Léon in the northwest, Cornouaille in the southwest, Domnonée in the north, and Bro-Waroc. The latter was the region around Vannes which came under the control of Breton leader Waroc in the second half of the sixth century (Broërec or Bro-Waroc means the territory of Waroc). But he had bigger plans and was soon pushing eastward, with plundering raids that drove the Franks to fury. Gregory, Bishop of Tours, is a major source for this hectic, violent period in his *Historia Francorum* (*History of the Franks*). He had jurisdiction over the Bishops of Nantes and Rennes, both towns then under the control of the Franks. He writes:

> In this year (579) the Bretons attacked Nantes and Rennes. They grabbed a huge amount of plunder, devastated the fields, seized the grape-harvest and captured many locals.

In the latter case, representations were made to the Bretons for restitution, but although promises were made, nothing came of it. Waroc's favorite tactic was to make an agreement when the heat was on and then ignore it.

> Waroc quickly forgot his oath and the pledge he'd made. He did not fulfil any of his promises. He seized all the vineyards, picked the grapes and carried the wine back to Vannes.

The Franks' reprisals consisted of extensive burning of Breton lands. Gregory tells us that Duke Beppolen was in charge of this punishment, but it only succeeded in stirring up the Bretons further. Vannes changed hands several times as Waroc was forced out and then forced his way back in.

Childebert as King of the Franks seems to have managed to remain on reasonable terms with the various Breton rulers (see Conomor, p.132), and St Samson of Dol-de-Bretagne visited him in Paris. His son Dagobert made a treaty with Judicaël, King of Domnonée, in 638, so the Marches enjoyed a brief period of peace and stability.

With the Carolingian dynasty controlling the Franks' empire, things became more organized. Pepin the Short determined to resume expansionist policies obscured by a century of Merovingian infighting. He established the Marches as a buffer zone in the mid-eighth century, supporting the authority of the Counts of Vannes, which he had taken, Rennes and Nantes, the latter being the base of the official in charge. Charlemagne continued the policy. The hero of *The Song of Roland* was Prefect of the Marches before his tragic demise in the campaign at Roncevaux. The story that he was Charlemagne's own nephew confirms the strategic important of this border territory, where armed impetus and reaction were equally important.

In the ninth century, the pendulum swung back. Louis Le Pieux, son of Charlemagne, waged two campaigns in Brittany against the leader Morvan from Langonnet before he saw the futility of guerrilla-style warfare, which suited the sinuous landscape and tough mentality of the Bretons. He decided to entrust the care of the region to a Breton, Nominoë, a Count of the Poher (see Chapter Six), who from c. 831 was *missus imperatoris*, the emperor's representative. As long as Louis lived, the arrangement was maintained without any conflict, although Nominoë's encouragement of the building of the new abbey at Redon when official sanction was reserved shows a willingness to go his own way.

With the weakened empire of the Franks following Louis' death in 840 and a divided inheritance putting Charles the Bald in charge in the west (but busily engaged in struggles with his siblings), the stage was set for the Marches to play a strong role in Brittany's development. Nominoë was now hell-bent on pushing out the frontiers of Breton territory, ready to secure the Marches once and for all. He had a willing ally in Lambert of Nantes, who held a grudge from the deprivation of his inheritance there as count. In 843 Nominoë was deep in the Franks' territory near Le Mans and his aggression could not be ignored for much longer. Charles the Bald, however, was a lesser man than his father. He underestimated the resources and determination of the Bretons, confident of a swift military demon-

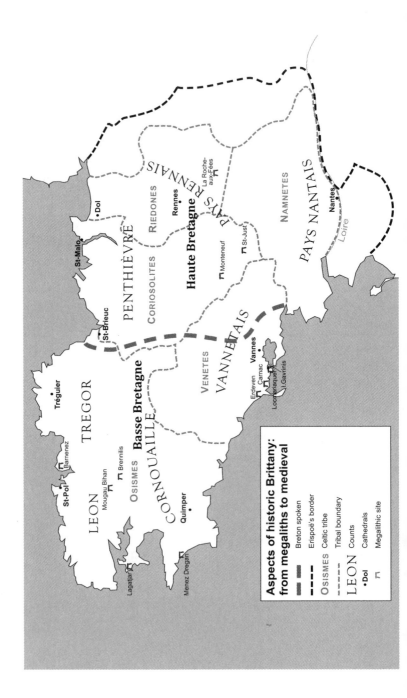

## Aspects of historic Brittany: from megaliths to medieval

| | Breton spoken |
| --- | --- |
| | Erispoë's border |
| OSISMES | Celtic tribe |
| | Tribal boundary |
| LEON | Counts |
| •Dol | Cathedrals |
| ⌐ | Megalithic site |

TREGOR

LEON

CORNOUAILLE

OSISMES

Basse Bretagne

PENTHIÈVRE

CORIOSOLITES

RIEDONES

Haute Bretagne

PAYS RENNAIS

NAMNETES

PAYS NANTAIS

VENETES

VANNETAIS

Tréguier

St-Pol

Barnenez

Mougau Bihan

Brennilis

Quimper

Lagatjar

Menez Dregan

St-Brieuc

St-Malo

Dol

Rennes

La Roche-
aux-Fées

Monteneuf

St-Just

Nantes

Loire

Erdeven

Camac

Vannes

Locmariaquer

I.Gavrinis

stration of supremacy. In 845 at Ballon, near Bains-sur-Oust, he was humiliatingly defeated in a two-day engagement by the swift agility of the Breton cavalry against his heavy infantry in marshy conditions well-known by his opponents.

The exact site of the battle is not known, but by the hamlet called La Bataille stands a memorial put there in 1983 by the Association Bretagne which quotes the words of Arthur de La Borderie (see p.80), the great nineteenth-century historian who was the first to give Nominoë his starring role in Breton history: "The old saints founded the Breton people. Nominoë made them into a nation."

In fact this was not the greatest victory against the Franks, and control of the Marches was not secured until 851 when Nominoë's son Erispoë defeated Charles at Jengland (Beslé) and forced a treaty in which he was acknowledged as King of Brittany, the first to hold that title, and ruler of lands from Mont St-Michel to Angers and the Loire.

Viking threats began as early as 843 when Nantes was sacked, with wholesale slaughter in the cathedral as Bishop Gohard was conducting mass. Raids took place all around the Breton coasts, but even inland sites on navigable rivers were not safe: Redon was attacked in 868 and Rennes itself seven years later. Many religious orders and important landowners anticipating destruction took their valuables and ran. Many fled to France, and their later return, when they were used to speaking French, had negative implications in the east, effectively preventing any expansion of the Breton language into new areas accrued by Nominoë and his successors. Later Viking expeditions may well have been seeking land for settlement, with some sites, like a camp near St-Suliac on the Rance, occupied for half a century. The Marches saw an important victory over the Vikings at Trans-la-Forêt near Dol-de-Bretagne in 939. The victor was Alain BarbeTorte, who ruled as Duke of a Brittany independent of France until his death in 952.

Alain had grown up in the English court, sent there for safety from Viking threats. These cross-Channel connections were increasingly important: Henry II Plantagenet was to be drawn, albeit willingly, into Brittany by Conan, who had been in England and received the dukedom of Richmond. On his return to Brittany as Duke Conan IV he soon needed the help of his powerful patron against a noble opponent, the lord of Fougères. Henry saw clearly the strategic advantage of controlling the northwest corner of the continent in his dispute with the French kings and came himself to teach the unruly Breton barons a lesson. An early version of the château of Fougères was destroyed in 1166, its stone base still visible inside the later fortress. Henry's son Geoffrey was established as duke by virtue of his marriage with Constance, daughter of Conan. This English influence in Brittany was a thorn in the side of the French and many Bretons. In the struggles for control after Henry's death, Geoffrey's son Arthur was murdered by the future King John (Lackland) of England. Philippe-Auguste, first of the French Capétien dynasty in Paris, was quick to take advantage of a power vacuum.

Pierre de Dreux, cousin of the King of France, became Duke of Brittany in 1213 through marriage and spent the next couple of decades trying to assert his position either against powerful Breton border nobles or with their support in political intrigues with England against France. He built the castle at St-Aubin-du-Cormier in 1225 to bolster his position against the lords of Fougères and Vitré as well as to protect the eastern frontier.

By the mid-thirteenth century, the main routes into Brittany were covered by a series of castles right across the Marches: Dinan, Combourg, Fougères, St-Aubin-du-Cormier, Vitré, Châteaugiron, La Guerche, Chateaubriand, Guérande, Ancenis. Facing them in French territory were Avranches, Mayenne, Laval, Pouancé, Angers and Champtoceaux among many others. These edifices were the physical embodiment of the tense, watchful profile of this border country.

The boundary of the Marches is impossible to define clearly. The River Sélune was the border between Brittany and Normandy around the year 1000 CE before the Couesnon further west took that role. Smaller streams marked the division elsewhere, or even special trees and rocks, with local traditions reflecting the politicization of the landscape. The Roche-au-Diable at La Potelais near Coglès is a formation of large stones standing across the trickle of the Tronçon, now the departmental border of Ille-et-Vilaine and Manche, an unmarked spot of remarkable atmosphere which has attracted a grotto and chapel above. There was also talk of a stone in the Couesnon with the arms of France engraved on one side and those of Brittany on the other. The *ruisseau français*, or "French stream," an affluent of the Airon, has borne that name since 1204 when the French King Philippe Auguste annexed Normandy.

The fourteenth century was a time of turmoil for much of Europe, all of Brittany and the Marches with their accessibility in particular. The Hundred Years' War and its contingent Wars of Succession for the Duchy of Brittany brought the menace of rapacious mercenaries, widespread destruction of property and crops and violent death to many thousands of people. English troops sent in support of Jean de Montfort's claim as duke in the main phase of the war were involved in numerous military actions. This also explains his serious unpopularity with many Breton nobles, and that of his son who became Duke Jean IV after the final victory at Auray in 1364. The great Breton soldier Bertrand du Guesclin from Broons near Dinan rose to the position of *connétable*—or commander-in-chief—of the French king's army. When Jean IV fled to England in 1373, the French saw a chance to seize Brittany. Du Guesclin was sent on a mission to regain strongholds in the Marches lost to the English. Châteaugiron fell in that year, to be followed by Rennes, Fougères, Dinan, and Guérande, before Jean IV returned to secure his position.

The Montfort dynasty held on for 125 years without significant challenge to the succession. François II, father of Anne de Bretagne, was not a popular duke during his thirty-year rule, especially with the high Breton nobility. Fearful of their motives he replaced them in his confidence and high offices with low-born men like Pierre Landais, a merchant's son from Vitré, and French allies, which openly exacerbated the simmering resentments. The French King Louis XI, greedy to take over Brittany, was only too keen to buy the allegiance of powerful Bretons with promises of position and pensions before his death in 1483.

In March 1487 sixty Breton nobles, thoroughly dissatisfied by the behavior and alliances of François II, decided to call on the Regent of France, Anne de Beaujeu, who was holding the kingdom for her young son Charles VIII. A spirited French campaign followed, with Dol, Vitré, La Guerche, and St-Aubin-du-Cormier falling to the French. Their commander Louis de la Trémoille, aged only twenty-eight, led as many as 11,000 battle-hardened troops, including a top quality Swiss contingent several thousand strong. Renewed French initiative saw Chateaubriand fall in April and Ancenis the following month. After a brief lull and more defections by Bretons to the French side, the last throw of the dice came in 1488.

The mighty fortress of Fougères was taken by the French on 19 July, and François II decided to counter this with an attempt to retake St-Aubin-du-Cormier. Nine days later the showdown took place on the gorsy plain just west of the town now called La Lande de la Rencontre. On the side of Brittany was Louis d'Orléans, future King of France and husband of Anne de Bretagne, but no response to the plea for support came from Henry VII of England or Maximilien, the Austrian emperor. The Breton cause lacked allies, numbers, and weaponry.

It was all over in a few hours, with almost 6,000 killed on the Breton side, and fewer than 1,500 on the French. Many of the dead were buried on site in the Bois d'Uzel. Among those lost was the future hope of one of the greatest Breton families, François de Rohan, son of the most implacable enemy of François II. As a result of this disastrous battle, the duke was forced to agree to the Treaty of Guérande, by which he could not arrange marriages for his two daughters without French agreement—this was ultimately to lead to the marriage of Anne to two French kings (not at the same time), and her own daughter yielding the duchy of Brittany to union with France in 1532.

Late-nineteenth-century interest in Breton history and nationalism brought new emphasis to the battle of St-Aubin-du-Cormier and it has become a shrine to the loss of independence and a focus of nationalistic sentiment. Visits today may be accompanied by a surreal symphony of cascading gunfire from army exercises on the military training ground which now places most of La Lande de la Recontre out of bounds, but there are two memorials to mark the significance of the site. A formal monument was placed in 1988 beside the main road (D794) for the 500th anniversary, with inscriptions to honor all those—including a contingent of English archers (probably from the Isle of Wight)—who fought for the Breton cause or, at least, on the side of the Duke of Brittany. The earlier memorial further into the Bois d'Uzel directly behind is much the more moving of the two, for its secretive location and simplicity, just a metal plaque fixed on the rocky outcrop which is surmounted by a plain cross.

There is a discrepancy between the actuality of this battle and its symbolic value in Breton nationalism, where it is seen as the moment when Breton independence came to an end. Many Breton nobles, including the Duke de Rohan, fought on the side of the French king and against the continuing hold on power of the Montfort dukes. François had the aid of two French princes contesting the authority of the French Regent, German mercenaries, troops from Gascony, and those English archers. Self-interest was the motivating force on both sides, the desire for power and influence, for what was seen as a hegemony of birthright by many of the Breton nobility, and their irrevocable entwinement with the French. Nationalism would have been an anachronism. François II himself was more French than Breton.

The following year the castle of St-Aubin-du-Cormier was semi-dismantled, that is to say, cut in half vertically, a dramatic sight today like a gaping wound with a huge fireplace standing bereft on the upper level. It is said that the ruined half faces west and Brittany, while the wall still standing is toward the east and France. Another symbol on a field already littered with them, a heroic fallen building among the many border castles that were as much participants in war as the men who strove to defend or destroy them.

## FOUGÈRES: LOVE, WAR, AND LITERATURE

> "Everywhere mountains of schist rise like an amphitheatre, ruddy faces disguised by woods of oak and dales full of freshness hidden by their slopes. These rocks form a vast enclosure, circular in appearance, at the bottom of which rolls an immense meadow designed like an English garden…"
>
> Honoré de Balzac, *Les Chouans*, 1829

Fougères and its memorable setting, almost characters in one of Balzac's novels, form a historic center of two halves: the ancient settlement in the valley of the Nançon and the eighteenth-century High Town perched way above, with the famously imposing château hovering somewhere in between. It is a strange sensation to look down on a castle of this magnitude, a perspective offered from the terrace of the park by the church of St-Leonard. Balzac wrote:

> There is a spot from where one can take in both part of the circle formed by a great valley and the pretty meanders of the little river that merges into its depth. This place, chosen by the inhabitants for their strolls, was precisely the theatre where the drama… was resolved.

The main streets of the High Town, rue Nationale and rue Chateaubriand (the eponymous writer used to visit his sisters here), are packed with beautifully balanced façades and windows adorned with ornate ironwork balconies. The old Porch house containing a museum dedicated to native impressionist painter Emmanuel de la Villéon, is something of a fossil remnant of the timer-framed medieval town before the great fire of 1710, but local pride of place goes to the Beffroi tower, built in 1397, although much reworked since, and evinced as symbolic of mercantile wealth.

After the French Revolution, Fougères was at the heart of anti-Revolutionary activity at all levels of society. Both Balzac and Victor Hugo used the town as a basis of research for their novels on that turbulent period. Balzac describes the area as "one of the most redoubtable centers of *chouannerie.*" The monarchist Catholic Chouans, a name said to derive from the owl call that was their signal, were strong in numbers in this area, which became the scene of repeated armed struggles with the new Republicans.

A statue created in 1993 in honor of Armand Tuffin, Marquis de La Rouërie, stands outside the Hôtel de la Bélinaye in place Aristide Briand, where he was born in 1751. This courageous and unusual aristocrat went to America—where he was known as Colonel Armand—to fight in the War of Independence, participating in the Battle of Yorktown and becoming a friend of George Washington. Back in Europe, he was one of a Breton deputation sent to Paris in 1788 to protest against edicts limiting the powers of the Parlement de Bretagne, arguing that these contravened the Treaty of Union between Brittany and France. The king refused to grant an audience and the deputation's members were subsequently arrested and imprisoned in the Bastille for more than a month before liberation and return home as heroes.

For all his liberal support for independence in America, La Rouërie remained a convinced monarchist in France, writing to George Washington that he feared "two great evils for this country: anarchy and despotism." He was also totally opposed to the civil oath for the clergy, the decree that did most to turn Bretons from the emergent Republic. In 1791 he founded the Association Bretonne, an aristocratic royalist group to raise anti-Revolutionary support in Brittany. One of his rallying cries illustrates his appeal to defend a fast vanishing past: "Bretons! You must recover your old privileges and your ancient rights, the bulwark of your liberty!"

In the same year he met Chateaubriand, who was off to America, and gave him a letter of introduction to George Washington. The writer has left a memorable description of the marquis: "He used to rummage about the woods in Brittany with an American major, and accompanied by a monkey sitting behind the saddle of his horse."

La Rouërie was eventually betrayed to the Republican army and had to flee from his home before soldiers arrived. After a time on the run, he went into hiding at the Château de la Guyomarais in Côtes-du-Nord, where he died of a fever. His body was buried secretly in the grounds and his death hushed up. When it became known, a relentless search by his enemies saw the corpse exhumed and decapitated.

There are various ways of passing from the High Town of Fougères into the valley far below, the scene of the town's main industrial activities, including the manufacture of shoes in recent times. The rue du Pinterie, the name itself evidence of a former pewter industry, descends steadily to the only remaining town-gate and the main castle entrance. Behind it is a more evocative footpath with views over the Nançon Valley gardens and the wittily sculpted hedge on the opposite height in the shape of battlements. An alternative route at the far end of the main street connects the

Fougères: finest fortress (Wendy Mewes)

two more steeply from below the Hôtel de Ville, a notable structure where the receptionist sits in a twelfth-century vaulted room, via the Escaliers de la Duchesse Anne, or as Balzac calls it, Escalier de la Reine—for Anne was also Queen of France twice over.

On the valley floor are the narrow winding streets of the medieval center around the place du Marchix. Little alleyways and bridges twist to and fro over the River Nançon and offer a footpath up to the Butte à Bigot for views of the fortress and Upper Town. The church of St-Sulpice beside the castle has a shrine to Our Lady of the Marshes, whose statue was found in the earth when the church was being extended, said to have been thrown there by the English soldiers of Henry II in the twelfth century.

Dominating the scene then as now was the château, a huge, formidable, gray stronghold ringed by menacing towers which represent the development of defensive works during the Middle Ages—"these magnificent medieval remains," as Balzac puts it. Only a stone base remains of the first (wooden) donjon, which may be that razed by Henry II during his destructive passage in 1166. The earliest round towers—the Tour des Gobelins and Tour Mélusine—in the same northwest corner date from the twelfth to the fourteenth centuries and form the final line of defense. Their compact triangular enclosure was separated from the massive inner court around the *logis* and wells, a space large enough to allow shelter for the town's inhabitants. In the fifteenth century Duke François II built two towers here in the new horseshoe shape designed to withstand heavy artillery, although his defeat by the French in 1488 soon made them redundant. At the eastern end is a heavily fortified outer court, which could be sealed off and flooded under enemy attack. The whole is one of the most impressive sights in Brittany, as Victor Hugo noted in a letter to his wife: "I am now in Fougères, in a town which ought to be visited religiously by artists, in a town which has an ancient château flanked by the finest old towers in the world..."

The castle had a crucial role to play in defending the Marches of Brittany during the struggles between Brittany and France, but it was also to witness a ferocious battle between Republicans and anti-Revolutionaries in November 1793. Fougères was on the route to St-Malo, a strategic target for the Chouans anxious to gain a port with access to Britain. A scratch Republican force failed to halt their advance and subsequently lost control of the château where a sizeable number of Chouan prisoners were incarcerated.

One Republican soldier described how he was treated on capture by the royalists:

> They wanted me to fight with them. When I refused to march against my own side, they sent me to the castle, where I stayed until Wednesday evening. They gave me a document… after making me promise that I would not fight against them again and making me shout "Long Live the King!" I did this in order to save my life because otherwise they would have shot me.

After pillaging and burning parts of the town, the new occupying force remained in the stronghold for only four days before going on, not as planned to St-Malo, but toward Granville in Normandy. There was to be a gory aftermath in Fougères: when the Republican army arrived soon after, they massacred all the sick and wounded male and female Chouans who had been left behind in the town's hospital.

Honoré de Balzac (1799–1850), one of France's great men of letters, was something of a Jack-of-all-trades in the literary world, producing romantic poetry, historical novels, gritty realism, and even dabbling with fantasy. He came to Fougères in 1828 in search of a setting for an already conceived novel about the Chouans and the Vendée uprising. He was looking in effect for a blockbuster to improve his ailing fortunes despite an already prodigious output of novels written under pseudonyms. This goal would be achieved by combining themes of social and political issues in post-Revolutionary France with a romance of intrigue between individuals on opposing sides in the conflict, "Le Gars," leader of the Chouans (actually the young Marquis de Montauran) and Marie de Verneuil, a Republican spy sent by Joseph Fouché, minister of the police, to seduce and betray him.

Making use of a family connection with the Baron de Pommereul, actual owner of the château at Fougères, Balzac came to stay with Gilbert de Pommereul in the house that today houses the presbytery, not far from the church of St-Leonard in the place Lariboisière. He spent a month in research, went back to Paris and published *Les Chouans* in the following year. It was to be the first volume in his major body of work given the overall title *La Comédie Humaine*.

The first section of the book, The Ambush, takes place in the vicinity of Fougères, as the Blues (Republicans), escorting Breton conscripts, advance from the Pellerine, a summit today on the border of Ille-et-Vilaine and Mayenne:

> The commander marched at the back, constantly looking behind him,
> so as to observe the smallest changes of this scene which nature made so
> exquisite and man so terrible.

They are attacked by a band of Chouans who rescue the conscripts, including the mysterious Marche-à-Terre, epitome of Balzac's lurid presentation of the semi-savage peasants fighting to save their way of life. He describes these men as dressed in goat-skin with their long matted locks concealing their faces so the animal hair could be mistaken for their own: "But through this hair one could soon see their eyes shining like drops of dew in a smooth green pasture."

Even great writers have their off days. Analysis not surprisingly takes second place to the atmospheric narrative and individual experience in what is after all a novel and not a political document. When the carriage driver Coupiau is asked by one passenger if he is a Chouan, he replies: "Not one thing nor the other. I'm a coachman and what's more a Breton. From that, I fear neither Blues nor gentlemen."

Chouan: defending the faith, 1795 (private collection)

The fixed polarization of the two sides is only occasionally relieved by a sense of ordinary lives still pursued outside the boiling cauldron of violence and bigotry. The plot, like all good spy stories, is full of misunderstandings, deception, and betrayal, whereas the romantic relationship of Marie and Le Gars is well used to illustrate the intensification of emotions under the stress of politically extreme circumstances and the constant threat of death. They are doomed, of course, to a bitter end. The landscape remains crucial to the atmosphere of the novel, setting the physical and emotional context of the Chouans who blend in and out of the concealing woods and rocks like shadowy phantoms.

The town of Fougères and its surroundings, full of twists and turns, made an immediate impression on the author. The public gardens with their sensational views over the oldest quarters and quarries were used for key scenes in the novel under the name La Promenade, with characters lurking in the mist and sounds echoing unnaturally between the heights and depths joined by winding stone steps. From here Marie glimpses the object of her affections across the valley; here also was the Tour Papegaut, a square stone structure on which was built the house where the heroine lodged. The "Château de la Vivetière," headquarters of the Chouan leaders, was possibly partly based on the extraordinary castle laid out before the visitor's gaze from this very park, although the Château de Marigny to the north of Fougères may be a closer model.

Fougères certainly made its mark on Balzac. He kept in contact with his host, who must have been dismayed to receive a letter from the author in April 1831 stating his intention of returning to the town to stand for election as a deputy: "you know my principles and will be there for me... like a veritable father you could serve as my patron before the voters." This was no time for tact. The baron said plainly that he doubted the locals would take kindly to a candidate from Paris. That seems to have been the end of Balzac's intimacy with Fougères.

Victor Hugo's attachment to Fougères was a more personal one. His mistress Juliette Drouet was a native of the town, born there in 1806 and brought up by her uncle Jean-Baptiste Drouet after her parents' death. In Paris she became the model and mistress of the sculptor James Pradier, with whom she had a child. She was performing on the stage in 1831 when she met Hugo, already an established literary celebrity. It was a relationship that would last throughout their lives.

The couple spent time together in Fougères in 1836, arriving at their hotel on 22 June. Within hours Hugo was making sketches of church gargoyles and the château's fortifications. They walked extensively, especially in the forest of Fougères where her mother's family had a farm. Hugo was much taken with the town, writing enthusiastically to the painter Louis Boulanger of its distinctive form:

> You really must see Fougères. Imagine a spoon: the bowl is the château, the handle is the town. Onto the castle, which is overwhelmed by greenery, place seven towers, all different in form and height and all the original article; on the handle of my spoon, heap up an inextricable complication of towers and turrets, of old medieval walls topped by thatched cottages, stepped gables, steep roofs, stone-traceried windows, fretted balconies, crenellations, terraced gardens…

The visit to Fougères was part of the inspiration for Hugo's novel *Quatre-vingt-treize*, published in 1874, a wide-ranging text about the rival values at stake in the Revolution, and Chouan activity in western France during the Revolution's nadir, the years of the Terror. The Marquis de Lantenac represents the royalists, his nephew Gauvain the forces of progress, a fervent, idealistic supporter of the nascent Republic. Some critics see a connection with Gawain and Arthurian chivalric values in the young man, but his name is that of Juliette Drouet's original family. Another chillier dimension is added by Gauvain's tutor Cimourdian, a former priest turned remorseless and implacable Republican, who sees the Revolution only as a clinical mission. The symbolic conflict of two ways of life takes place in the siege of La Tourgue, "a stone monster" of a tower probably based on Fougères castle's Tour Mélusine but displaced to the edge of the forest for dramatic purposes. Here the Blues besiege the Chouans and take the tower, but Gauvain, whose political opinions are tempered by *humanitas*, decides to spare his uncle's life. For this he is condemned to death himself, the casting vote given by his own mentor. The guillotine is set up at La Tourgue and Gauvain goes to his death with the words "Vive la République" on his lips. Cimourdian witnesses the fatal blow and then shoots himself.

Fougères and its striking setting played an integral part in these literary works, even if most of their action is not situated in the town. The different levels of physical geography make it an ideal theatrical context for the diverse scenes of warring ambitions and desires, an essential backdrop for the clash of cultures played out during early years of the Republic and the Breton backlash it provoked.

Let the last words, despite their historic futility, go to local hero of this resistance, the Marquis de la Rouërie, whose statue in the town bears the modern inscription "Defender of Breton Identity":

> I am only taking up arms to defend you and your properties. And Bretons, my dear friends, I want to help you recover your ancient liberties and those ancient rights which were both the most solid defence of your political and religious liberty, and the surest guarantee of the peace of the region and the prosperity this has produced.

## COMBOURG: THE INVENTION OF BOREDOM, A RAMBLING WOODEN LEG, AND SCARY DEAD CATS

> "In the woods of Combourg, I became who I am."
>
> Chateaubriand

Although born and buried in St-Malo, François-René de Chateaubriand (1768–1848), high priest of French Romanticism, remains an eternal child of Combourg thanks to his early experiences of living at the château, recounted at the end of his life in a vast autobiographical work, *Mémoires d'outre-tombe*. In Volume I he describes his arrival at Combourg for the first time—"I still remember the moment when I entered the shade of the avenue and the terrifying joy I felt"—and the increasing hold the place exercised over his imagination. After several school holiday visits, he was to pass a lonely and tormented two years there between the ages of sixteen and eighteen.

Combourg today is an idyllic little spot, the solid castle on an eminence overlooking the lake to which Chateaubriand gave its epithet *tranquille*, streets lined by the handsome architecture of a prosperous late medieval bourgeoisie: the Relais des Princes, a sixteenth-century, half-timbered, former staging post, is a reminder that Combourg was on the main routes to Rennes, Fougères, Dol, and Dinan; La Maison de la Lanterne, built in 1597 in Renaissance style, its name referring to the function of watchmen who kept order on the many market and fair days; and La Maison des Templiers, complete with courtyard on a former Knights Templar site.

The château was built originally in the eleventh century as a means of defense for the lands of the cathedral at Dol-de-Bretagne. The bishop there set up his brother Rivallon as the earliest lord, an event commemorated in the nineteenth-century interior decoration. The castle's lopsided, square-turreted form is shaped, as Chateaubriand later said, like a cart with four wheels. He also recalled the façade as sad and severe, clear architectural evidence that its purpose was first a military one, and he states its role: "Combourg defended Brittany in the marches." Although the moat was filled in long before the author's time and the drawbridge replaced by a monumental exterior stair, the thickness of the walls, the crenellated *chemin du ronde*, and arrow-slits all attest to a function unconnected with comfortable habitation. The boy Chateaubriand reveled in the castle atmosphere, its passages and secret staircases, dungeons, labyrinth of galleries, and mysterious underground reaches. Everywhere silence, darkness, and a face of stone: "voilà le château de Combourg." The original keep, the Tour du Maure (Moor), on the north face dates from the thirteenth century, linked in the fifteenth with the Tour du Croisé, while the southern wing developed during the fourteenth. This added the Tour Sybil and the Tour du Chat, so vividly memorable from Chateaubriand's account.

His childhood bedroom was in this latter tower, reached in those days by the turret staircase from the internal courtyard. "I had my nest up in a sort of isolated cell," he wrote, and described how he used to revel in summer storms when rain battered the tower and lightning flared across the night sky. It is certainly a Spartan space, dim and remote, now with the histrionic addition of a mummified cat in a glass case, found during the renovations. It was common medieval practice to bury a cat, symbolizing the Devil, in the wall-cavity of a new build to ward off evil, but there is a connection with a famous legend of the castle. It was said that the ghost of a previous owner, the Marquis de Coëtquen, haunted the premises, often in the form of his wooden leg which had a tendency to tap-tap itself down the staircase at night accompanied by a black cat.

Chateaubriand himself claimed an ancestral connection with the Coëtquen owners of Combourg in the sixteenth century, but the château actually came into the Chateaubriand family in 1761, bought by the

Seat of the Romantic imagination: Combourg (Calips/Wikimedia Commons)

author's father René-Auguste who had restored the financial fortunes of the family as a prosperous St-Malo-based ship-owner or *armateur*, trading with the West Indies. The *Mémoires* laboriously outline the ancient nobility of the family, whose name was originally written Brien, or Brient/Briand. The first eleventh-century ancestor was lord of a large castle in the Marches of Brittany in a strategically important position between Nantes and Rennes. When a settlement grew up around this defensive point, it took the name Chateaubriand. Both town and château still exist, although technically outside Brittany in Loire-Atlantique today. In the following centuries three distinct branches of the Chateaubriand lineage appear, with the Beaufort/Guérande dynasties relating to the author.

He describes the great state of confusion of claims of nobility in the seventeenth century and Louis XIV's attempts to sort it out with a definitive etiquette. In 1669 this confirmed that "Christophe de Chateaubriand, lord of Guérande... issue of ancient nobility... is permitted to take the rank of knight."

The writer's father set great store by the family's rank—"one sole passion possessed my father, that of his name"—and in the whole history of the Chateaubriand family we see all the pride and problems of the Breton *petite noblesse*: the falls in fortune from one generation to the next, the complex division of rent incomes between siblings, the marriage market, and the cost of maintaining vast properties like the château at Combourg. His father's exhortation at their final interview was to behave like a man and never dishonor the family name, but Chateaubriand himself claimed to prefer his own personal name to the title of viscount.

Chateaubriand was born during a terrible a storm at St-Malo on 4 September, date of the great annual Fête de L'Angevine in Combourg, which continues in the town to this day. "At least once a year, you can see something resembling joy at Combourg," he later wrote. He saw himself "like the last witness of feudal customs," observing the behavior of his father's vassals arriving at the château, carrying arms, and ready to raise the lord's banner. The viscount stood on his rights as lord of the domain at Combourg, with tenants and dependents held strictly to their duties. They had to keep order during the fair and the cattle market as crowds wandered everywhere, through the gardens and woods. His son remembers these peasants in their clogs and country-style trousers participating in traditional games, "men of a France that exists no longer," when he was writing long after the Revolution.

Chateaubriand senior was a silent, severe man: "The gloomy calm of the Château of Combourg was increased by the taciturnity and unsociability of my father." A telling scene in the *Mémoires* has the young François-René and his sister Lucile constrained from whispering in a corner for fear of attracting the attention of their father, who paced metronomically around the huge salon after dinner, appearing on each circuit out of the gloom like a ghost. As soon as he had left the room, brother and sister and their mother, a vivacious and highly imaginative woman who hated the château, began to chatter in sheer relief before going off, terrified by thoughts of their haunted home, to bed in lonely rooms. On other occasions, after yet another dinner in total silence, Chateaubriand would have to go outside and rush about the grounds, running, jumping, and gambolling about in an excess of emotion. Despite describing his father's habitual state as "a profound sadness," he felt some instinct for the man behind the manners after his death. Treatment that had seemed harsh and unfeeling at the time in retrospect looked more like lessons in courage, with the unwitting benefit of a spur to his highly colored imagination.

There was little in common between the two men in character and interests.

It was the serious, religiously intense Lucile who was the beloved companion of Chateaubriand's time at Combourg. In the grounds she would become fixed in spiritual contemplation before a rough stone cross that still stands a little distance from the monumental staircase. Her suggestion that he should capture the spirit of the place that became their imaginative world was the first impetus he had towards self-expression, but in words rather than paint. It was the wooded land of the castle that was the scene of self-discovery, the ecstatic combination of solitude and wild imagination, melancholy and passion, for the writer. Here he developed the fantasies of his ideal woman—an amalgam of real and legendary heroines and deities—and constantly imagined himself in the company of this goddess, the château grounds becoming Venice or Rome or Athens, Jerusalem or Carthage in such idylls.

As the prototype Romantic figure, Chateaubriand is credited with giving form to and verbalizing that state of teenage angst, of ecstasy teamed with *ennui* and interspersed with a maudlin frisson of despair and instinct for self-destruction—"this sadness which has been my torment and my happiness," as he put it. The intensity of his fluctuating emotions is played out in the château and its environs. Supper in the Salle des Gardes on their arrival "finished for me the first happy day of my life." The following day, exploration of the grounds celebrated "my accession to solitude," that essential mood of Romanticism, and provided the perks of nature—birds, trees, and weather—so vital to the yearnings of the Romantic soul. Later he was to toy with killing himself with a gun on the grounds he loved so much.

Chateaubriand went on to extraordinary things: from Combourg to the life of a Romantic hero, with travel to America and later the Near East, an impoverished exile in England serving a traditional apprenticeship for writers by starving in a garret in Holborn, dashing public roles as ambassador abroad in Sweden and London, literary triumphs, amorous highs and lows, political hopes and disillusions. A final fall from grace with his opposition to the new monarchy of 1830 gave him the time and concentration to return to his memoirs, largely written in seclusion at his retreat called the "Valley of Wolves" near Paris. With that came a reliving of those formative years in Combourg.

Here he remembers every detail of the décor, the furniture, and the paintings he knew as a boy there, although all that remained in his possession through the years was one canvas from the castle chapel, *La Sainte Famille* by Francesco Albani. In 1786, on the death of Chateaubriand senior, ownership of the château passed to Jean-Baptiste, the eldest son. Chateaubriand himself went to America in 1791, taking a last brief look at Combourg before departure. He found the place abandoned and had to call upon the manager, but it proved too painful to pursue a visit as he looked along the avenue toward the deserted outside stair, where once the family sat silently in early evening, his father taking shots at owls emerging from the woods. He left the village in the middle of the night to avoid more harrowing memories.

When Jean-Baptiste and his wife were guillotined in 1794, the property was seized and pillaged, before being restored to the dead owner's eldest son who was only seven and never visited again. The estate fell into disuse and ill-repair: such was its condition when another great luminary of French literature, Gustave Flaubert, visited on his tour of Brittany in the company of Maxime du Camp in 1847.

An account of their travels was published later, usually called *Par les champs et par les grèves*. The great French novelist was then only twenty-six and more of a young Romantic than the realist he was to become. Nature and landscape are described in minute detail, the setting of the castle at Combourg as significant as the building itself, in a state of sad neglect at that time. As the manager was not available to take them round, it fell to his assistant to escort the two young men. This man brought his dog along, puffed away at his pipe throughout the tour, and spat on the floor at regular intervals. Flaubert likened the lack of light in the internal courtyard to that of a prison exercise yard. He noted that the coat of arms over the fireplace had been smashed. Nothing here to conjure up the infant François-René.

As evening fell the two young men sat by the lake and read Chateaubriand:

> As shadows fell on the pages of the book, the bitter-sweetness of the phrases won our hearts and we steeped ourselves with delight in I don't know what depths of melancholy and sweetness.

The château was finally restored in phases between 1866 and 1878 by the descendants of Chateaubriand's eldest brother. The famous architect Viollet-Le-Duc's pupil Ernest Thrile was employed and, with scant regard for the existing inner structure—where a large internal courtyard had featured—he redivided the space unsympathetically to add a dining room and created the impressive oak staircase, ensuring the impossibility of connecting to any atmosphere from the days of young François-Réne. The adult Chateaubriand memorabilia, like his marble portrait bust in the entrance hall or his bed and square writing table brought in from other places, rather obscure the writer's childhood connections. One can only grasp at hints of former simplicity like a curved stone window seat with a view over the park to picture a boy and his imagination at work in a castle of legends.

Staying at the Château de Montboissier in 1817, the song of a thrush triggered instant nostalgic memories for Chateaubriand of a similar song in the woods of Combourg and the childhood happiness he had felt there. Time finally airbrushed the grim strictures of his father to leave an impression of liberty, his pleasure in the surroundings internalized into a growing sense of self and a particular place in the world.

The grounds at Combourg were included in the nineteenth-century renovation program with an English-style landscaped park courtesy of the Buhler brothers—well known for their arrangement of the beautiful Thabor gardens in Rennes. Attractive though the new setting of the château undoubtedly is, it bears little resemblance to the more densely wooded scene that met Chateaubriand's eyes on his first visit. "Les bois" referred to in his seminal statement of identity at the head of this section refer to this earlier woodland and the sense of freedom and discovery, but also the secrecy they engendered in the child Chateaubriand and his beloved sister and companion Lucile.

Trees were always important to Chateaubriand. In later life he likened the château at Combourg denuded of its friends the woods to himself despoiled after the loss of so many of his family. In the "Valley of Wolves" property near Paris purchased in 1806, which became his second true emotional connection to place, he planted many trees and came to form companionable relationships with them, even giving individual specimens names. Although the park at Combourg is irrevocably changed from the days of the author's formative years, perhaps the extraordinarily shaped

Lawson cypress near the north front of the château, by Lucile's cross, its lower bare trunk convoluted into the limbs of some bizarre marsh monster and said to be over 250 years old, was young alongside him and a valued companion in the 1780s.

## MAN OF THE MARCHES: HISTORY, PATRIOTISM, AND A PROPHET IN HIS OWN COUNTRY

It is odd that there is no statue or memorial in Vitré to Louis-Arthur Le Moyne de La Borderie (1827–1901), the great Breton historian who was born and lived there nearly all his adult life. He is a prime example of the intellectual movement in Brittany in the late nineteenth century: one of the founders of the Archaeological Society of Ille-et-Vilaine and the review *Revue de Bretagne et Vendée*, he was also the initiator of the museum in the château in 1876. As an *homme politique*, a conservative hostile to Republican principles, he served as a monarchist deputy for Vitré from 1871 to 1876. In this vein La Borderie re-founded the Association Bretonne started by Armand de la Rouërie in 1791 and dissolved in 1859 by Napoléon III.

After studying law at university in Rennes, he had pursued research into historical methodology and then worked during the 1850s as an archivist in Nantes, where access to centuries of ducal documents inspired his own serious enquiries. He was fortunate that a substantial inheritance subsequently left him free to devote his time to the reconstruction of the Breton past. Among many other publications, his *Histoire de Bretagne* was a monumental and monumentally influential work, incomplete at his death and finished for publication in 1914 by Barthélemy Pocquet.

It was La Borderie who first emphasized the role of the immigrants from Britain in the formation of Brittany and the Breton saints in its Christianization. He argued that this made a "new start" for the region rather than a continuation of Gallo–Romano society. Rejecting Conan Meriadec as a legend of political creation, he stressed the historical role of Nominoë in the ninth century and gave him the image of *pater patriae* (father of his country) of the Breton state, which emerged from La Borderie's work as a coherent entity for the first time.

The importance of Nominoë as a symbol of Breton strength, defiance, and independence has been maintained in nationalist thought (witness a glum statue of 1952 in Bains-sur-Oust) and popular tradition. In the *Barzaz Breiz* (see p.20), La Villemarqué recorded *Le Tribut de Nominoë*—

an account of Nominoë's action on behalf of a bereaved father whose son carried tribute to the Franks and had his head cut off to make up the due weight. George Sand regarded this account of the vengeance carried out by Nominoë as "greater than the Iliad"! In more recent times the bard Glenmor (see p.151) wrote *La Marche de Nominoë*, the name a rallying cry for Bretons to throw off the yoke of the French (just as King Arthur is said to sleep in readiness for the national crisis that will see him rise again). Certainly he achieved a degree of unified support among the Bretons and saw off the Franks.

Two contrasting events make the Marches a crucial ideological territory for Breton nationalists: the remarkable triumph over the Franks in 845 at Ballon (although this was probably a lesser engagement than La Borderie claimed) and the final defeat of the Bretons by the French army in 1488 at St-Aubin-du-Cormier. Both are marked by nationalistic monuments, and the statue in Bains-sur-Oust by Raffig Tullou depicts Nominoë as "Tad ar Vro," a Breton epithet echoing La Borderie's *pater patriae*. At the hamlet still called La Bataille there is a cross and plaque placed in 1983 by the association Bretagne 845. The latter bears a quotation from La Borderie mentioned earlier: "The old saints founded the Breton people: Nominoë made them into a state, thus ensuring for long centuries their existence, independence, persistence and the development of their genius and national character."

For all that he regarded history as "patriotic science," it was also an affair of the heart for the historian, who was a veritable product of the Marches in his allegiance to both Brittany and France, and in his attitude to the Breton language, which he saw as but one of the constituent elements of a nation and not the *raison d'être*. He described the exceptional character and achievement of the Bretons as adding a tributary to the "great and splendid river of the history of France," seeing the Bretons as quite distinct in their Celtic origins, customs, and ancestral language, a people who had remarkably retained this ancestral heritage through all the waves of invasion and imposition. He summed up his assessment of the Breton character in the inaugural lecture for his history of Brittany course at the University of Rennes in 1890:

> One imagines a frank, loyal character, with strong personal relationships, independent, an enemy of oppression and base behaviour,

The Historian's house: Vitré (Wendy Mewes)

showing an open spirit and generous heart, but above all a tenacious will—very tenacious, sometimes to the point of obstinacy, even stubbornness…

La Borderie's history of Brittany is one of great figures like Nominoë, du Guesclin (whose mission was to drive the English from France during the Hundred Years' War), and Anne de Bretagne. In contrast to the prevailing spirit of research into popular oral traditions in the late nineteenth century, he placed more emphasis on heroic history and the theme of resistance than on the concerns of ordinary people. What he did do was to establish a strong basis for the study of Brittany's history, formalizing the stages of the country's development, forging a sense of pride and discrete identity, creating belief in a national character formed from pioneering ancestors and vivid energy in the face of adversity.

Breton nationalists may have adopted La Borderie for his stature and emphasis on the puissance of the origins of the Breton state, but it is a strange evocation considering that his attitude to France is absolute anathema to their ethos. He wrote to Léon Séché, urging him not to support a new regionalist move: "The day we are no longer French is the day we will cease to be Bretons."

There is little sense of La Borderie and his vital role in the town of Vitré. A pseudo-triumphal arch has been added to the entrance to his house off the place du Marchix, with a terse inscription bearing his name, dates, and key roles: historian of Brittany, curator of the town's museums and library. Strange in a place with the label "Ville d'Art et d'Histoire" that the seventeenth-century society lady Madame de Sévigné—whose copious correspondence remains—is made more of than one of the greatest figures in the establishment and interpretation of Brittany's history. Political hot potatoes aside, he deserves better.

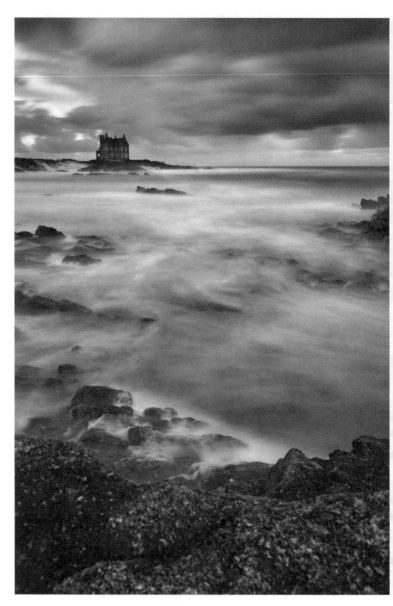

Quiberon seascape
(Mario Bono/Shutterstock)

*Chapter Four*

# SEA

## A WAY OF LIFE AND DEATH

The sea is often considered the dominant element in Brittany's personality. Over the centuries it has been a source of wealth and sustenance, the playground of pirates and explorers, a Janus portal, opening to the wider world and exposing the Breton shores for good or ill. As a connective principle it has made a small region into a place of international significance, and Breton skills and manpower have always been crucial to the French Navy. Received images of Brittany today often revolve around the sea and coastal scenery: ports, lighthouses, fishing boats, and sailing competitions, all reflecting an essential skill base and experience in which the Bretons excel. The modern economy also derives much from boat-building and marine technology, although it is pleasure ports that proliferate nowadays as the fishing industry declines. Add to all this those less tangible marine characteristics like the prevailing scent of brine, the savor of seafood, and the call of the gulls carried on the breeze.

Life on the sea often breeds a kind of fatalism, acceptance of the incontestably superlative and always unpredictable nature of this unruly element, but it also inspires courage and a kind of instinctive rebelliousness against conventional mores. It certainly seems that coastal Bretons have subliminally learned the lesson of the sea, which accepts no authority and follows no orders. For all the blessings of ships and religious processions to pray for safety on the ocean, it also retains a pre-Christian mysticism in legends of death and transformation.

### THREATS FROM THE SEA: SEA WOLVES, ABDUCTION, A FAMOUS SINKING, AND BLACK TIDES

The sea provides a way in as much as a way out, and visitors who arrive by the blue road are not always welcome. They are not always human either: proximity to major shipping routes and turbulent waters means Brittany has suffered more than its fair share of environmental disasters.

The openness of this maritime location is a mixed blessing, weighing the possibilities of beneficial exploitation with permanent potential danger.

Early threats from the sea may still be enshrined in folk memory through songs passed down in the oral tradition. François-Marie Luzel's ballad "Bleizi Mor" (Sea Wolves) could be an historical echo of the Viking raids which hammered the Breton shores in the ninth century.

> Here come the ships of the Wolves of the Sea
> Carrying their war into Brittany
> They've taken a village, Yaudet by name,
> Destroying the church by fire and by flame.

Another tale relates how a young woman of Plougasnou was snatched by men from a Saxon ship (*Saoz* means English in Breton) as she strolled by the shore. When they sailed away she resolved to avoid a fate worse than death and threw herself overboard rather than submit to the lechery of the captain. A typical Breton mixture of legend and fairy tale adds the detail that a little fish saved her as she sank into the ocean, pushing her up to the surface of the waves and then towards her home on a favorable breeze. But there is no happy ending: reaching her father's dwelling, she walks three times around the house, then falls down dead.

Adolphus Trollope heard many such stories during his mid-nineteenth-century visit to the area around Paimpol:

> During the early part of the middle ages [such precautions] were most especially necessary on this wild and remote coast… Never could any man there lay his head upon his pillow without a great probability of being waked by the attack of a gang of Norman pirates.

In better documented times it was to be the Royal Navy which harried and harmed the Breton coasts, using their supremacy to patrol and blockade, and often hemming the French Navy in port. Brest was especially vulnerable to this maneuver, lying within the Rade de Brest, separated from the ocean by a long, narrow channel called Le Goulet. Trying to get out into the Atlantic here against the currents was hard enough at the best of times, but facing a parade of enemy ships made it well-nigh impossible without a fight. Chance encounters could also be just as lethal, as the fate of the *Cordelière* shows.

The sinking of this enormous ship in 1512 is the naval disaster most enshrined in popular memory. The 200-cannon vessel was built on the orders of Anne de Bretagne at Dourduff near Morlaix around 1495, and had already seen active service in the Mediterranean. It was in harbor at Brest on 15 August with an onboard celebration of the feast of St Laurent, all the notables of Léon and their families there to toast the occasion with music and dancing. Accompanied by about twenty other ships of the French Navy, they left the relative safety of the harbor in Brest for a jaunt along Le Goulet towards the Atlantic. Off Berthaume, an English fleet was sighted on the open sea.

Henry VIII's recent marriage with Catherine of Aragon had brought England into alliance with Spain, reinforcing the English king's position of hostility towards France. As regaining Calais was one of Henry's objectives, harrying the French coasts wherever possible was a strategic part of the plan to deplete the enemy's resources. On that summer day in 1512 the marauding vessels led by Edward Howard included the *Mary Rose, Sovereign,* and *Regent.* They were keen to lock horns with the French ships and an engagement began which was to last for hours. At the denouement, the *Cordelière* was involved in a deadly tussle with the *Regent.* When the two ships were grappled together and no escape was possible, the Breton commander, Hervé de Porzmoguer, had his own ship blown up—with the words (allegedly), "So let us celebrate St Laurent who died by fire!"—to take the English to the bottom with him. The loss of so many local families was felt for a long time in the area, but the event remains to this day the epitome of valiant action in popular tradition, a heroic sacrifice by the patriotic commander in order to save Brest (and therefore his country). The incident was later lauded in a song by the bard Théodore Botrel (see p.103):

> We must not forget to tell our children
> Of the twelve hundred lads
> Sunk with the Cordelière
> Taking with them three thousand English…

The English naval historian William Laird Clowes (1856–1905) sums up a common Breton cultural phenomenon: "The fight of the Cordelière…

has thanks to patriotism, poetry, and vulgar tradition, been clouded over with the rosy mist of myth."

Although the painful fact of English raids on these shores over centuries remains strong in Breton memory, the events did not always turn out in favor of the attackers. The "Combat de St-Cast" is a song from the *Barzaz Breiz* relating the heroics of the battle of St-Cast-le-Guildo in 1758, when an English force tried to reembark there, having failed to take St-Malo. When troops from Basse-Bretagne arrive to join the fight they are already singing in Breton a victory song about recent triumphs over English aggression:

> At Camaret just now the English landed; they were parading on the sea, under their billowing white sails.
>
> They fell on the shore, struck down by our shot like so many wood-pigeons; of the four thousand who disembarked not a single one got back home safely.
>
> At Guidel they landed, at Guidel in the district of Vannes, at Guidel they were dead and buried as they had been at Camaret.
>
> In Léon opposite the Green Isle once they landed too; they lost so much blood, the sea turned red.
>
> There's not a hill or hillock in Brittany that doesn't bear their bones for the dogs and crows to fight over, for the wind and rain to whiten.

There is an interesting twist in what follows: the "English" archers appeared to understand this strange language and stopped fighting. In response to the remonstrance of their captain, they replied: "We are Bretons like them." In fact, they were Welsh.

In more recent times the destructive gifts of the tides have been not bloodshed but waves of pollution from a series of wrecked oil-tankers, bringing environmental devastation in the form of *marées noires* to the coasts of Brittany. In 1976 there were two separate incidents in the Atlantic, with *Olympic Bravery* breaking up near Ouesssant and the *Boehlen* floundering in turbulent waters off the Ile de Sein.

The most infamous disaster happened in 1978 when the *Amococ Cadiz* hit rocks off the north coast of Brittany near Portsall during a severe storm. Hazardous attempts were made to drag the ship away to open water but it proved impossible and the ripped hull began to hemorrhage oil: all

220,000 tons were lost after the ship broke in two the next day. More than 300 kilometers of Breton shoreline felt the damage of these "black tides," with great loss of wildlife and coastal pollution. In a grim reminder of the disaster, the anchor of the *Amoco Cadiz* today stands on the harbor at Port-sall.

The south coast was to suffer the same sort of damage in December 1999 when the oil-tanker *Erika*, on its way from Dunkerque to Italy, got into difficulties off St-Nazaire. Initially the captain canceled his distress call, feeling the crew had dealt with the severe listing which was threatening the cargo. They wanted to make for Donges (where there are oil refineries) but the port authorities refused as the proximity of a leaking ship and the currents of the Loire made such a maneuver too dangerous. Overnight the situation worsened and it became clear that it would be necessary to abandon ship as the hull broke asunder. Eleven days later the first oil slicks hit the shores of Morbihan. The Ile de Groix was particularly badly affected, but in total 400 kilometers of shore from Finistère to Charente-Maritime endured deadly damage.

This series of disasters, cruel injustices for a maritime people, have marked the Breton consciousness in the traditional way—through songs. Tri Yann, one of the early wave of traditional Breton groups formed in 1970 in Nantes, added two songs on the *Amoco Cadiz* to their repertoire: "Le Soleil est Noir" and "Gwerz Porsal." The Goristes, founded in Brest in the 1990s and noted satirical specialists, released an album with the title song "Bretagne is beauty fuel."

## LEGENDS: A DOTING FATHER, SIRENS, AND THE NIGHT BOAT

The destructive power of the sea sadly has no shortage of examples, but it is also seen as a transformative element, symbolizing a different kind of potency. The Breton Atlantis story of the city of Ys, smothered by waves to punish the wickedness of Dahut, daughter of King Gradlon of Quimper, leads to such a metamorphosis in legend and popular culture. This doting father had agreed to build the girl a special abode where she could live free from all strictures, a youthful reaction to the increasing holiness of a Quimper controlled by those worthy Breton saints Corentin and Guenolé, the king's advisors. Dahut was keen on fun and lascivious frolics (Christian version) or loyal to the old polytheistic religion that was being forced out by this pushy newcomer (pagan version). Maybe she just

Gradlon riding high on Quimper's cathedral (The supermat/Wikimedia Commons)

wanted to laugh and dance without the old boys tutting. In Ys, surrounded by waves at high tide, she was free to indulge her passions, whatever they were. Lovers figured high on the list of tales told about the iniquity of her behavior and the saints pressured poor Gradlon to put an end to this licentiousness, which could only draw God's punishment.

On the very night he rode across the sand to the city with St Guenolé in tow to remonstrate with Dahut, she was busily embroiled with a new lover—the Devil in disguise—who persuaded her to steal from her sleeping father the keys to the gates which kept the waves at bay. This mysterious figure then opened the sluices and let the water in. As levels began to rise and submerge the city, Gradlon and Guenolé escaped on their horses, but, despite the saint's warnings, the king insisted on dragging his beloved daughter up onto the saddle behind him. This slowed the horse to a pace destined to lose the battle with the rising tide, and Guenolé urged Gradlon to throw Dahut into the waves. In anguish, he finally he did so (in other versions she plunged in willingly), and so the two men escaped from the wholesale destruction of the city of Ys and all its people.

The tension between Christian teachings and Celtic mythology is clear in the story, where Dahut can be either heroine martyred in the cause of the old religion or the epitome of pagan degradation, the kind of moral ill-discipline Catholicism had come to Amorica to stamp out. Pagans had the last laugh, however. Dahut rose from the waves an immortal, transformed into the sea spirit Ahès, a siren figure with powers to calm a stormy wind if she so desired.

Similar stories of a flooded city are told in the oral traditions of Wales and Ireland, indicating a rite of cultural passage important in the Celtic tradition. In the *Barzaz Breiz*, La Villemarqué gives the text of a song on the theme: at the end a forester hears the king's horse pass to safety, and a fisherman, asked if he has had sight of "the daughter of the sea" replies, "I have seen the white daughter of the sea and heard her singing, refrains as plaintive as the passing billows." It is also recorded that in the sixteenth century fishermen claimed to have glimpsed the remains of a lost city in the Bay of Douarnenez at the lowest tides.

The semi-mysticism of the sea is also marked in a transitory stage between life and death for coastal peoples who know only too well the dominating element on which they depend. The Baie des Trépassés near the Pointe du Raz (see p.2) has long been associated with death and the dead. The place is powerfully atmospheric, a bay inset between two rocky headlands, deep enough for the Atlantic to roll in forcibly: "Each wave which passes carries a soul seaching everywhere for his lost brother, friend or beloved, and when the two come face to face, they lament with a sad murmur and drift apart, forcibly carried away on the tide which they are compelled to follow," wrote Émile Souvestre.

The night boat (*Bag Noz*) carries properly shriven dead souls out to sea to the Île de Sein and on out westwards into the blue distance where the Blessed Isles and tranquility await. Ankou—a role perhaps taken by the last defunct of the old year—officiates at the helm. Many on the shore claim to have seen the night boat or even to have recognized dead relatives on board, but when they cry out there is no response and the phantom boat passes without a trace in the water. Sometimes it is taken for a vessel in distress by other ships in the vicinity, but if they come near to offer rescue, the *Bag Noz* makes a sudden effortless shift to the horizon.

Others less fortunate who have drowned and been denied a proper burial by the merciless sea are destined to shift endlessly on the waves, waiting for contact which will bring them peace. If they can persuade a sailor or fishermen to arrange (and pay for) funeral mass for them back home, their souls will be allowed to depart in peace for eternal rest.

In all the intense seriousness of man's partnership with the sea, there was also room for humor. The mischievous strain of little people in Breton folklore enters maritime tradition with the activities of *lutins* (imps or elves), described by Paul Sébillot, who collected the tales of Haute-Bretagne at the end of the nineteenth century. One such *lutin*, Nicole, was a constant torment to sailors around the Bay of St-Brieuc, tangling the nets of fishermen or making holes to let the fish out. He would release the anchor of oyster boats so that their masters in light skiffs along the oyster banks would have to rush back and resecure their craft. He also liked to move boats from where they were left or twist the cables of different vessels together. Many sailors claimed to have heard Nicole's hearty laughter as he played yet another joke on the mariners. He once made the oars of a boat fall into the sea, leaving the vessel hopelessly adrift far from shore, but when the fisherman called on Nicole to stop messing about and take him back to harbor, the *lutin* obligingly did so.

Stories of sirens, again linked to the concept of transformation and the lure of death and very much part of the imaginative world of mariners, abound in the Breton tradition, with Mari Morgan the name given to these watery beings who may be associated with the open sea or deep echoing caves (or *houles*) along the shore, as in various other tales collected from the Gallo tradition of the north coast by Sébillot. They are usually female (although the island of Ouessant preserves stories of males—the Morganed, see p.257), sometimes predatory in their search for human souls to confine under the sea, sometimes victims of tragic former lives on earth.

Luzel's long and involved tale of the Hawk and the Siren shows the deadly and unpredictable power of these sea spirits who can help and harm mankind at will, and the battle of wits needed to outmaneuver them. It is an amalgam of various folk traditions, but the essential story begins with a mermaid caught in a fishing net. She rewards the man who releases her back into the sea with a gold coin which will increase overnight into a fortune. All she asks is that he brings his newborn son to the shore for her to kiss the baby, promising that no harm will come to him. Instead the siren snatches the child and dives into the sea, only to be followed by the fisherman who wrestles his son back from her arms and returns home.

Despite thwarting the siren, undreamed of riches do materialize for the man and his wife, and they are able to bring up the boy, Fanch, for a prosperous future. But the siren has not forgotten the loss and awaits her chance, even though the boy has grown to manhood before she can find him by the sea again. What she does not know is that Fanch is by now in possession of extraordinary powers of transformation given to him by various animals. When finally he is seized from the shore and confined to a non-life underwater with the mermaid, he eventually feigns resignation, begging for one last look at the land that was his home. She carries him to the surface and he turns into a hawk and flies away to freedom.

A sadder story relates the fate of a girl from the Ile d'Arz who had the most beautiful voice and always sang as she worked. This attracted the attention of a young man from the neighboring island, and as a causeway then joined the two places, the couple were able to meet and fall in love. His parents, however, thought the girl beneath their precious son, and had him shut away by monks near his home. Every day the heartbroken girl crossed over to his island and the walls of the monastery where she sang to her imprisoned beloved. All work on the island stopped as the

Siren lure, Vitré (Wendy Mewes)

inhabitants were enchanted by her voice, but the prior eventually intervened against what he saw as a gift of the Devil: one night saw the disappearance of the causeway and there was no longer a way for the girl to remain close to her lover. In despair for her loss, she finally she hurled herself into the waters of the Gulf of Morbihan, but her lament remained audible forever, carried to the ears of passing sailors on the sea breeze.

The motif of the siren as a Christian symbol of vice and temptation in medieval religious art can also be seen adorning many Breton churches (and not necessarily those by the coast—there is a fine example to be seen in Vitré), but the mysterious and potentially fatal power of these half-women is inextricably linked to Celtic legends of the sea.

## ST-MALO: MEN AT SEA, AN INFERNAL MACHINE, AND HIGH ADVENTURE

Despite the defiant enclosure of the famous walled city—rebuilt in full detail after the World War II bombardment—with all its claustrophobic passages funneling the searing channel winds, the relation between St-Malo and the sea has been one long history of outgoing opportunity. Few people have taken better advantage of this active energy than the Malouins or townspeople, making a mark all over the world with their seamanship, enterprise, and commercial instincts as explorers and discoverers, master-traders and wily predators. Such was their swashbuckling reputation that everyone understood the implications of the simple phrase "les messieurs de St Malo."

The ship owners did not do so badly either, and houses from the mid-seventeenth to mid-eighteenth centuries in the surrounding area—the Clos Poulet, a name meaning the country around Alet, the original settlement of St Malo—reflect the wealth of these *armateurs* and also merit their own epithet, *Malounières*, by a distinctive symmetrical style and palatial gardens. Those which are open to the public (the Manoir de Belle Noë, once the home of famous corsair Robert Surcouf, even offers *chambres d'hôtes*) present the affluent lifestyle and valuable possessions that were the fruits of maritime investment.

Today the town is still all about the sea which dominates the view, the senses and the illustrious history of its adventurers. These days adventure takes the form of competitive sailing, with the famous Route du Rhum, a grueling, solo cross-Atlantic race, starting from the harbor every

"Wasps' nest": St-Malo (Wendy Mewes)

four years. The town oversees many yachting contests and the annual international Tall Ships race also uses the port as a venue. Every two years St-Malo hosts its own Raid des Corsaires event, the name an echo of the form of sailing for which the town has the greatest reputation.

Such enterprising spirit goes hand in hand with the city's long-held reputation for independence, its stance during the Wars of Religion being the prime example. Between 1590 and 1594 St-Malo declared itself an autonomous republic, summed up in the dictum *ni Français, ni Breton, Malouin suis* (I'm neither French nor Breton, but Malouin—the last words being the crux of the matter), before being forced to come to terms with the French king. It goes back a lot further than that. St Malo himself, one of the seven founding saints of Brittany, failed to get along with his own congregation and had to run off when things got too hot to handle. Nothing and no one is important enough to boss the Malouins. One of the towers of the château—which houses a fine museum, a real eye-opener for those interested in maritime history and artifacts—is the oddly named Quic-en-Groigne ("never mind who complains"), a reference to local opposition to Anne de Bretagne's restoration of the building at the end of the fifteenth century.

In 1534 Jacques Cartier set off from his native port charged by the King of France to find passage to India and China after being presented to François I by the Bishop of St-Malo. A straightforward voyage led the expedition to the Gulf of St-Laurence (so named on the second voyage in 1535 when they arrived on 10 August, the saint's feast day) where Cartier put his mark on the territory by erecting a cross at Gaspé to stake France's claim to what would become Canada. Two sons of Donnacona, chief of the Autochtones tribe, returned to France with the expedition. Cartier made two further voyages, but the last in 1541 was disastrous as attempts to create a colony proved unsuccessful in the face of harsh conditions and sickness.

Home town mementos of Cartier and his achievements include a replica of the Gaspé cross at the Tour Solidor, a fourteenth-century donjon in the St-Servan area of St-Malo. The famously imaginative Auguste Lemoine portrait of Cartier gazing pensively on deck hangs in the château museum, together with paintings recording his encounters with the Native Americans, with whom he exchanged goods. Cartier's house, the Manoir de Limoëlou in nearby Rotheneuf, is now a museum devoted to the explorer's life and career.

The English were long the Malouins' naval rivals, the city being regarded as such a "wasps' nest" of potential trouble by sea that the *Infernal Machine*, a ship packed with explosives, was launched on the tide towards the walls in 1693, during the War of the Grand Alliance between Louis XIV and pretty much all the other European powers. The intention was to fire it below the walls and catch the Tour Bidouane where the town's powder store was held, hoping to destroy the corsair stronghold once and for all. It all came to nothing, except a host of broken windows, when a sudden change in the wind drove the boat to the rocks well off target and the fuse was lit more in desperation than hope of success. The vessel exploded, causing loss of life only on the small English escort boat.

The north coast of Brittany was well-placed for access to commercial shipping routes and St-Malo was not the only port to nurture corsairs, those who were given official permission through "letters of the course" to capture the ships of official enemies of the French state—the English being the most constant and popular targets. Roscoff and Morlaix had many of these licensed privateers but the range and expertise of Malouin adventurers was second to none. The Channel was their highway to prizes and glory, the theater for running battles between corsairs from Britain and Brittany. Seizure of rich cargoes was the aim, although the necessary accompaniment of disabling opponents' ships was also a measure of success. Scores were kept and many successes against astonishing odds were lauded. The profit from this officially endorsed piracy benefited the state as well as rewarding the daring of individual commanders. There were rules to be followed—including no unnecessary violence against individuals—but plenty of scope for the unscrupulous.

The spirit of St-Malo is personified in many a *corsaire* and adventurer, none more vivid and remarkable than René Duguay-Trouin (1673–1736). He has left his own account of a career that encapsulates the full flavor of marine experience from banal to gruesome and from disaster to glorious triumph. His very first excursion on the frigate *La Trinité* at the age of sixteen was inauspicious: he suffered from severe seasickness and witnessed the revolting sight of a comrade crushed to death after falling between two ships and smattering the contents of his skull over young René's clothes. He comments later that that if such a thing could happen to an old hand, he did not see how he himself would ever manage to avoid the same fate.

They had captured an English ship loaded with sugar and indigo and managed to get it back to St-Malo despite a terrible storm on the way in which all had feared death. Putting out to sea again they met another corsair ship from Flessingue (Vlissingen) and were preparing to board when the awful accident occurred. Neither of these lessons in the hazards of life at sea put Duguay-Trouin off. Within two years he had his own corsair vessel, and in ten years he was in command of three ships and wreaking havoc among Dutch and English merchant convoys.

His good luck ran out in 1694 when he was finally captured by the English after an unequal fight in which he was surrounded by four ships and forced to surrender. Taken to Plymouth, he was treated with all respect and privileges accorded to gentlemen prisoners in that epoch and managed to get about the port and town. His escape was something of a burlesque episode: he offered to act as the go-between for two aspiring lovers, a female merchant and a French Protestant serving in the English army. If they could arrange his liberty to visit a local inn he would organize everything for their rendezvous. Despite the frivolous pretext, Duguay-Trouin's plans had been carefully laid. He had arranged with a Swedish merchant for a vessel to be waiting at the port and he was soon back in Brittany. The following year, as commander of the *François* he took twelve merchant ships and two English war vessels.

And yet such bravado and such brilliance did not breed arrogance. Duguay-Trouin was a moderate, disciplined man, deeply loyal to his king and detached in assessment of his own exploits. He was reluctant to write memoirs but gave in to the pressure of his brother and many friends, on condition that they were not to be published. The account is frank and unconcerned with presenting the personal glory of a distinguished career. It was only by mischance that the manuscript fell into the hands of a Monsieur de Villepontoux, who took it upon himself to publish in Amsterdam without permission to the author, adding a groveling dedication to the great man: "Allow me to have the honour of offering you your own work!" Duguay-Trouin had previously agreed to let Cardinal Dubois see the only copy of the text, which lingered in the cardinal's papers when he died in 1723. It took a month for the author to resecure his property, but during that time a hasty copy had been made and sent to Villepontoux, who went so far as to encourage Duguay-Trouin to correct of any of the unknown copyist's mistakes.

Greatest of all Duguay-Trouin's exploits was the capture of Rio de Janeiro in 1711, a feat achieved with only fifteen ships and fewer than 4,000 men. The city was held by the Portuguese, who had already fended off a French attack the previous year, but the governor ignored English warnings of the Malouin's arrival and defense was perfunctory. Seven Portuguese ships in the harbor were soon disabled and after three days of cannon bombardment, Duguay-Trouin was able to land his troops and force a surrender to avoid the total annihilation of Rio. A vast ransom was paid: for a start more than a ton of gold was brought back to Brest in February the following year. The success was an astonishingly bold and morale-boosting achievement for the French.

For all the cult of individualism fostered in Malouin tradition, Duguay-Trouin saw himself primarily as a servant of the state. He was touched by Louis XIV's appreciation in words and in career terms, for the brilliant commander was to be appointed *chef d'escadre* and given a pension of 2,000 pounds. His pleasure was marred only by a realization that Louis was very ill: "I can't express the sadness I felt: he deigned to honour me with a kindness and trust which made me ready to sacrifice my own life a thousand times to prolong his days."

After the king's death, he remained in favor, named Lieutenant General and Commander of the Order of St Louis in 1728. Even at the age of sixty he agreed to a command when war with England threatened, hurrying to Brest to carry out his duties. The crisis passed without action, but the Malouin hero was already a dying man. When the end came in 1736, he was initially buried in Paris—his last letter spoke of his devotion to the state of France—but his remains now lie more fittingly in the St-Vincent Cathedral in St-Malo, the town whose enterprise and spirit he exemplified.

Duguay-Trouin was followed by other illustrious Malouin adventurers, like Jacques Gouin de Beauchesne (1652–1730), who navigated the Straits of Magellan, was the first French sailor to round Cap Horn from west to east (1701) and opened up trade with South America; or Bertrand-François Mahé de la Bourdonnais (1699–1753), who took Madras in 1746 and extorted ransom from the English incumbent rather than destroy the city as other French commanders advocated. Robert Surcouf (1773–1827), scourge of the English in the Indian Ocean, was given the epithet "Roi des Corsaires" for his daring and determined exploits. In 1800, in command of the aptly named *Confiance*, he took the *Kent*, an East Indies Company vessel on the way to Bengal, despite being vastly inferior in tonnage, cannon-fire, and manpower. After a swift success, he refused to let his crew run amok and saw that the passengers on the captured ship were well-treated.

The Malouin legend was well-served by all these men, who amassed glory and riches in equal measure, but in the end perhaps the most extraordinary thing about them, so much larger than life in the memory of the town and bringing St-Malo to worldwide renown, is that despite the most valiant deeds and incalculable risks, they all died in their beds.

### PAIMPOL: SAD WOMEN, SALT COD, AND SUPERHEROES

Paimpol is an unprepossessing sort of town, lacking the natural beauty of Binic, another port on the Côte de Goëlo, north of St-Brieuc. The Bay of St-Brieuc has one of the largest tide recoils in the world, leaving up to seven kilometers of exposed bed at times of the highest tides. Just north of Paimpol is the Bréhat archipelago, a scattering of small islands including Lavret, once home to the famous monastery of St-Budoc. At Kerity just south of the town is the Abbaye de Beauport, which well deserves its name for its location and is an exceptionally interesting monument to an Augustinian community much exercised in extending hospitality to travelers, especially pilgrims on the Santiago de Compostela trail.

Breton fishermen were after cod in Newfoundland as early as 1500, boats leaving from Roscoff, St-Malo, and other ports on the north coast. St-Malo launched fishing for the *morue* and made it an important European commodity, but the enduring memory of North Sea long-haul fishing—*la grande aventure*—is of the ships of Paimpol, active around Iceland for about eighty years.

*L'Occasion*, the first ship to make the trip, was kitted out in 1852 by owner Louis Morand, one of the many *armateurs* who were to reap a fine profit from the cod trade. Each year between forty and eighty two-masted *goélettes* left Paimpol at the end of winter, with about twenty-five men on board (the *Islandais* as they were called) including a young boy apprentice or *mousse*. A small advance was set against earnings according to numbers of fish caught, but the pay was little compared to the level of risk and hardship involved. From 1884 a third of the money from the campaign was divided between the crew according to their grades.

Their goal was huge shoals of cod passing through the icy waters of Iceland or *Islande* as the French called it. Tens of thousands of fish were gutted, salted, and dried, brought back not only to Brittany but then taken on beyond to the warm south—Spain and Marseille—in a contrastingly soft stage of a working journey of six to nine months a year. They collected salt in preparation for the next voyage on their way back home to rest in Paimpol for a few months and greet the offspring born in their long absence. The pay hardly compensated for the grueling labor and unhealthy isolation in primitive conditions, but it was better than that of a farm laborer, and there was considerable *kudos* to be won, thanks to a surprising source—literature.

They were not the first Frenchmen in those waters, with Dunkirk already sending about eighty vessels a year, the first in 1737, before the Paimpolais turned up, and Boulogne and Calais also sent lesser numbers of ships. Other ports in Brittany—like Binic and Erquy—were there too, but why the abiding impression that it was the distinct province of the Bretons? The answer lies in Brittany's great forte, the power of popular culture. The pure chance of a single novel and single derivative song created an image and traditional identity so powerful that the memory of any others who suffered and died on the same haul has seeped away.

The boats left earlier and earlier as the economic stakes grew, and the state withdrew sensible restrictions in the face of pressure from the *armateurs*. Instead of waiting until the end of winter to lessen the navigational dangers in threatening seas off Iceland, the departure became fixed in February and ships often ran into severe conditions with heavy losses. Sometimes the weather conditions prevented any fishing for weeks after arrival. It was a calculated risk.

The port of Paimpol was smaller than it is today, consisting only of what is now the quai Morand. In 1857 the first Pardon des Islandais was held to celebrate the departure of the fishing fleet, a religious festival with boat blessing, the statue of Notre-Dame des Bonnes-Nouvelles carried on high by sailors in the procession. An elaborate altar decorated with raised oars was constructed on the quay for outdoor mass, and the Bishop of St-Brieuc no less came to give it. As they sailed from the harbor, the sailors took off their caps and sang the canticle "Salut, Étoile de la mer" for the protection of the Virgin Mary.

A dispute over dates between the mayor and the local priest saw the religious element of the Pardon withdrawn in 1904 to be replaced by a secular festival, Fête Laïque des Islandais et du Commerce, the new name giving a good idea of the motivation. The *Journal de Paimpol* published anticlerical articles to keep the ball rolling, but popular opinion was on the side of tradition, if not religion, and the original form was restored in 1913.

The *grande époque* of Icelandic fishing at the end of the nineteenth century found its bard in Pierre Loti. Born Julien Viaud in 1850 in Rochefort, Charente-Maritime, he pursued a naval career, visiting many exotic places portrayed by his burgeoning alternative author persona. His Breton connection came through a stay at the naval school in Brest and at Lorient where he met his future close friend Pierre Le Cor (the subject of Loti's novel *Mon frère Yves,* sometimes regarded as a homosexual hymn) who lived in Rosporden in southern Finistère after marriage to a local girl. Loti often visited Le Cor and his wife there and dressed in Breton costume for local events. He wrote, "At first Brittany felt an oppressive and very sad place, but mon frère Yves began to make me understand its melancholic charm."

During his first visit to Paimpol in 1868 he stayed at the Hôtel Le Richard, on the corner of place Martray, and returned later with Le Cor. In Brest in 1882 he met the sister of a sailor, Guillaume Floury, from little Pors-Even just north of Paimpol. His fascination with both was to be Paimpol's great good fortune. Loti followed the girl back to Paimpol in 1882, but she refused his offer of marriage, being already engaged to an *Islandais*. He tried again two years later, but the only productive outcome of the encounter was to be the character of Gaud, heroine of Loti's novel *Pêcheur d'Islande*, a storming popular success from the moment of its publication in 1886.

The book tells of the love affair of Gaud, daughter of a wealthy merchant, and *Islandais* Yann Goas, a primitive giant of a man, based on Guillaume Floury (who was to die at sea in the Bay of Paimpol in 1899), whose cottage, much changed from its original simplicity of form, can still be seen in Pors-Even, where steep terraces of small houses rise above the tiny harbor. In Paimpol itself, the little turreted room of the hotel in the place Martray, where Loti himself stayed, is made into Gaud's bedroom. (Today, unfortunately, it houses commercial premises.) After a long, fraught, and uncertain relationship, when Gaud despairs of his attraction to her, they finally reach an understanding and marry, but happiness is devastatingly brief—Yann never returns from his next trip to Iceland.

The book was an immediate hit, and has remained so, with several films including a TV version in 1996, as well as an opera and a play. It won the Prix Vitet for Loti. Paimpol's tributes to the author have been various. In 1901 a *goélette* was named the *Pierre Loti*, but it was wrecked in Iceland four years later. There has long been a project to erect a copy of the sculptor François Renaud's 1920s statue of Gaud and her grandmother, in homage to Loti, in the port at Paimpol. At the time of writing, a public subscription is on the go.

Loti caught the spirit of the time. To Brittany's own particular brand of exoticism was added the mystery of the sea and the romance of the remote. The rapid expansion of the railway had opened the way for mass tourism and the coast was a natural magnet for city dwellers. The book put Paimpol on the map, with its clearly delineated locations and picturesque allure. Everyone wanted to see the scenes of the novel, and to admire the virile fishermen and beautiful women. For Parisians, Loti's main audience, *Pêcheur d'Islande* was a nautical fantasy, combining a specifically Breton mythology with daring high sea adventure.

The cultural seed sown by Loti's novel might have had a short season of bloom were it not for a further piece of extraordinary good fortune that was to ensure Paimpol's immortality in popular culture.

At the age of thirty, Théodore Botrel (1868–1925), an artist-composer from Dinan with a theatrical background, read *Pêcheur d'Islande* and was inspired to write "La Paimpolaise," a six-verse song summarizing the story. It was a stunning success: an addictively simple tune with a cleverly adapted chorus for each verse earned the song the nickname "La Marseillaise de la mer," such was its impact.

*J'aime Paimpol et sa falaise*
*Son église et son grand Pardon*
*J'aime surtout la Pampolaise*
*Qui m'attend en pays breton*

I love Paimpol and its cliffs,
The church and Grand Pardon,
But above all I love the girl from Paimpol
Who is waiting for me in lands Breton

The hordes of cultural sightseers who surged to Paimpol will have looked in vain for any cliff, but Botrel was not one to let facts interfere with a heaven-sent rhyme. The nearest thing to it is the pimple of Krec'h Mahaf on which stands the Tour Kerroc'h, a chess rook structure based on the Tower of David in Jerusalem (the idea of Bishop Augustin David of St-Brieuc) that gives wide views back to town and out to sea. Botrel has his own monument in the old town of Paimpol opposite the tower which is all that remains of the ancient church.

The *armateurs* must have rubbed their hands in glee at the circulation of Loti's novel and Botrel's song. There lay a permanent inspiration for an endless supply of aspirant labor and a forcefully romantic public image that would draw—and still draws—many thousands each year, to the immense commercial benefit of the town. The peddling of this image of the "superman" sailor/fisher with his exceptional physique and rude exterior concealing a sensitive heart saw a cliché in the making, quenching the contemporary thirst for all things Breton and out of the ordinary.

The economy of Paimpol was made strong by the Icelandic fishing operations, and there were spin-offs in naval construction like the successful Chantiers Bonne at Kérity at the very end of the century (1899). Local construction of the ships was important for adaptation to specific requirements, not least the fact that many harbors were dry at low tide before the development of locks and sea walls.

Paimpol, as a port, was a Republican outpost in the conservative department of Côtes du Nord, and even *armateurs* who might well have had conservative tendencies and were often local officials—providing various mayors from 1892 to 1910—looked to work with Republicans where there was profit to be had. State grants courtesy of the Third Republic were to provide a new harbor in the 1890s.

The shipowners were hard-nosed businessmen, powerful through their wealth and economic success. They were not at all averse to sending their ships out laden with the alcohol that was to ruin the health and concentration of many an *Islandais*. The *Journal de Paimpol*, here on 27 May 1894, was very much an organ of support for these men who were charitably presented:

> The *armateurs* are mostly from the ranks of peaceful bourgeoisie, benevolent, former administrative officials who have changed course to in-

crease their incomes, landlords who seek to place their modest resources more profitably. They have but one passion—the sea.

The *Journal* also echoed the sentiments of Loti and Botrel's work, heightening the glamour and elevating the popular status of the fishermen. Rarely have cultural trope and reality been so divorced. What is surprising about Paimpol and its literary advertising is the false message almost willfully perpetrated, the cultivation of an image of the *Islandais* fishermen that elevated them from men with an economic imperative to go on a dangerous voyage away from their families for half the year to hulking supermen, marked out for a starring role in a cultural spectacle by preternatural bravery and courage. If we believe the hype these were strong, silent Hollywood-style heroes; according to Botrel, "His heart is proud, his spirit immense, but gentle at the same time…" The reality was never so romantic, even though it was a social and economic truth understood but accepted in the balance of commercial advantage at the time.

During the eighty years of activity nearly 120 ships were lost, at a cost of 2,000 lives from the Paimpol area. The Mur des Disparus (Wall of the Lost at Sea) in the cemetery at Ploubazlanec, on the way to the Pointe d'Accourest, is a memorial to the inglorious realities of the world of the *Islandais*. Originally this was a larger display with many individual memorials, an aspect of the cult of the dead so common in Brittany, but the creation of a larger cemetery in 1939 caused its dismantlement. In the 1950s when centenary "celebrations" of the Icelandic fishing were underway, the wall was restored in a basic fashion with a line of black wooden boards listing the ships and numbers of men lost. Last recorded is the *Butterfly*, one of two ships from the final year of the trade in 1935. The *Glycine* returned with 40,000 fish on board, but the *Butterfly* never came home. There are also a few plain individual commemorative plaques in simple language: *Disparus en mer… Regrets*. Few words do the work of many. Old photos show widows in their huge black hooded cloaks kneeling in futile prayer. A similarly moving display can be seen in the south porch of the Chapelle de Perros-Hamon nearby.

Loti dubbed a granite cross on the headland at Ploubazlanec La Croix des Veuves or Widows' Cross, where women waited with fear in their hearts for a sight of the returning ships, as Gaud lingered vainly for Yann.

Lonely vigil: Widows' Cross (Wendy Mewes)

It is a place of sad longing, even on a sunny spring day, the inscrutable sea stretching out its dismally beautiful trail of hope and loss.

In reality the women were probably so desperately occupied in working to support their children and stay alive that they had little time for the indulgent hanging around suggested by many posed paintings and photos of local women in their white *coiffes* and aprons. The chronic strains of absentee fathers and husbands, daily privations, and constant uncertainty of the financial and emotional future must have taken its physical and mental toll on these long-suffering women. Public and private charitable efforts did exist to succor the bereaved families, but the women get little mention in the aftermath of the mythology of the *Islandais*.

The *Islandais* themselves labored in the terrible conditions of one of the harshest environments on earth, with the eternal roar of the wind and screech of gulls pounding in their ears. Penetrating cold, humidity, disconcerting fog, ferocious storms from the northwest, and icy winds thrashed them as they worked, heaving up cod of enormous size and weight. A photograph shows a fisherman with a cod carcasse over his shoulders: the fish is almost equal to his height. The work was hazardous at best, demanding extreme physical exertions, the scrape of salt engrained in every crevice of their skin.

Iceland itself had suffered from volcanic eruptions during the eighteenth century and as many as 10,000 died following a famine in 1784. There was little in place for aid and support during the period of French fishing involvement. Ports were undeveloped, farms remote, and help in case of shipwreck unlikely. The *Islandais* were picked by shipowners more for their fishing abilities than maritime skills, a factor that contributed to many a wreck and a practice that drew censure from the marine authorities.

The constant curse of alcohol was another. "A quarter of the captains were in a permanent state of inebriation," says one report. In 1905, 232,923 liters of wine (usually the cheapest and heavily acidic), 42,763 of cider, and a good supply of eau-de-vie were loaded for three months for 1,504 men. The *armateurs* maintained that alcohol provided nourishment for the men as well as keeping out the cold and fighting fatigue, and ignored regular remonstrations from the *Commissaires* and administrators who recorded the fleet's resources on departure. In such extremes of danger, fatigue, and isolation it is not surprising that the crews turned increasingly to drink, with the inevitable toll on their health and safety. Their food— salted pork and potatoes as long as stores lasted, then dry biscuits and endless soups made from the plentiful fish heads—contained little enough nutrition for the grueling, endless work they had to do. As long as the fish were there the men worked around the clock. Evidence recorded by Dr Dubois Saint-Séverin affirmed that many accidents and violent scenes were caused by the abuse of alcohol, quite apart from the dreadful malnutrition, exhaustion, scurvy, and rotting teeth of these superheroes. Many photos from the Icelandic fishing fields bear witness to the harshness of conditions. Bare-headed, heavily moustached men stand in morose groups in the snow as a comrade is buried in the icy earth of lonely cemeteries on the barren coast. The *Paimpolais* make up a goodly number of the French graves.

Factual objections, moral values, the destruction of health, fractured families, and loss of life weighed little in the balance against an immense commercial incentive, political pressures by those who sought to profit from the inhumane activity and the popular cult of the *Islandais*. Cultural celebrity enhanced the status and self-worth of these men out of all proportion to their reward and quality of life and death.

And yet... For all the romantic melancholy of the literature, this is no superficial phenomenon. There is a profundity of attachment in Brittany to the sea as a canvas of life, a source of commodities, a theater of adventure, a working out of the unequal partnership of man and nature. Botrel could tread the line with the best of nineteenth-century sentimentality, but there is more to *La Paimpolaise* than mawkishness. The young girl from Paimpol stands for all women waiting for their fishermen, anxious not only for an emotional attachment but from fear of destitution. She also stands for Brittany itself, tugging the umbilical cord between every Breton and his own special corner of this land. And she stands for the strength and depth of a popular tradition that has cemented social bonds over centuries in a community-based culture.

There is no better example of the enduring power of song in Brittany. You will be hard pushed to find someone who cannot sing you *La Paimpolaise*, or the chorus at the very least. The second and third verses with their religious references seem to have dropped out of fashion and performances go straight from departure from Paimpol to chucking the harpoons about, but the drowning enacted in the final stanza can still moisten the eyes of many an audience.

The enormously successful biennial Festival du Chant de Marin at Paimpol has evolved considerably from its beginnings anchored in the traditional sea shanty and religious prayer for salvation and now includes big international names like Sinead O'Connor, whose maritime connection is obscure to say the least. Like so many of the big Breton festivals it has been internationalized to include maritime traditions from all over the world, bringing a variety of culture and sailing ships to the port, but the best performances are often those to be found in the street where sailors' songs reflect the solidarity and shared experience that unites maritime communities wherever.

*Chapter Five*

# COAST

## ON THE THRESHOLD

Coast is the meeting point of land and sea, a place where boundaries may be blurred; an exceptional tidal range can make it hard to distinguish where mainland really ends and ocean begins, a no-man's land subject to both the muffled obscurity of marine mist and a startling clarity of light. In terms of tourism, the coast has been Brittany's calling card for over 150 years, with its unrivaled beaches, small fishing villages, sailing, and water sports acting as a magnet for French and foreign visitors. Idyllic seaside holiday memories are as firmly ingrained in the Breton ethos as the noisy consumption of *fruits de mer* in many harborside restaurants. If coastal industries have declined, fishing holds on in ports that have expanded to embrace a lucrative pleasure craft trade, and the widespread cultivation of oysters and mussels is much in evidence, along with seaweed scavengers and *pêche à pied* on beaches deserted by the tide.

The coastal path is a glorious resource for walkers, nearly 2,000 kilometers of cliffs, headlands, sand, dunes, bays, and estuaries, following the old *sentier des douaniers* route where customs officers struggled against smugglers in the nineteenth century. For the coast is also the sharp edge of Brittany, a place of tension and danger, first stop for invaders and environmental disasters, scene of shipwrecks and daring maneuvers during the Resistance. Protection has taken the form of lighthouses, from the earliest fire-towers manned by monks to solid sentinels pounded by the waves. The forts designed by Louis XIV's military genius Vauban and the Germans' Atlantic Wall from World War II are both still much in evidence, presenting the first line of defense for the Kingdom of France and then occupied territory.

Through it all the coastal people have struggled on, working hard, adapting and making do with changing conditions and priorities. Their lives and habits have been a major attraction for artists drawn to activities

109

carried out along the shore, a place more capable of definition than the ineffable sea.

## DOUARNENEZ: SARDINES, COMMUNISTS, AND BUTTER CAKE

"…le Naples Breton…"
                    Max Jacob

The wide Bay of Douarnenez on the Atlantic coast is the most favored location for one of Brittany's seminal stories, the destruction of the city of Ys (see p.89). It was also the scene of the arrival of St Ronan, skimming along on his stone boat among the fishing craft, before being driven inland by angry natives to the settlement now bearing his name, Locronan. The locals did not appreciate his action in causing a great light to shine on the coast to put an end to the evil habits of wreckers. The prickly and awkward Ronan, like many other Breton saints, often had trouble getting along with folk.

He picked a good spot, however. This shallow bay stretches for over twenty kilometers, between the more rugged arms of the Crozon peninsula and Cap Sizun, softly edged by rounded hills and low cliffs. The height of Menez Hom looms to the north, marking the end of the Montagnes Noires. This adds to the rich religious mythology of the area: the height was once a pagan pinnacle. King Marc'h (horse in Breton), who had equine ears, was said to be buried there and an apparently Celticized statue of Minerva, transformed into the goddess Brigitte and dating from the first century CE, was unearthed in 1913.

By contrast one of the *hauts lieux* of Breton Catholicism in Brittany also borders this bay. The shrine of Ste-Anne-la-Palud still attracts many thousands for the Pardon on the last weekend of August. Legend holds that Ste Anne, female patron saint of Brittany and mother of Mary, whose role in the story of Christ is relayed in the Apocrypha, actually came from Brittany and went to the Holy Land only to escape an abusive marriage. Later in life, she returned to visit her native shores at this spot—some say with her grandson Jesus in tow. A canticle sung at the festival includes the words:

*Mirit tud an Arvor*
*War zouar ha war vor*

Protect the people of the coast
On sea and on land

The town of Douarnenez, folded unobtrusively into the southern rim of the bay, was an important fishing settlement at least as long ago as the Roman period. At its northern tip lies the green strip of idyllic calm known as the Plomarc'h, which retains the rather fine (restored) remains of a Roman fish sauce factory, the pungent *garum* made from rotting entrails, a most desirable condiment shipped all over the empire. The oily sardine was perhaps ideal for this purpose and this shimmery little fish has continued its significance in the history of the town right up to the present day. The chapel of St-Hélène above the port of Rosmeur has an unusual carving high up on the street façade: a diving *fou de bassan* (northern gannet) looks set to beat the little fishing boat to a shoal of sardines. Indeed, the epithet *penn sardin* (sardine head) was given mainly to the female workers who processed the catch in the canning factories that gave

Sardine capital: Douarnenez (Wendy Mewes)

111

the town its prosperity in the nineteenth century. The firm of Chancerelle, established in the town in 1853, is still functioning at the time of writing. By 1880 there were forty similar establishments providing significant employment for the local population. During that century the number of inhabitants rose from fewer than 1,500 to 11,500, a sign of the success of the fishing industry and its associated processes.

Douarnenez, like Concarneau on the south coast, was highly dependent on its annual sardine catch. The shoals arrived in early summer to feast on the rich plankton of the bay, the shallowness of the water compacting the fish into a mass which boosted the volume of the catch. When sardines suddenly deserted the Breton coast in 1902, it was a social and economic catastrophe, bringing incredible hardship to all those whose living was directly or indirectly linked to the trade. In Concarneau, which suffered a similar trauma, the first Filets Bleus festival in 1905 was set up with the aim of raising funds and support for the fishermen and their families. In Douarnenez aid was also forthcoming, but the fishermen were forced to adapt to survive, chasing mackerel and deep-sea fish like tuna further afield or even langoustines off the coast of Africa. Those who got rich from the latter were locally referred to as "Mauretanians" who built large showy houses and whose wives put on airs.

Douarnenez has a history of radical sociopolitical action, much of it stemming from its role as a major sardine port. The factory owners were reaping great profits from the processing and conserving industry, based on the grueling work of women in poor conditions with minimal pay. Girls went into the factories as young as ten, and up to eighteen hours a day of labor was expected in high season. Little wonder they sang together at their work to alleviate the toil. Pay was according to the number of sardines processed, an unsatisfactory system given it was not the workers themselves who assessed their tally. A strike in 1905 was initially successful in gaining hourly rates, but relations between management and staff were poor.

The rise of socialism in the early twentieth century, highlighting inequalities and injustices in the workplace, sprang from just such situations. In Douarnenez a socialist triumph at the polls in 1919 was followed by the first communist municipal success for the party of Sébastien Velly two years later. When he died soon after Daniel Le Flanchec took over the mantle and his support was invaluable to the women at the Carnaud factory who took strike action in 1924, soon followed by other factory-workers. Their slogan was *Pemp real a vo*—"it will be 1.25 francs" (the hourly rate they demanded). This time the cannery bosses played hardball, calling in notorious strike-breaker Léon Raynier.

The mounting tension in the port was followed all over France, with publicity stirred by the communist press, and the enforced new perception of a traditional rural society like western Brittany was now one of "Zola-ism"—the struggle of the proletariat. As the months dragged on, families left without any income were hard-pressed to survive but they continued even in the face of ruthless tactics by owners determined to ride roughshod over the women on whose work their wealth was founded. Matters came to a violent height when Le Flanchec and his nephew were fired on and wounded at a café with friends during New Year celebrations. The mayor survived but the outrage that followed the attack led to a speedy settlement of the dispute in the workers' favor. One woman at the forefront of this struggle, Josephine Pencalet (an apt name meaning "hard-headed"), was named on the mayor's list for the elections of 1925. Her success at the polls was symbolic: at that time women were ineligible for the vote, never mind standing for election, and her political post was declared invalid.

There is even a genre of tales—*les histoires douarnenistes*—that illustrates the town's strong personality and the duality of strong Catholic faith and radical politics. These may need to be savored, like the sardine, with a large pinch of salt, but nevertheless offer an insight into the essential character of Douarnenez. There is the man who wanted to name his boat *A bas la calotte*, an anticlerical slogan—"Down with the skull cap" (worn by priests)—frequently chanted during political demonstrations. His devout wife says she will leave him and go back to her mother's house if he does such a thing. He asks if he may name the boat after their children instead. His wife is delighted. So the boat is named the *Louise Michel*—which just happens to be the name of a nineteenth-century French feminist anarchist and militant. Imagine the bishop's reaction at the annual blessing of boats! (It was naming a street in the town after her which got Sébastien Velly censured by the departmental Prefect.)

Today Douarnenez comprises three ports: the fishing harbor of Rosmeur; Port Rhu, where an important boat museum is located; and Tréboul, once a quiet coastal village, now the mecca for pleasure craft. Just offshore at the mouth of the estuary which leads past the museum to Pouldavid, an important harbor in medieval times, the Île Tristan may in fact have been the site of the original settlement, as the name of the town means "land of the island." Associations with the Tristan of Arthurian cycle fame are unlikely, as earlier versions of the name like Tutual seem to be derived from St Tugdual, one of the founding saints of Brittany, and the little island was once farmed by monks from the monastery at Marmoutier. In fact it has seen many changes of use over the centuries, being fortified at various times, the site of a fish-processing factory in the nineteenth century, and given a lighthouse in 1845.

In 1595 the island was the stronghold of the notorious young noble brigand Guy Eder de La Fontenelle. With his ruthless band of about 400 men, he was the scourge of many areas of western Brittany during the Wars of the League, taking advantage of the unsettled times for personal mayhem. He was renowned for his swift, savage raids such as at Penmarc'h (see p.119) and Pont-Croix, pillaging and burning whole settlements as he went. A contemporary, Canon Jean Moreau, described him as "Christian in name and infidel in effect… a perjurer and traitor." A large force of peasants tried to dislodge him from Île Tristan but a thousand are said to have lost their lives in the showdown at Kerlaz.

In many ways La Fontenelle personified the bold and violent times, cutting a colorful figure in oral tradition in later years, especially courtesy of what passes for the "romantic" side of his life. La Villemarqué and Luzel both record songs relating to the snatching of a young noblewoman aged twelve (some say seven) to be his bride. Married at fourteen, Marie de Chévoir was apparently devoted to her wild husband and a son was born before La Fontenelle was finally captured, accused of conspiring with the Spanish (who had supported the Catholic cause in the wars of religion). Marie went to Paris to plead with the king for La Fontenelle's freedom but he had already been broken on the wheel as a traitor. According to popular tradition, she died of a broken heart within the year.

The coastal scenery and activity around Douarnenez inspired many artists. Eugène Boudin described the landscape as "the object of my dreams" and wished he had discovered the area earlier. Max Jacob (see p.179) and his friend the young British painter Kit Wood spent two summers here just before the latter's death back in England in 1930. Wood had entered the Parisian scene and the world of opium through a meeting with Jean Cocteau, which led him to other influential figures like Jacob and Picasso. In his works inspired by those Breton visits he manages to get beyond the romanticized cliché to a natural appreciation of the slow, rhythmic scenes of life on the littoral, even if the heaviness of portrayal hints at a certain underlying sadness. In Douarnenez his subjects reflect those self-contained maritime routines—a fisherman with his nets, the building of a boat (with a hint of coffin about it)—yet with odd twists like a woman in traditional dress and *coiffe* carrying timber, or naked sunbathers beside some artfully arranged lobster baskets. Wood returned to England as his problems with drugs increased. Accidentally or by intention, he fell under a train in Salisbury Station in August 1930.

Douarnenez was also a place of less direct inspiration for the surrealist painter, the mad-haired Yves Tanguy (1900–55). Born in Paris to Breton parents, he spent much time during his childhood around the Bay of Douarnenez, his mother having a house in Locronan. Through acquaintance with André Breton, doyen of Parisian surrealists, Tanguy began a commitment to life as an artist. He frequently spent his vacations in this area in the 1920s with his first wife Jeanne Ducrocq and friends like Pierre Matisse, son of Henri, and the influence of the landscape may be discerned even in this most elusive of painters. André Cariou, former curator of Quimper's Musée des Beaux-Arts, described his work as "a reflection of the internalized image he held of Brittany."

Tanguy never explained or offered an analysis of his own work and even asked friends to come up with titles for his paintings, a strange obfuscation. It is clear, however, that the tidal shore, the expandable boundary between land and sea, inspired many canvases, where shadowy beaches peopled by bizarre objects recede into the murky horizon. One or two scenes also seem to suggest tidal waves and a sense of lingering menace on these fantasized shores, relevant to the local mythology of Douarnenez, but to look for coherence or "meaning" is perhaps a futile game.

Tanguy's second marriage was to the American artist Kay Sage, and he took dual American nationality in 1948 before dying suddenly of a brain hemorrhage in the US in 1955. After organizing and cataloguing the collection of her husband's work, his wife shot herself. In 1964 lifelong friend Pierre Matisse scattered their ashes, according to their wishes, in the waters of the Bay of Douarnenez.

Douarnenez is not all sardines and surrealism. The signature Breton butter cake, *kouign amann,* is said to have been invented by a local baker named Yves-René Scordia in about 1860. The method involves extensive folding of dough with sugar and butter slathered between the layers each time to produce a flaky cake crusty on the outside and softly succulent within. The number of calories may be obscene, but sometimes one must be prepared to suffer for authentic local experience.

Here is a recipe:

3 cups / 400g flour
2 tsp / 1 packet / 10g yeast
3 ½ sticks / 14 oz / 400g softened butter
1 cup / 250 ml warm water
1 ¾ / 350g sugar

1) Develop the yeast in the water for ten minutes. Then mix into flour to form a dough. Rest it for thirty minutes. 2) Roll out into a rectangle. Spread with ¼ of the softened butter almost up to the edges and cover with ¼ of the sugar. 3) Fold over four times, then rest the dough for twenty minutes. 4) Repeat stages 2 and 3 three times, resting for twenty minutes between each. 5) Finally shape into a round and bake in a buttered cake pan for forty minutes at 400°F / 200°C.

## AROUND PENMARC'H: DARK AND DANGEROUS COAST, CHAUCER, AND A BEACON OF LIGHT

"The Pointe de Penmarc'h is the most desolate, wild, depressing place we have ever visited. All we can say is that a day passed there throws one into such a state of sadness and a sort of stupor that it takes several more days to get over it."

Émile Souvestre

"The approaches to Penmarc'h are magnificent… heathland, Druidic stones, bell towers, sea and rocks, all the essence of Brittany is there.

Fortuné du Boisgobey

This strange flat coastline, pounded by Atlantic waves and winds, has a wild grandeur all of its own, lying at the southwest tip of Brittany in the far corner of Pays Bigouden, which has its capital at Pont l'Abbé. The

Pointe de Penmarc'h (or Cap Caval, both meaning horse's head) is one of the most dangerous coasts imaginable, serrated by low files of segmented granite rocks, compressed by tectonic plate movement billions of years ago. The result is a treacherous layer of the hard stuff just below the water when the tide is up and exposed for the potential death trap it poses the rest of the time. Behind this savage shore lies a large area of marsh and loch, aptly described by René de Sourdeac, Governor of Brest in the late sixteenth century, as a "terrestrial archipelago," separated from the sea today by strips of low, salt-encrusted white houses. The *bourg* of Penmarc'h, once named Tréoultré, is inland, fringed by three ports: Kérity on the south coast, St-Pierre and St-Guénolé on the west.

Geoffrey Chaucer, writing *The Canterbury Tales* in the second half of the fourteenth century, based "The Franklin's Tale" on the coastal scenery at Penmarc'h, in "Amorik that is called Britayne." Dorigen is terrified that her beloved husband Arveragus, who has gone to gain glory in tournaments in England, will be shipwrecked as he returns home. She walks with her friends on the coast where their castle is situated, watching "many a ship and barge sail their course" and sees the danger of the "rokkes blake" that have ripped the hulls of countless vessels. Dorigen resorts to using the services of a magician—despite a fateful promise in exchange—to make the black rocks disappear, and her husband does indeed come home safely. The price she must pay for this is to leave him for another man, but all eventually ends honorably with the couple reunited.

Sailing has been a way of life throughout Penmarc'h's history but even local sailors in recent times have been undone by these cruel traps. Twenty-seven people died in 1925 as two lifeboats were lost attempting to save sailors from a wreck. In 1967 the *Kreiz ar Pin* struck the Étocs (Stacks), a line of offshore rocks. The disaster was visible to those on land in St-Guénolé and St-Pierre, but despite attempts at rescue all the crew drowned. Incredibly, the ship's dog, Milou, was found alive, surviving in an air pocket under the boat.

It is not only those at sea who are in danger. The dark Rochers de St-Guénolé nearby are notorious for fatal accidents. Almost every year someone is swept away by a sudden greedy wave. In 1870 the family of the Prefect of Finistère was enjoying a picnic on a fine day on these rocks when tragedy struck. The archaeologist and artist Paul du Chatellier, whose little studio used to stand nearby, witnessed the event but was powerless to help.

Only three of the five bodies were ever recovered. An iron cross set into the stone now marks the inauspicious spot, and there are railings to cling on to for those daring enough to mount the same mass of granite. The element of danger remains as exceptional spring tides on this flat coast draw many to the spectacle of thunderous watery mountains looming over the low land and the curious phenomenon of thick white foam filling creeks and inlets like heavy snow drifts.

The busyness of shipping traffic around the Pointe de Penmarc'h noted by Chaucer's Dorigen in medieval times reflects the importance of this trade route between the Mediterranean and northern Europe. The skill of local navigators and seamen was legendary, and unsurprising after an upbringing on this deceptive coast exposed to the full might of the Atlantic. In addition to fishing for sardine, mackerel, ling, and hake, the major occupation here was *cabotage*, the transfer of goods by sea along the coast from one port to another. This was a staging post on the wine route between Bordeaux and England: the depression known as Toul Gwin (wine hole) behind the beautiful beach at Pors Carn is a reminder of barrels snatched from a ship beached on the shore, doubtless a prize much appreciated by the locals. Salt from the southeastern coast of Brittany passed through in large quantities, a vital ingredient in the preservation of fish and always in demand. A more unusual commodity for transport was *pastel de Toulouse*, the blue dye derived from woad, but this trade lessened in the seventeenth century after indigo became widely available, and later became redundant when blues could be chemically produced. At the end of the nineteenth century, the last period of significant *cabotage*, ships were heading to Swansea with pit props from Quimper and to Cardiff with potatoes from Pont l'Abbé.

Penmarc'h is a remote area, not somewhere passed through by land travel today any more than in earlier epochs. For this reason, ships' captains were the local "nobility" and some solid stone houses still to be found in the backstreets of Kérity reflect a considerable degree of prosperity from maritime trade. (Gentry preferred the comparative comforts of Pont l'Abbé.) The local churches—St-Nonna (1509) at Penmarc'h and the Tour Carrée (1488), all that is left of the former structure in St-Guénolé—have exterior decoration of ships in relief carving, a proud statement of the source of wealth that built them. The fifteenth-century Chapelle de Notre-Dame de la Joie between St-Pierre and St-Guénolé has long been a focus of thanks for survival from the sea, as the votive gifts of model ships in the interior illustrate.

This chapel is unusually situated right on the sea front, almost a challenge to the forces of nature and a symbol of faith's power against elemental wrath. In 1896 when the dunes were breached causing extensive inland flooding, the church was filled with seaweed and pebbles but not structurally damaged.

The height of Penmarc'h trade was between 1450 and 1560, carried out by as many as 400 small boats (usually about seventy tons, with a fifteen-man crew) and individual enterprise. The area was devastated by La Fontenelle in 1596, with hundreds of boats seized or burned and a massacre of the population who had taken refuge in the church of Penmarc'h. To add to the misery of these losses, economic pressures began to bite in the seventeenth century, with Louis XIV's demands for taxation to finance his wars and compulsory service in the Navy. Absentee aristocratic landowners began to insist on their rights as they too felt the pinch, but when the Duchy of Penthièvre sent sergeants to collect their dues here in this far corner of land, the unfortunate men were thrown into the sea by the tough local skippers.

As time passed, however, the rest of the maritime commercial world began to build much larger vessels and to become organized in syndicates for more effective working practices, to the detriment of Penmarc'h, which remained the domain of small family businesses. Fishing held its importance, and nine canneries providing much-needed employment—primarily for women—were established in Penmarc'h by the end of the nineteenth century. The collection and processing of seaweed (see p.125) also provided jobs. There was once a large factory for this coastal industry near the lighthouse, and old photos shows stacks of seaweed being burned alongside the Chapelle de la Joie, clouds of smoke driven inland by the sea breeze.

There were those unconnected with maritime exploitation: behind the coast peasants in their small houses surrounded by dry-stone walls eked out a living on soil fertilized by the readily available seaweed. Before the nineteenth century they grew grains and vegetables, but the potato gradually took over and became the staple crop. One of Mathurin Méheut's paintings (see p.123) shows Bigoudene women harvesting the crop in St-Guénolé. A railway line over the marshy interior once ran little "potato trains" across to market in Pont l'Abbé: it is now a cycle path bisecting this tree-starved interior. The station was "manned" by a Bigoudene, complete with tall white *coiffe* and whistle, in the late 1950s.

The extremes of this coast have resulted in grief for many ships over the centuries, and accusations of deliberate wrecking. There were stories of lanterns hung on cows' horns along the paths above the shore, and popular tradition preserves the "Gwerz Penmarc'h," a song in which the people of Penmarc'h are lambasted for intentionally luring ships onto the rocks by lighting their church towers at night.

A fleet on its way back from Bordeaux had a calm journey until rounding the Pointe de Penmarc'h when the winds grew strong and the ships found themselves by the Étocs, confused by unexpected lights:

> Who will take the news to Audierne
> That all the fleet but one is lost?
> …
> A curse on you folk of Penmarc'h
> For lighting your steeples at night

As with any other coastal people, booty brought in on the tide from wrecks was reckoned fair game and had to be snatched away quickly before the nobility or royal officers started asserting their rights. Deliberately causing the deaths of other mariners was quite another story and many brave attempts at rescue were made. There was also ready help for the stranded. During World War I, a German U-boat patrolled this stretch of coast, intent on intercepting Allied convoys. The Americans called this submarine "Penmarch Pete" (and another farther north "Armen Archie"). When one of their ships, the *Alcedo*, was hit, some of the crew escaped in a lifeboat and made their way towards the beam of the lighthouse.

An unnamed "bluejacket" later told the *New York Times* reporter:

> We were too exhausted to continue rowing. Luckily one of those brown-sailed sardine fishing boats sighted us and came alongside. The fishermen took us into a typical Brittany village. We will never forget the welcome those fishermen and fisherwomen gave us. They even gave us their stockings.

It must have been quite a culture shock to meet these Breton-speaking locals in strange clothes, and a further disquieting surprise for their American comrades when the survivors turned up dressed in "peasant frocks, caps and clogs."

The construction of lighthouses put an end to tales of wrecking. Brittany's ragged coastline is littered with these marine *menhirs* standing sentinel over a heavily indented rocky shore ruled by the strong tides and currents which have shaped its tortuous edges. These offshore and coastal lighthouses, for many the ultimate symbol of a region dominated by the sea, have their own history and legends like the Île Vierge off Plouguerneau in north Finistère, which is the tallest in Europe with 10,000 opaline plaques lining the inner walls, or Tévennec, near the Pointe du Raz, haunted by a violent ghostly presence once making the job of guardian a veritable curse.

At Penmarc'h the Phare d'Eckmühl is the most handsome and sophisticated of them all, built of Kersanton stone with an octagonal tower, sixty-six meters high, a frieze of stylized waves decorating the base. It was constructed between 1893 and 1897 to replace a more functional version

Light on a dark coast: the Phare Eckmühl (Fafner/Wikimedia Commons)

set up in 1835 (now a marine center). The tiny chapel in its shadow may itself have once been used as a primitive fire tower to warn sailors of the dangerous rocks. Eckmühl towers over that and the little port of St-Pierre, its modern lantern with a phenomenal range of forty-four kilometers.

The money to build it came from a bequest by the daughter of Louis-Nicolas Davout, given the title Prince d'Eckmühl by Napoleon for his role in the battle of that name in 1809 against the Austrians in Bavaria. She wanted a placement on the "dark and dangerous Breton coast" in a location of particular peril, with a view to saving significant numbers of lives at sea, a way of balancing those lost in war. It was the first to be a veritable architectural design, with Paul Marbeau, a Parisian architect, enlisted for the plans. The lighthouse soon became a tourist attraction and the emblem of the Pointe de Penmarc'h. It even found its way into literature, in a work by Quimper poet and artist Max Jacob.

> The Phare d'Eckmühl is a great beacon of light. If you are lost on the land, look left or right and you will see where St-Guénolé is…
>
> Marie Guiziou! For me Life is like the land and for me you are like the lighthouse of Eckmühl.
>
> Marie Guiziou! My life is like the sea around Penmarc'h! And if I don't see your eyes, I am but a shipwrecked soul on the rocks.

Now open to the public, the Phare d'Eckmühl is one of most visited sites in Finistère. There is a popular annual race where individuals are timed as they run up the 307 steps and back down again. The record set in 2013 by Quentin Thomas, a medical student from Quimper, is forty-seven seconds.

To get a sense of the innate wildness of this coastal area, a short walk up from Pors-Carn leads to the spectacular peninsula of Pointe de la Torche, famous for staging the world surfing championships. Here a sizeable Neolithic *dolmen* sits on the tip of the headland, in what must have seemed a commanding position over the ocean. Today it is cheek by jowl with a German defensive structure from the World War II. The Musée de la Préhistoire Finistérienne in St-Guenolé contains finds from all the major excavations in recent times. Local examples of the Neolithic still in situ also include the Menhir de Kerscaven, less impressive since the top broke off but representative of what was a widespread megalithic presence in this area until about 200 years ago—some say in alignments to rival those which have survived at Carnac—but the demands of agriculture and the greed of treasure seekers have been the instruments of their destruction.

Something even more remarkable because of its archaeological rarity lies under the grassy dunes at St-Urnel: a cemetery dating from the early years of settlement by the Britons (Penmarc'h's patron St Nonna is said to have arrived on this shore from Ireland in his stone boat) as Amorica became Brittany and the Dark Ages gave way to the development of the Breton state. This burial ground was once attached to a parish now disappeared and became covered by the encroachment of the dunes during the Middle Ages. The outline of a chapel dating from the eleventh century was found during excavation by Pierre-Roland Giot during the 1940s. The burials date from c. 500-1100: one could say that the earliest Bretons we know of in the intimate detail of death are from the singular area around Penmarc'h.

ART AND GRAFT: THE WORKING MAN'S ARTIST, SORROW, AND SEAWEED

The coast was once much more a place of activity than it is now, when walkers on the magnificent coastal path are the busiest sign of life away from actual ports. A man whose work encapsulates an older rhythm of working-day existence along the shore is Mathurin Méheut. Brittany may have attracted and inspired countless artists from elsewhere, but Méheut is arguably the one great homegrown talent.

He was born in 1882 in Lamballe, Côtes d'Armor, where a museum honors him today. His father was a carpenter with a large workshop, and as a boy the future artist not only passed a lot of time in practical tasks around this type of work but also in observation of the artisans themselves. A clear interest in *métiers* or trades—in how people do things—is evident within the very large body of work he accomplished over a long career: in 1944 he was to illustrate a seminal book by Florian Le Roy called *Vieux métiers bretons*. Subjects range all over Brittany from onion sellers in Roscoff, salt producers in Guérande, and stone cutters in Maël-Carhaix to a preponderance of sea-related scenes from Brittany's southwest coast.

His interest in marine subjects began with an assignment for a Parisian decorative arts magazine which took him to Roscoff, where he ended up staying for two years, meticulously studying all aspects of this new universe: paintings of fish, crabs, seabirds, and seaweed show the sort of scrupulous attention to detail that was to be transferred into a new style for the human form. The result was an exhibition which attracted much attention, and a book, *Étude de la mer, flore et faune de la Manche et de l'océan*, published in 1913.

He was in Japan (as a result of winning an artistic prize) when World War I broke out and he made a hurried return to France. After serving on the front at Arras, where he sketched continuously between military engagements, he was called on to put his talent to practical use in "works of observation" which could be used by army tacticians. In this way the war could be said to have nurtured his development as an artist—he was also decorated for bravery in action in 1915.

Teaching posts later took up much of his time, but Méheut's real desire was to develop the artistic love affair he had started with his home region, and particularly the littoral. He even carried this into the decorative arts, designing a dinner service called *La Mer* for the Henriot pottery in Quimper in the 1920s. Even though he never lived in Brittany he made many long visits, sketching compulsively as was his lifelong habit. He passed the summer of 1919 at Penmarc'h, and was to be drawn again and again to the southwestern coast of Finistère. The resulting scenes show a tender respect for the activities that occupied the bodies and hearts of the people, from men at sea or raking seaweed to women picking potatoes at St-Guénolé or packed like the sardines themselves along tables in a factory, their *coiffes* a rank of white blobs like the heads of the fish they are processing.

Méheut is well-known as an artist of seascapes—in 1921 he became an official artist of the French Navy—but his portfolio is effectively a documentary tribute to the working man. There is no sentimentality or romance in his portrayal of men and women going about their business, but an inherent acknowledgment of the effort of physical work, the bodily rhythms it imposes and—as always in Brittany—the necessary partnership with the elements. His meticulous observation extends to all the traditional activities of the coast from fishing, boat building, and net mending to salt and seaweed production. His effortless ability to convey quiet concentration in just a few dark strokes, even in portrayal of suspended activity, is memorable. One of his most famous images is a back view of three sailors on board ship, each in blue beret and *vareuse* (smock) above bright yellow trousers, hands in pockets, legs braced against the roll of the waves. It is a moment of inactivity enforced by conditions: they watch and wait, both relaxed and alert, at total ease in their natural *métier*. The picture is called *La vie à bord: en route*.

One less well-known traditional *métier* well-illustrated by Méheut is that of the *goémoniers* or seaweed collectors. Found mainly—but by no means exclusively—in northern Finistère, this industry was vitally important to the region's economy and employed both men and women in a series of labor-intensive tasks. Seaweed was a free natural resource which would yield a basic income in return for hard work. There was no need even to have a boat as the beaches provided a steady supply after each tide. Seaweed was used extensively for fuel and fertilizer before the early nineteenth-century discovery of iodine, derived from its ashes.

The laborious practice of amassing and processing the seaweed from the seabed or the beach was entirely manual. Horses plodded out into the shallows for carts to be loaded using wooden rakes directly from small boats. The seaweed was then dried out on top of the cliffs or dunes before

Seaweed oven (Wendy Mewes)

being burned, with clouds of yellow sulphurous smoke obscuring sections of the coast. Echoes of the processes involved still litter the shoreline: the notched stones used for pulley cables to lift loads of seaweed up from the beach and the remains of seaweed ovens, looking for all the world like divided stone coffins sunk into the ground, are widely in evidence. From these structures blocks of *pain de soude* (sodium carbonate) were lifted out and transported to factories for iodine extraction. Many industries—paper, glass, and soap—relied on seaweed products.

The work, particularly harsh and unrelenting in physical labor, naturally figures in the oral tradition of Brittany which is keenly linked with occupations. The modern *gwerz ar vezhinerien*, Lament of the Seaweed Workers, was written in 1974 by Denez Abernot, whose grandfather was in the profession all his life. It figures in the repertoire of various contemporary singers, including that most Breton of performers Denez Prigent. The song describes the sadness of a young man whose girl is off to the islands (Molène archipelago) to work as a seaweed gatherer.

> Every night and every day in sorrow
> The seaweed gatherers are a cursed breed
>
> In their boat, early in the morning
> They strip the rocks
> Hands split by the scythe
> Backs broken by the ladder

Méheut offers a meticulous observation of the *goémoniers*, both working in groups, their bodies aligned to a task, and as individuals. The tools of the trade are almost extensions of the physique in action: rakes and the long staff (*perche*) used for propelling rafts of seaweed or *drômes* back to shore. A sketch from 1910 portrays a seaweed gatherer's widow, standing upright in front of a large rock, clad in traditional black, arms folded across her precious *perche*, eyes fixed on the beach, the domain of her kind. Other illustrations present men and women up to their thighs in seawater collecting the bounty of the tides, a woman with shoulders squared as she hauls a hand cart, a team putting their backs into bringing in the *drômes*. All these scenes are in shades of blue, black, and endless greys, the colors of sky, sea, and clothes uniting the elements with human toil, harmonizing the labor with its context. The object of all the effort, the seaweed itself, is marked out in russet browns.

The seaweed industry is still very much alive in Brittany. Lanildut on the northwest coast is the main port in Europe, handling over 35,000 tons each year. There are more than 600 varieties to be found along the Breton coasts, and although the traditional usage for fertilizer remains significant, cosmetic and culinary applications are increasingly important today. The processes are all mechanized: where once the *laminaires* were harvested from the seabed with a *falz hir* (long scythe) and hauled up onto the boats by human muscle, now a hydraulic arm called a *skoubidou* has transformed the speed and capacity of the task. Tractors and trailers have replaced the horse and cart, and mechanization has virtually cut manpower from the later stages of transformation. To appreciate Méheut's sense of people at the heart of process it is necessary to attend the annual celebration of the old craft at the Fête des Goémoniers at Plouguerneau in north Finistère, where all the former methods are reenacted with typical Breton pride in a way of life that lives on in cultural tradition.

## CARANTEC: THE BRAVE BOAT BUILDER AND *THE SHARK*

"No port in France can boast a prouder record in those sombre years of defeat and humiliation than the villages of Carantec and Pont de la Corde."

Brook Richards, *Secret Flotillas*, 2004

One very important coastal activity which has stood the test of time is boat-building, even if the emphasis may have changed from war, trading, and fishing to safety vessels and leisure craft. At Carantec on the Channel coast near Roscoff the business of the Sibiril family began at the time of the Revolution, although Sibiril Technologies, still functioning in the rue Lamotte Picquet today, finally passed into other hands in 2011. A stele beside the coastal path dedicated to Ernest Sibiril—the man the Allies called The Ferryman—is a reminder that his boatyard was the center of a remarkable Resistance network during World War II, responsible for evacuating 193 British servicemen and French volunteers.

Sibiril was not the first. This area became a significant escape route right at the beginning of the Occupation, after Jacques Guéguen, a fisherman from nearby Pont de la Corde, used his boat the *Pourquoi Pas* to smuggle British soldiers and French *résistants* across the Channel from June 1940. He made several more trips before being interned for seven months in 1941. Clearly under threat again in 1942, he was forced to leave Brittany himself, helped by Ernest Sibiril.

This was the start of a coherent and courageous venture of skillful evasion right under the noses of the occupying German forces, a pattern repeated along this Channel coast of Brittany, where small boats and experienced sailors were plentiful. After General de Gaulle's appeal in 1940, more than 350 people from just one area around Plougasnou left to join him in London. Equally daring were those Allied agents and *résistants* coming in, and farther east the Var network operated on their behalf around Beg an Fry between January and April 1944, despite a German post on the headland directly above.

Brittany was not short of brave men during the war years and the Resistance *maquis* involved many local networks, organized to varying degrees, in addition to or conjunction with the FFI (Forces françaises de l'intérieur). These were active all over the region (an evocative museum in Morbihan at St-Marcel gives a detailed presentation of one particular battle fought in the countryside there which brings home the terrible realities of occupied Brittany) but the north coast with its proximity to England was a crucial line of communication and transportation that could only be kept open by the fearless commitment of Breton sailors and the local population. It was also a treacherous piece of littoral to navigate safely, especially at night, and the long tidal recoil also placed limitations on the timings of embarkation.

In Carantec, Sibiril's business was a great advantage in his clandestine work, and the quality of construction was not a small factor in the success of operations, although it also naturally attracted the attention of the Germans. He painted all the small boats from his yard black to help avoid detection on the water at night and, because the Germans were capable of counting and checking the number of craft he possessed, bits of broken up boat were always kept ready to account for discrepancies. Those in the know were his family and trusted friends, a network of maybe thirty people, all risking their lives for the sake of freedom.

Many spoke later of Sibiril's physical bravery and exceptional moral strength, as well as his courteously hospitable dealings with all those he helped. His "calm courage and intelligence" are highlighted in Sir Brook Richards' book about secret naval activity in Brittany between 1940 and 1944. In addition to obvious dangers on the water, there were many other complex logistics of hiding, housing, feeding, and transporting the escapees. And if a projected mission failed to take place through sea conditions or enemy activity the extra organization involved in aborting and rearranging a voyage became even more hazardous.

The dramatic chances taken by all those involved in Sibiril's escape network are underlined by the experience of Olivier Le Borgne, who in 1943, at the age of twenty, was entrusted with a mission. He recounted later how they had left Carantec at midnight and then had the misfortune to encounter a German convoy just north of the Ile de Batz off Roscoff. They were fired on and the frightened passengers wanted to go back but Le Borgne was confident of getting away and refused. Nature rewarded his decision as mist soon engulfed them, preventing alerted enemy aircraft from using the little boat for target practice. "It was this mist that saved us," he acknowledged. They reached Fowey in Cornwall safely after a journey of twenty-three hours. His attitude in later years—"I just did my duty like the others"—sums up the selfless dedication of all those unassuming and remarkable individuals who came together in the cause of liberation.

Sibiril himself eventually became a marked man but was warned by a neighbor after mass that the Germans were waiting at his house. He and his wife joined their young son Alain, already in hiding in Henvic, and later moved to Brest and various other locations before returning to Carantec for his last very personal mission. On the night of 31 October, eight men set sail under cover of darkness in *Le Requin* (*The Shark*), a boat hastily assembled by Sibiril's father and helpers at the boatyard. The party included Sibiril and his brother Léon and an Englishman, George Wood. This pilot from the 263rd Squadron had miraculously escaped death when his plane took a direct hit and exploded above Ploujean, near Morlaix. Wood survived and was nurtured by local members of the Resistance before being moved to Carantec, ready to join Sibiril's last voyage. They reached Plymouth twenty-one hours later.

Wood went back to RAF duties for the remainder of the war, but later fulfilled a vow made at the time of his miraculous survival and became a minister of the Church. So it was the Rev George Wood who returned to revisit Morlaix and Carantec in 2010 at the age of ninety. The false identity papers of a deaf and dumb person provided for him as cover in 1943 can be seen in the museum at Carantec which has a detailed section devoted to the Resistance movement in the area and—prime exhibit—Sibiril's boat, *Le Requin*.

Ernest Sibiril returned to Carantec and his boat-building business after the war. General de Gaulle, whose wife and children had stayed in Carantec in 1940 before their escape on one of the last ships to sail from Brest, paid him a visit there in 1950. He also received official honors for his extraordinary part in Resistance activity, but a safe return to the Bay of Morlaix and a life following the marine traditions of his ancestors probably meant most of all to this self-contained, reluctant hero. As remarkable as the success of Sibiril's network—no boats or men were lost during any operations—was his quiet, unassuming, and matter-of-fact conduct. It was for others to speak of his profound bravery and sense of duty.

A poignant irony: he eventually died by drowning in 1967, aged sixty-two.

*Chapter Six*

# LAND

## THE HEART OF THINGS

Émile Souvestre writes in *Les derniers Bretons* of walking in the country-side in the evening and hearing peasants, seated far apart on different rocks, exchanging the lines of a *cantique,* or religious song. For him the rural setting is the cradle of song, with its "poetic, dreamy and enchanted" at-mosphere. Everywhere, he claims, one can hear the voice of a child or old woman giving snatches of ballads (*gwerziou*) dating back perhaps centuries with their themes of miracles, lost love, and local events. The innate poetic sense of the Bretons stems from a retained closeness to the land, their songs as natural as speech but communicative of higher emotions than the every-day. He cites the example of a cholera epidemic when official notices posted to be read by the population were ignored, but as soon as someone gave them voice in the form of a song, the preventive advice spread rapidly through the countryside and was finally given attention.

In Brittany the words of poems and the steps of dance have emanated from the landscape, an expression of the relationship between a people and their environment. Place names today evoke the richness of the Breton language and the beloved nature of rock, moor, hill, wood, and valley. These are the ties of the heart, the simple song of connection that roots an identity beyond need of further definition.

As life has moved further and further from the land in the last fifty years, with changes in agricultural practice and migration from the countryside, so has it become more important than ever to preserve the culture that sprang from close association with the natural world and develop the old traditions in new and meaningful ways for the next generations to understand and contribute to the continuity of this inestimably valuable Breton legacy.

### POHER: ROMANS, RED CAPS, AND RAILWAYS

The ancient region of the Poher (*pou-kaer,* territory of the fortified place) lies at the eastern end of the Aulne basin, a corner of Finistère where the

131

Montagnes Noires curve north to meet the high hills of central Brittany, reaching east toward Maël-Carhaix in Côtes d'Armor and south toward Gourin, Le Faouët, and Langonnet in Morbihan. The countryside flows around low hills and wooded valleys, the kind of folded terrain suited to guerrilla warfare, as Breton chief Morvan used to his advantage in conducting his defense against the Franks in the early ninth century before succumbing near Langonnet. Here the outlaw Marion le Faouët ("Marie the Redhead" of oral tradition) with her band of highwaymen had little trouble in leading the authorities on a merry dance in the mid-eighteenth century. It is deeply rural territory: even today there are no large towns in central Brittany, and dairy farms blend into a landscape of rolling views, heavy with trees.

The capital Carhaix-Plouguer stands on a plateau above the Hyères river, the finials of St-Trémeur's square church tower visible from afar. Recent discovery of a Bronze Age village on the edge of the town indicates a long-used site which was part of the territory of the Osismes Celtic tribe, before becoming a Roman regional center, Vorgium. Archaeological digs in the last decade have furnished much information on the grandiose first-century town of 138 hectares with its houses, shops, and extensive aqueduct structures, bringing water from twenty-seven kilometers away, a fine advertisement to the local nobility of the benefits of Roman civilization. Standing at the central gateway to the west of Brittany, it was at the heart of a network of Roman roads, with many routes linking the north coast at Morlaix and Kerilien, Quimperlé to the south, the west at Camaret, and the southern center of Aquilonia (Quimper). The name Carhaix (Karaes) probably derives from the Latin for "crossroads."

During the Dark Ages, Carhaix was one of the powerbases of Conomor, a brutal warlord transformed by legend into the Breton Bluebeard who murdered a series of wives and buried them in a cellar. The oral tradition maintains that, heeding a prophecy that he would lose power to his son, he decapitated young Trémeur, whose statue, head in hands, adorns the façade of the main church.

Conomor's story also provides a link with Cornwall, his probable place of origin: some see the name Carhaix as an echo of Carhays, near Falmouth. He is also equated in one tradition with King Mark, father of Tristan (of *Tristan and Isolde* fame), following the inscription on a stone found near Fowey: "DRUSTANS HIC IACIT CUNOMORI FILIUS" (here lies Drustanus (Tristan) son of Conomor).

Established in Brittany as an early "count" of Poher, Conomor used this central base to pursue his own ambitious plans of expansion, and to fulfill the mission assigned to him by Childebert, Emperor of the Franks, as *praefectus classis*, admiral of the fleet, protecting the coasts and Channel crossing, which explains his other coastal holdings. The mineral resources of the Poher and surrounding lands—lead, silver, tin, iron ore, and alluvial gold—provided another motive for Conomor to establish control over an important place of passage.

The Poher was to provide an even more significant figure in Brittany's history. Around 830, Count Nominoë was chosen by Louis Le Pieux, Emperor of the Franks, as *missus imperatoris*, the emperor's representative in Brittany. Following numerous attempts at dominance over the surprisingly stubborn Breton military leaders, Louis went for the subtler strategy of keeping the peace by using a native in a supervisory role. It worked for his lifetime, but Nominoë was soon at loggerheads with Louis' successor, as we have seen. As the Breton state developed, Carhaix remained a ducal possession, and later a royal one after the union with France.

Maison du Sénéschal, Carhaix, the glamorous tourist office (Wendy Mewes)

Medieval Carhaix had a population of only about 2,000, well down on its Roman heyday. A few half-timbered houses remain from the end of this period, including the magnificent so-called Maison du Sénéchal, once the house of some dignitary, now somewhat fallen in the world to lodge the tourist office. Henri IV financed its restoration in 1606 in gratitude for the town's support during the Wars of Religion. At the other end of the social scale, the *faubourg* of Petit Carhaix and Kergroaz, around the eighteenth-century bridge over the Hyères, retains many small stone houses of the artisans who were active here right up to the twentieth century—cobblers, rope makers, and those who cleaned and dried animal skins to be sent to the tanneries.

The bridge carried the route to Morlaix, on the line of an old Roman road. The lord of Ty Meur (the Great House) near Poullaouen was responsible for its upkeep and also held lucrative control over rights of passage to and from a busy commercial center. And Ty Meur was to play a decisive role in one of the most telling events in the Poher's history—the revolt of the *Bonnets rouges*.

The exploitation of the *ancien régime* began to bite in Brittany as Louis XIV pursued his lavish lifestyle and trade wars with Holland in the mid-seventeenth century. The economic downturn was keenly felt by 1670 as revenues started falling. When wealthy landowners felt the pinch, they began to demand their rights to the fullest degree and often further, an extra pressure on peasants who were already struggling to make ends meet. Events starting elsewhere were to find a resounding echo of resentment and despair in the countryside of the Poher.

There had been little evolution in a peculiar medieval system of landholding in western Brittany which did nothing to encourage good relationships between landowners and peasants. The burdensome *domaine congéable* affected thousands of poor rural laborers. By this contract the local lord retained possession of the land they worked, while the buildings, walls, banks, hedges, and fruit trees were owned by the peasant. It did not stop there. So-called "noble" trees (those that produced an income) of oak, beech, and elm remained the property of the *seigneur*, who sought to wring every scrap of profit from the system, and the peasants had to pay for the privilege of using the mills and ovens of their overlord. He could also demand the *corvée* (days of unpaid labor on his own land) and the *champart*, a percentage of the harvests of the peasant's farm. If the peasant moved or was put off the land, he was entitled to a fair price for all the improvements he had made, but he might have to go to law to get it. It was little wonder that such a system gave rise to constant disputes, and, as the judicial structure was in the hands of the landowner, justice was hard to come by.

The anger came to a head with the revolt of the *Bonnets rouges* (Red Caps) in the summer of 1675, when simmering discontent against landowners reached boiling point in central Brittany. What began as an urban protest in Rennes against new taxes on tobacco and the stamped paper used in legal documents imposed by Louis XIV's finance minster, Colbert, without the consent of the États de Bretagne, lit a touch-paper of dissatisfaction in the countryside. The main areas of rural rebellion were Pays Bigouden, southwest of Quimper, where the "Blue Caps" proclaimed their grievances in a Peasant Code, and the Poher, scene of a large-scale peasant uprising.

The outbreak of rage and revenge wreaked its toll on the châteaux and *manoirs* in the area as these were looted and burned, destroying archive evidence of landownership and obligations. The first attacks in early July were on the residence of a tax collector, and then in Spezet, the house of Henri Porcher, a *notaire* (lawyer) for aristocratic judicial officers, where archives were destroyed and stamped paper stolen. These measures were clearly a response to the injustice felt at the new taxes, but the heat soon turned on the lords and landowners themselves, repayment for their abuses of the system. Many houses were attacked: La Haie-Douar at Locmaria-Berrien, the Manoirs de Keromen, Kerbiquet and Kéranforest in Plouyé. On July 11, the Château de Kergoat at St-Hernin was sacked and burned with some loss of life among the resident staff. The owner himself, Toussaint de Trévigny, who was noted for his harsh treatment of peasants, was away from home.

The enigmatic figure of Sébastien Le Balp, a *notaire* from Kergloff, near Carhaix, emerged as a leader, giving focus and direction to disparate groups. He moved around the countryside accompanied by several thousand armed men, and was able to muster as many as 30,000 for a projected march on Carhaix. He knew that the Duc de Chaulnes, Governor of Brittany, would soon be on the scene with a trained army, and that the insurgents needed powerful allies and military experience if they were not to be brushed aside like flies. It is possible that Le Balp thought of alliance with the Dutch, whose fleet was in the Channel, and he certainly considered a move on Morlaix, a river port providing a link with the outside world.

He already had connections with the Marquis de Montgaillard of Ty-Meur, having acted as *notaire* for the *marquise*. On 2 September Le Balp had a meeting at the château in this hidden valley location with Charles de Montgaillard and his brother Claude. The former had already been in correspondence with the Governor of Morlaix, who suggested that if the leader were captured or killed, the revolt would soon fizzle out. Le Balp left safely enough to organize a huge gathering at Poullaouen to march on Carhaix. But he returned to Ty Meur later the same night, never to leave it alive. Accounts of motives and true circumstances are contradictory, but it is certain that Le Balp was run through by the sword of Claude de Montgaillard.

The peasant army dispersed in disarray and proved no trouble for the vengeful royal army when the Duc de Chaulnes arrived. It took only two weeks to subdue the Poher region, hanging ringleaders or breaking them on the wheel, and sending thousands to the galleys or prison at Brest for

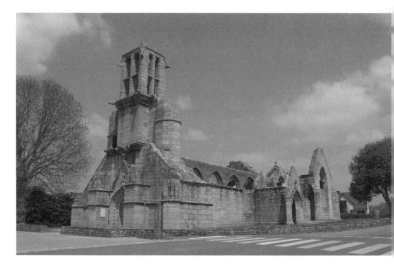

Truncated bell tower: Lambour, Pont l'Abbé (Yann Gwilhoù/Wikimedia Commons)

hard labor. The reprisals were savage. Madame de Sevigné wrote: "all the soldiers in Brittany do nothing but rape and murder." In Pays Bigouden the church bell towers that had summoned peasants to revolt were truncated or decapitated, as can be seen at Lambour in Pont-l'Abbé.

The revolt of the *Bonnets rouges* was an epitome of the divisions and conflicts in Brittany in the final century of the *ancien régime*: an exploitative French administration, ruthless aristocrats, urban unrest, rural poverty and suffering. Even the Duc de Chaulnes acknowledged the misery of the peasants in a letter to Colbert: "their wretchedness is so great that we must understand the consequences of their rage and their brutality."

It is not hard to see why the French Revolution in 1789 was eagerly supported by those looking for a change in their standard of life and security of control over their possessions. The peasants of the Poher had no reason to love their king or the Church that offered no defense against the harsh realities of everyday life.

Sébastien Le Balp himself has been transformed into a martyr of the abused "liberté armorique," the rights enshrined in the union of France and Brittany in 1532, and a symbol of class struggle. His politicization has been resisted by the powers that be: in 2006 a proposed tourist panel on the road into Carhaix was rejected by the Conseil Général because it showed the figure of Le Balp. He has, however, found his place with a large plaque in Spézet.

The new departmental divisions established in December 1789 were a blow to Carhaix. Right on the edge of Finistère, near the boundary with both Côtes du Nord and Morbihan, it was left in no-man's land, cut off from its traditional sphere of influence. The town was even denied the status of subprefecture for the central zone, that honor later going to Châteaulin. Overlooked and out on a limb, the town showed signs of decline. Jacques Cambry, visiting in 1794, described the general character of the inhabitants as "cold and indifferent," only showing signs of life under the influence of *eau-de-vie*. He found the roads deserted and gardens growing wild as the people fell back into the apathy of "Spaniards and savages." A lack of investment and resources took its toll. Even the construction of the Nantes-Brest Canal three kilometers to the south, which saw the establishment of Port de Carhaix with its wharfs and warehouses, did little to revive Carhaix's fortunes.

In an account of his wolf-hunting trip to Brittany published in 1875, a Welsh visitor, Edward William Lewis Davies, gives this impression of the town:

> Surrounded by woods and till lately approached only by a precipitous and rugged route, it stands on a high and bold eminence overlooking the country far and wide, and by its isolation seems to have bidden a successful defiance to the inroads of commerce and civilization.
>
> Carhaix is a very primitive town and, as long as the railways keep their distance, is likely to continue so for many a year to come. Beyond a couple of water mills to grind corn here are no other mills or manufactories to induce commercial visits and increase the wealth of the place.

The coming of the railway in the late nineteenth century did indeed lead to a change in fortunes in the form of an economic boost, allowing the town to reclaim its role as a center of communications, forming the hub of the *Réseau Breton* narrow-gauge railway system.

Lines stretched in all directions, most significantly linking the north coast with the interior. Up to fifty trains a day passed through in the railway's heyday and there were significant employment benefits for Carhaix, with more than 500 people needed to run and maintain the trainyards. Areas of housing for the railway workers grew up—one called *nègre* from the drivers and stokers who returned black with soot. Despite the fact that many *cheminots* (railway workers) were non-Breton speaking, so developing the use of the French language, there was strong social solidarity and socialist political activity, including the formation of unions or syndicates. In 1948 it was railway workers who formed the first nonmilitary *bagad* (musical band), consisting of *biniou* (Breton bagpipes), *bombardes,* and percussion.

Yet even the railway struggled in the post-war era as truck transport became more common and offered more precise transportation of goods. Investment to upgrade the lines to normal gauge was not forthcoming, and only the Carhaix-Guingamp route—still in use today—made the leap to the modern world. The issue of road improvements also proved a difficult one for Carhaix. It was the railway situation all over again as the state favored the north and south *routes nationales* (RN12 and RN165), leaving the central axe from Rennes to Châteaulin largely a standard two-lane highway. The vital importance of high-speed road links for economic development was not lost on the town and vigorous campaigns were waged for upgrades to bring businesses to the area. The Paris-based government was seen as hostile—or at best, indifferent—to the economic development of central Brittany. Despite a degree of decentralization of power in the 1980s, the RN164 dual-carriageway is still not complete at the time of writing.

Carhaix still fights today to maintain a high-profile identity, making much of its central location and cultural assets. The area has tried to re-brand itself as a discrete district with a daily newspaper, and there is a sharp image consciousness in the town. The main protagonist in the reassertion of Carhaix's status has been the controversial figure of Christian Troadec, former journalist and mayor since 2001. He started *Le Poher* newspaper before selling it to the Télégramme group and buying the Coreff brewery, once located in Morlaix but now in Carhaix, and he was one of the founders of the Vieilles Charrues rock festival, which has become Brittany's Glastonbury, attracting nearly a quarter of a million people in recent years. He has also been keen to emphasize the Breton heritage and future of Carhaix, which houses a Diwan *lycée* and the Office de la Langue Bretonne.

Troadec is a radical socialist, pugnacious and articulate, a dominant personality who has become identified with the image of Carhaix itself and the re-Bretonization of the Poher. His letter to François Hollande demanding an urgent explanation of the president's failure to fulfill a promise to ratify the European charter of minority languages gives the flavor of Troadec's pet theme—insistence on the particular economic problems of central Brittany, so often overlooked and discriminated against by the Parisian powers. A vigorous campaign to keep the local hospital open in 2008 and his recent part in encouraging Chinese company Synutra to invest in building a milk-product factory in the hope of saving jobs at the struggling Entremont plant have been in line with all his much-publicized activities in the name of progress and economic development. In late 2013 he orchestrated a new *Bonnets rouges* movement, with thousands of red knitted hats bobbing through the streets of the town in protest against the Parisian government's ecotaxes and a mixed bag of other issues bringing together strange bedfellows of left and right. His instinct for show is certainly effective, whatever one thinks of his political methods or personal image making.

Under Troadec's leadership, rather than looking west to Finistère, Carhaix's attention is firmly in the direction of ancient Poher and engagement with central Brittany. After all, being at the center has always been key to the town's character: people from Carhaix used to say they could understand all four Breton dialects thanks to their particular geographical position.

## *BLÉ NOIR*: A HUMBLE FOODSTUFF FOR EATING AND DRINKING

*Paneved gand mez*
*E-tiwanje en eun nozvez*

What would grow up in a single night
Were it not for shyness?
>                   Riddle posed by Visant Favé, Bishop of Quimper, 1957–77

The thin, acidic soil of central Brittany is not conducive to a plentiful supply of varied food. Away from the coastal areas and vegetable-producing Golden Belt of the north with its seaweed-enriched earth, poor soil accounts for the abject poverty in many areas, especially in the nineteenth century as progress rocked the towns while the rural population fell victim to epidemics and starvation when crops failed.

Breton cuisine is about simple ingredients offered by nature. Simplest of all is *blé noir* (black wheat or buckwheat, *gwiniz du* or *ed du* in Breton) and its eponymous dark flour. The flower is white or very pale pink as it flourishes on green stems, then turns grey as the stems redden toward the moment of harvest.

But Brittany is never simple, as we have seen. This is not a grain at all but a member of the *polygonaceae* family of plants, related to sorrel and rhubarb. The botanical name *Fagopyrum* is from the shape of the seed, like beech mast (*fagus* being the Latin for the beech tree). *Blé noir* is also called *sarrasin* from its supposed origins in the east—linked in some stories with the return of Crusaders—but pollen from this plant dating from the Iron Age has been found in marshes in Brittany by archaeologists. It appears that the use of *sarrasin* here died out in the fourth century CE and these plants were reintroduced between the tenth and twelfth centuries, from northeast Asia via Russia and Turkey. There is no word for it given in the

*Catholicon* of 1499, the first Latin/French/Breton lexicon, but it was certainly widely grown in the sixteenth century—a bizarre popular tradition ascribes this important development to the ubiquitous positive influence of Anne de Bretagne!

In reality it is admirably suited to growth in poor earth, being hardy, resistant to disease, and even fertilizing the soil in which it is sown. Its speedy growth—a hundred days from seed to harvest, as the saying goes—proved the value of *blé noir* in the subsistence diet of peasants. It was filling, nutritious—incidentally, gluten-free—and could be ground into flour in the home rather than at the mill, making *blé noir* a most economical commodity. The discarded "straw" was used as bedding for animals or in compost.

The *conteur* Ernest du Laurens de la Barre (1819–81) tells a story of birds, trees, and flowers trying to protect themselves from a savage storm, horrified that the *blé noir* plants insisted on standing proud to face the hail and thunder. Afterwards, its stems were bent and so remain in lasting punishment for the plant's hubris.

In its most basic state, *blé noir* flour mixed with water and salt provided a thin gruel, or *bouillie,* the staple food in very poor households. The people of Huelgoat were said to have offered this unappetizing dish to the giant Gargantua, who did not forget the insult. When he was given creamy oat porridge (*youd*) in Plouarzel, he obligingly tore up all the huge rocks from the inhabitants' land and chucked them back at Huelgoat—the legendary origin of the famous granite Chaos there today. Émile Souvestre records a song about the ogre's preferences for a cannibalistic meal:

First I love (to eat) the Leonard
Nurtured on fatty meat;
Then those from Trégor
Tasting of crêpes and fresh milk;
But I'll keep those buckwheat boys
From Cornouaille and round Vannes
Until later.

Noel du Fail, writing in Rennes in the sixteenth century, said of *blé noir*: "In truth, without this grain [*sic*] which arrived sixty years ago, poor people would have suffered greatly." Nearly 300 years later, the traveler

Adolphus Trollope described the resources of a solitary farmhouse in the Méne hills: "their only food was a small quantity of black bread made of sarazin, eked out with potatoes, and buttermilk from the churn, whose produce they could not afford to eat" (in line with the peasant policy of "sell the best and eat the rest"). He added that many did not even get the dark bread, but only pancakes made with gruel in a hot frying-pan, shuddering at the memory of their leathery consistency.

The crêpe was a step up the culinary scale, but still a domestic dish. Peasants would have been astonished that today it is a ubiquitous symbol of Breton cuisine, and a feature of dining out. At one time crêpes served with anything other than just butter were referred to as *krampouez bourc'hizien* (bourgeois). It was a custom even in the 1960s to arrive at the crêperie with your own plate and pats of butter according to the number of pancakes you wanted to eat. The *crêpe* remains at its best when closest to its roots and served with the sort of basic accompaniments that would have been produced by the household and land: butter, eggs, ham, mushrooms, apples, and pears.

It is a fallacy to call savory pancakes *galettes* and sweet ones—made with white wheat flour or *froment*—crêpes. Crêpes are historically both sweet and savory in Breton-speaking territory, where the French word is nearest to the Breton *krampouez*. The French term *galette* for the savory version comes from parts of eastern Brittany where Breton was not spoken, although it is true that today the boundaries of usage are blurred.

Haute-Bretagne has also given us another version, a sausage rolled in a crêpe. It is a favorite pre- or post-match snack for soccer fans in Rennes at the Stade Rennais: a popular chant from the terraces starts "galette saucisse je t'aime…" I well remember my first taste of this "Breton hotdog," recommended by friends long ago at the Crêperie L'Akène in Redon, with a perfect accompaniment in Breton beer.

The crêpe inevitably has its place in oral tradition, witnessed by this piece of doggerel from Théodore Botrel:

> Some, seeing the moon
> High in the peaceful evening sky
> Have taken it for a sarrasin crêpe.

The humble crêpe has come a long way from the cottage hearth. Exported to Paris and other parts of France by Breton emigrants, it also made the jump from filler to main course in the 1950s, from the home to the public arena in crêperies all over Brittany, and much further afield. Families often sent homemade crêpes to relatives abroad (although the US customs might confiscate them) or to students in university towns like Rennes. Although it may seem incongruous—and a creation for tourists in search of Breton experience since the nineteenth century—to go out and pay for simple peasant food, it does seem that the practice is older than many think. Documents listing assets at death include references to *galetterie* in eighteenth-century Rennes.

Inevitably there have been attempts to gourmandize the crêpe. Unholy fillings like duck and *foie gras* or health-conscious choices such as smoked salmon and chives now produce endless lists of possibilities on crepêrie menus. A short list is often a sign of quality, with the taste resting on an excellent batter. Whatever the choice of filling, crêpes are best washed down with a *bolée* (pottery cup) or two or three of local cider.

I had my one and only crêpe-making lesson from a master, Yannick Colas, then a retired chef and gifted advocate of all things Breton, now sadly deceased. My initial attempt at his house was predictably disastrous, an event so regular as to have a name: the first one is the *crêpe du chien*. In this case it was literally so, being gobbled up by my optimistic dog, Brian. I wish I could say after that it got easier, but I struggled with the wrist dexterity and lightness of application of the *rozell* to spread a lacy sheet of batter over the hot surface of the *billig*. It became easier to let Yannick cook, and concentrate on eating. The first crêpe was, as tradition demands, plain with butter only, an intense flavor of *blé noir*, followed by more filled with ham, eggs, and sausage before the homemade preserves were brought out ready for a sweet session. I gave up at this point, a greater disappointment to him than my inability to master the technique.

The skills of production can be seen at any festival anywhere in Brittany, but en masse at the Fête de la Crêpe at the Château of Tronjoly in Gourin, the effect is mesmerizing. Behind a great line of electric plates, women and a few men effortlessly roll out crêpes in their hundreds to feed to crowds watching the production line in admiration.

*Farz* is the generic name for flour-based dishes, and *blé noir* figures in another Breton classic, *kig ha farz,* or meat and stuffing. This is the traditional dish of Léon, the northwest region of Finistère famed for its veg-

143

etable production. It comprises meat—pork knuckle and bacon originally, later with beef and sausage added—cabbage and other vegetables like turnips or carrots, and the *farz*, a compote of *blé noir* mixed with cream and butter, is cooked in a cloth bag (a reminder of Léon's lucrative linen trade with England) alongside the other ingredients. Everything is simmered together for hours, making a dish that could be left to cook while work continued in the fields. *Kig ha farz* is regarded as something of a treat and features regularly on local menus today, often once a week, which is about the time it will take before you are hungry again.

*Blé noir* has recently taken on a new character in contemporary brewing, a growth industry in Brittany, first revived in 1985 by Breton partners under the guidance of English brewer Peter Austin. Coreff Brasserie was set up in Morlaix but moved to Carhaix in 2005. Other breweries such as An Alarc'h (the swan, named from a chant recorded in the *Barzaz Breiz*) in Huelgoat and Britt in Telgrunc also produce dark beers from organic *blé noir* with names like Aour Du (Black Gold) or Gwiniz Du. And Brittany now even has its own whisky, made in Plomelin by the Distillerie des Menhirs—the name Eddu gives away its origin.

After years of neglect during the expansion of agricultural production, *blé noir* today is regaining its place, becoming something of a symbol of Breton-ness. It is perhaps not surprising that a group, L'Association Blé Noir Tradition Bretagne in Ploërmel, is devoted to relaunching production and developing the full gamut of this humble plant. Faithful performance in an important supporting role in the social history of Brittany has proved its worth and adaptability in the past and there is plenty of scope for diversification in the future.

## *FEST NOZ*: FROM FARMING TO FÊTE, OR DANCING WITH THE DEVIL

Working the land is all about cooperation, laboring in line with the moon and the weather, sharing laborious tasks with fellow humans as the seasons demand. The threshing of grain (*battage*) was a ritual of impeccably timed rhythmic movement carried out by neighbors working together, relying on a community of spirit and effort that welded rural society together in good times and bad. After the graft came relaxation, a time of eating, drinking, and dancing, for here was the origin of what has become emblematic of Breton culture, the *fest noz*, a celebration in music and the movement of the dance. The beat of the *gavotte* seems born into the Bretons of Basse-Bretagne, letting their bodies speak naturally of an ancestral way of life.

The creation or annual restitution of the threshing floors in farm courtyards was a process of dance, earth flattened by the bare feet or wooden clogs of the dancers, a ritual described as *fest al leur nevez* (*l'aire neuve* in French). In the Trégor, the *frikadeg boloh* was a dance on *blé noir* to extract seeds from the dry husks. In the Poher region, the September harvest of potatoes and beets was a time of work followed by play in the evening popular with young people from all over the district. These festivities would certainly have included many games and a few bouts of *gouren* (*la lutte*), a special Breton wrestling, but the group dance was the best reflection of a society that thought—and often still thinks—of itself in communal terms.

Other rural tasks led to festivities even on winter evenings. The *filages* or *fileries* were dances after long days of spinning and carding in the home. The word is used even now in the Montagnes Noires as a generic term for evening events. Social celebrations like weddings were also the theater of the dance, as many nineteenth-century paintings and travelers' accounts of Brittany show.

Henry Blackburn describes a *gavotte* he witnessed in Châteauneuf-du-Faou in an account published in 1881:

> They jog along the earthen floor in shoes, clogs, and sabots to the music
> of a flageolet and a bagpipe, varied by an occasional few bars of the voice.

He goes on to note the costumes, the "gravity of manner" which marks the women dancing in the round, and the ordered regularity of the movement despite the apparent rollicking and unrestrained character of this dance. The main types of dance are named for their locality, like the *fisel* (the area around Rostrenen and the hat worn by men there) and the *plinn* (between Maël-Carhaix and Loudeac), but hundreds of different dances are practiced today, reflecting not only various old forms, regional differences, and local specialties, but also modern innovation.

Edward William Lewis Davies was fascinated by the *jabadao*, which took place after a wrestling match he watched in Pleyben: he called it "the Breton Fandango" with its pirouettes, jigging, and complex patterning, a dance "utterly unknown beyond the region of Cornouaille."

Dance, like everything else, reflects social changes, so scope for individuality in performance by groups of four or pairs has increased. Some involve spectacular acrobatic leaps, like the *gavotte pourlet*, a reference to the area around Guéméné-sur-Scorff where the style seems to have originated. Even a minor amendment like starting on the left foot instead of the right marked a particularity of a village or commune.

The earliest dances were communal, with long chains of participants, or two facing lines, men on one side, women on the other, or dancing in the round, a perfect expression of unity and collective sentiment. This circle or *korall* is familiar from the world of legend, the chosen form of the *korrigans*, those imps of Basse-Bretagne who sing and dance on the moors at night, and woe betide the hapless traveler drawn into the ring, for he may literally find himself danced to death.

There is no doubt that Brittany was an original source for this creative art from early on, in a period when it was a pastime for all social classes. The accessible oral tradition deals almost exclusively with peasant practice in the nineteenth century, but Madame de Sevigné, writing in the seventeenth, saw aristocrats here performing dances that had never been seen at court in Versailles.

Dancing was the work of the Devil in the eyes of the Church, and in the region of Léon, where priests wielded a controlling influence on society at all levels, such laxity of manners was severely frowned upon. It would surely lead to corruption at best and damnation in extreme cases. The cautionary tale of Katell Gollet who loved to dance and drink all night only to finally meet her match when partnered by the Devil and dragged off into the jaws of Hell by diabolic monsters (see p.49) gives the flavor of clerical rhetoric on this subject. Even in the 1950s young people in Léon were forbidden to go to dances. Heaven forbid that they should get involved in the licentious *kof ha kof* (belly to belly) dance. Another story from Pays Bigouden tells of the *Sonerien Du* (Black Pipers—a reference to their dark costumes), who were hung in the eighteenth century in place of two robbers, a punishment orchestrated by the Church authorities in retribution for the pagan pleasures they incited with their musical invitation to the dance. A group formed in 1971 took their name and is still going strong on the *fest noz* and concert circuit.

Today the *fest noz* (night festival) or *fest deiz* (day festival) with music

Rural dancing, 1950s (Yves Marhic)

and dancing and a communal meal is the ultimate manifestation of Breton culture, designated in December 2012 by UNESCO as part of the "patrimoine immateriel de l'humanité" and distinguished by its conviviality and social inclusiveness.

The Poher lies at the heart of an area of Haute-Cornouaille with a distinctive form of dance, accompanied by two (or three) singers whose call and counter-call gives the name *kan ha diskan*. This unique unaccompanied *a capella* form is a cross between a song and a chant, the essence being the beat to lead the footwork of the dancers. They chant in turn, sharing the final note of each phrase, so that the voices blend for an instant, and can create an intensely emphatic vibration echoed in the passage of the dance. Originally these directors physically led the dancers at the head of a moving chain, but modern developments usually see them placed apart, on a platform in the village hall or square. Elsewhere, especially in Haute-Bretagne, it was usual for *sonneurs*, a duo of bagpipe and *bombarde,* or sometimes an accordion player, to set the rhythm of the dance.

There is nothing mechanical about the *kan ha diskan*, springing as it does from the singing that naturally accompanied everyday life in rural

Breton society, regardless of the opportunity for dancing. It is the expression of a connection with one's land and locality, with appreciation of the continuity of experience that is the strength of Breton communal values.

The survival of *kan ha diskan* into the modern world can be attributed largely to the passionate commitment and perceptive strategy of a man from Poullaouen. This unprepossessing village was the birthplace in 1921 of Loeiz Ropars, a highly significant figure in the resuscitation of the culture of Basse-Bretagne after the First World War. As a child he had witnessed dancing at his grandfather's farm at Restangoff, with an uncle leading the chain of dancers and singing the words of the dance. He went on to study in Rennes, and later as a teacher of French, Breton, Latin, and Greek came to settle in Quimper, where he organized the first *bal Breton* in the town and was involved in the foundation of the Bagad de Quimper and the city's *cercle celtique*. The Confédération Kendalc'h, started in 1950 and today still a strong cultural force, was also close to his heart. A singer and *sonneur* himself, he wanted to revive the music and dances of traditional festivities in western Brittany, and even before the war when the *fest noz* was gradually dying out, Ropars formed the intention of reviving the *kan ha diskan*, starting up a group Mesaerien Poullaouen in July of 1939. They began to perform at events and festivals outside their immediate area, like the fishermen's festival of the Filets Bleus in Concarneau, introducing this little known practice to many admiring converts.

After the war, Ropars was living in Quimper, but well aware that the rural world was changing fast, with young people leaving their homes to make a living in the towns. He continued to organize and promote training and opportunities for singers and dancers, alongside a fervent campaign for the teaching of the Breton language. In 1949 he started a *cercle celtique* in Poullaouen, encouraging older people to come and sing and perform their traditional dances to inspire and instruct the young. This foundation was to be drawn on significantly in the years to come.

In 1954 Ropars returned to Poullaouen, with its supply of talent and experience, in his quest to create a new context to publicize and popularize the *kan ha diskan* dances. On 26 December, a contest—won by eighty-year-old singer Katrin Guern—was held in the community hall, and the *fest noz* was reborn. The second contest the following year, when the dancing was followed by a feast of *crêpes*, attracted a crowd of 3,000 people, as well as a spate of recordings by radio, music producers, and the Musée des Arts et Traditions. This renewed interest in *kan ha diskan* ensured a supply of singing pairs to animate the revival of the *fest noz*.

One of the iconic partnerships of *kan ha diskan* were the Soeurs Goadec who regularly performed with Ropars. Maryvonne, Anastasie, and Eugénie, three sisters from Treffrin near Carhaix, were to appear at *festoù noz* all over Brittany for decades. Like the equally famous Frères Morvan, their appeal was lasting—for age is a benefit in the transmission of oral tradition—translating even to rapturous receptions on the grander scene like the Vieilles Charrues festival in Carhaix in 2009. Both sets of siblings learned songs and chants at an early age from their parents and grandparents, a modern illustration of the powerful principle of family transmission that has nurtured Breton culture over centuries.

Ropars had the idea of going right back to the roots of the *fest noz* by organizing events once again on farms. It got off a good start but in the second year demand dwindled: too much had changed in the countryside. Farms were modernizing and moving towards an open field system in areas where the soil yielded good harvests. Machines were taking over from humans, with the old sharing of labor dying out. Less emphasis was placed on coppicing of wood for heating or fencing as the banks and hedges were ploughed out of existence. Arguments for biodiversity, so widely voiced today in Brittany, were almost unheard of. Between 1955 and 1965 at least 3,600 kilometers of hedgerow and banks were lost in Finistère alone, as mechanized farming moved to large-scale exploitation of the land. Some were concerned by such wholesale remolding of the landscape. The Terroir Breton association tried to mobilize defense for the traditional *bocage*, and Ropars was an activist in this context too. Fanch Postic's article in *Armen* magazine (April 1998) gives the words of Ropars' *Chanson du TACO*, dedicated to the "technocrate-araseur en chef official" (chief official technocrat-leveler). This song was a powerful denunciation of such mindless rural destruction, reflecting another strong Breton tradition—the protest song. It is aimed at the urban-based official who does not understand that the result of these lost boundaries in the countryside will be the flooding of towns, and who badly needs "a kick up the backside to clarify his thinking." Ropars also supported other associations connected with environmental issues, like the SEPNB (Société pour l'Étude de la Protection de la Nature en Bretagne). This was created in 1959, originally for the running of bird reserves in the region, but soon found itself involved in a variety of wider concerns. Changed in name in 1998 to Bretagne Vivante-SEPNB, it is still a major force in conservation and environmental education, and organizes many events to promote understanding and awareness among the general public.

Thanks to the commitment of Ropars and other like-minded individuals, the *fest noz* redeveloped all over Brittany in hundreds of venues over the next decade. "Nous sommes en plein coeur de la tradition," said Jean-Michel Guilcher, author of an exhaustive study of dance in the popular tradition of Basse-Bretagne, in an interview with the *Ouest-France* newspaper. The work of association DASTUM, committed to collecting songs and tunes still known to the older generation in order to record them for posterity, has also been significant, as its researchers continue to discover new versions to this day.

In 1986 the association Dans Tro was founded in Poullaouen to set up the festival La Nuit de la Gavotte, a twelve-hour non-stop marathon of the traditional dance. Today the event each September incorporates concerts, training courses, and a *fest deiz* in addition to the Saturday night dance where hundreds of people come together to honor the *gavotte*. They also pay a fitting tribute to Loeiz Ropars, who received the distinguished Ordre de l'Hermine (Order of the Ermine) in 1995 for his service to Breton culture. He died in 2007, leaving a vast legacy of *fest noz* celebrations all over Brittany, from tiny hamlet parties to huge public events.

If you really want to get the supreme *fest noz* effect, join the crowds of thousands at St-Thégonnec on New Year's Eve. It is the antidote for those who wonder at the unpeopled, silent streets as they drive through Breton villages. It feels as if the whole world is here, and having a great time. It is not just the music and huge circles of dance—it is greeting friendly faces, smiling, and feeling part of a community at ease with itself and the world.

The *fest noz* is the epitome of Breton life. Dance, music, and food bring together all sections of a community in an expression of social connection. Everyone is welcome, and foreigners frequently are drawn into the circle. There is nothing showy or artificial here, only the reality of life in what remain small, essentially rural communities. The rhythm of the celebration retains an echo of much earlier rituals when the contrast between work and play was significantly greater than it is today.

ONE BARD AFTER ANOTHER

150

Langonnet, a large *commune* on the edge of Poher territory, is well-known for its former Cistercian abbey, which still retains the thirteenth-century chapter-house, despite being used as national stud-farm for a time in the nineteenth century. A curiosity on site is the African Museum, indicative of the abbey's role as a missionary rest home. The area was subject of a late 1950s song written by Émile Le Scanff, much better known by the bardic name Glenmor ("land and sea"), a weighty figure in twentieth-century Breton culture. From a poor background in Maël-Carhaix, he made a name for himself in the Breton cultural world of Paris, notably at the restaurant Ti-Jos in Montparnasse (which is still going strong today). In the capital Glenmor began a relationship with a girl from Langonnet, and composed *O Langoned ma bro garet* ("Langonnet, My Well-loved Land") in her honor. Although their connection did not last, the song remains a favorite in the Breton repertoire.

Glenmor himself, a prolific writer and composer, became prominent in the Breton nationalist movement in the 1970s, a figurehead and standard-bearer in his songs and texts, such as the "Song for the March of the Breton Revolutionary Army." He went on hunger strike for the release of Breton political prisoners after an attack on the château at Versailles in 1979. He was a close friend of Xavier Grall (see p.182), both founders of the journal *Nation Bretonne*, both passionate disseminators of the Breton word.

Glenmor represents the politicization of Breton culture as a struggle for the pride and standing of a nation, the word defense used frequently as a response to the perceived attacks of the French government and the oppression of the Breton language. (Unusually enough, however, he did not see language as an absolute essential of Breton identity, an issue discussed in an interview with the sociologist Ronan Le Coadic toward the end of his life.) But his championing of his native country was a life-long crusade: the heroes of his earliest work, an operetta of 1952, were Nominoë and Lez-Breiz (Morvan), essential figures from Brittany's beginnings used widely in the twentieth century in promoting the notion of Breton identity.

Glenmor was to die of cancer in 1996. He gave his final concert in 1990 at the Fête de la Langue Bretonne in Carhaix, where the largest conference and performance venue is now named after him.

Langonnet was also for many years the home of Alan Stivell, the musician most credited with the renewal of Breton culture during the 1970s. He too first appeared on the Breton music scene in Paris, one of his earliest performances as a harpist with Glenmor, but their future routes were to be very different. Stivell's album *Reflets* (1970) was the first to bridge the world of folk and pop with his electrification of traditional Celtic music. This was an international musical genre in the making, an immediate influence on the new generation and a kick-start for the astonishing revitalization of Breton culture that took place in that decade.

*E Langonned* (1974) was the first of his records to be produced in Brittany itself. It indicates the whole range of Celtic influences: a *gavotte pourlet*, Irish, Scottish and Welsh airs including "*Bwthyn fy nain*" ("My Grandmother's Farm"), which evokes in Stivell a nostalgia for his ancestral roots, and tales from the *Barzaz Breiz*. "*Jenovefa*" tells the tragic story of a girl who kills herself when her love is forced by his parents to become a priest.

Stivell's family came from near Gourin, and although he was born in the Auvergne and grew up in Paris, the hold of Brittany was the heart of his cultural upbringing. He learnt the harp from an instrument made by his father—one modeled on those played by the monks who came to Brittany from Great Britain in the Dark Ages, similar to that shown in a statue found in Paule near Carhaix. After a full musical and linguistic education, he pursued a performing career, taking the surname Stivell ("a lively source" in Breton) in place of his own, Cochevelou, in 1966.

His immense influence both in Brittany and abroad led to an explosion of Celtic pop and a growing interest in what Stivell sees as "world music," where diverse exchanges lead to enrichment without any sacrifice of integrity or authenticity. The giving of new life to old forms was a great gift to Breton music, an exciting challenge to a new generation of *chanteurs* and *sonneurs*. He was also fully involved in the so-called second wave of Celtic music in the 1990s, with the album *Again* reviving the success and reaching out to an ever-expanding fan base.

My friend Yvonne has been a devout admirer of Stivell since 1973, attending his concerts here, there, and everywhere over the last forty years, and we went together to his concert at the Glenmor in Carhaix in 2012. One remarkable thing about Stivell is that while he is without question a cult figure in the Celtic world, it is a cult of music rather than of personality. He has tweaked old music into something modern and popular, but remained himself. He appears at the start of a concert checking the gear with technicians, a slight figure in dark shirt and jeans, the trademark ponytail a 1970s survivor, along with the triskell (which has become from its Manx origins a Breton symbol par excellence largely thanks to Stivell's personal choice of ornamentation). He sits down on the edge of the stage and begins to speak quietly. The atmosphere in the packed hall is of a large family gathering, with an audience spanning the generations in typical Breton fashion. Everyone has grown up with Stivell in one way or another. They know what to expect, greeting each song with the rapture of recognition. Any opportunity to sing along in Breton, in French or even in English on occasion is seized eagerly, because this event is as much about collectivity as any *fest noz*. There is no strutting or exhibitionism; indeed the performance is understated in personal terms, outstanding in musicianship. Stivell surrounds himself with young talent to nurture the future development of this extraordinary electro-folk phenomenon that he began forty years ago, a facilitator more than an egoist.

He has avoided the excesses of Breton nationalist politics, being a man of considerably wider vision and experience, a democrat in favor of autonomy, but his modest manner belies a fiery sense of purpose, with Stivell memorably described by the poet Yvon Le Men as "un timide intimidant" (intimidatingly timid). He is a man of words too, and an ardent advocate of the Breton language: "*heb brezoneg Breiz ebed*," he says—"there's no Brittany without the Breton language."

Allegorical statue of Law, Parlement de Bretagne, Rennes (Pymouss/Wikimedia Commons)

*Chapter Seven*

# TOWN

## WALLS THAT BIND

RENNES: SERIOUS ARCHITECTURE, BEWARE OF FIRE (AND
FIREWORKS)

> "When I found out that Rennes had been entirely destroyed by fire in
> 1720, I didn't expect to find much of interest in the way of architecture.
> I have been pleasantly surprised."
>
> Stendhal, 1837

Rennes is a visually intense and demanding place, full of relatively large
buildings in relatively small spaces. Walking around can feel like observing an architects' orgy at close hand, as the streets rattle off period detail
like machine-gun fire, a volley of half-timbered beauties of wondrous dimensions followed by a blast of grand neoclassical homes of seventeenth-
century political big-wigs. There is also the famous Parlement de Bretagne
building, a glorious expression of political pride, which ironically escaped
Rennes' most famous disaster, the great fire of 1720, but was seriously
damaged in a major conflagration in 1994 after a firework was thrown
during a fishermen's demonstration. Altogether there is a surfeit of
grandeur, *dignitas,* and sculptural eye-candy, fitting for a regional capital
that takes itself very seriously indeed. But traces of more humble modes
of existence remain, and there cannot be many cities where tower blocks
from the 1960s and 1970s are rightly some of the most alluring draws for
visitors.

The first settlement Condate ("confluence" in Gaulish) sat on a slight
rise above the Ille and Vilaine rivers, and this developed into the small,
hexagonal *ville close*, based around the cathedral. Roman maps call Rennes
the city of the Riedones, the Celtic tribe occupying this area, and it is in
the Roman period that archaeological studies suggest a place of significant
status, with traces of Roman walls remaining near the Tour Duchesne and

the Portes Mordelaises.

Rennes was part of the Marches of Brittany (see Chapter Three) established by the Franks, only coming directly into Breton hands after the time of Nominoë. It was never colonized by incomers from across the Channel and hence was not part of the Breton-speaking area. There was a bishop from the fourth century, although nothing remains of early versions of the cathedral, the current building being essentially nineteenth-century. The town was pillaged by Vikings in 875, when the abbey of St-Melaine, then outside the walls, was sacked, a feat repeated around 920. Our earliest "view" of Rennes is from the Bayeux Tapestry—as Conan fled there having escaped from William of Normandy in Dinan—but this is little more than a stylized fortified place. The twelfth-century château has disappeared: when later dukes visited they stayed in the Hôtel de la Garde-Robe in rue St-Yves, and the important event of Anne de Bretagne's proxy marriage to Maximilian of Austria was sealed here. When Charles VIII forced an annulment by threatening to take Rennes, his engagement to Anne was celebrated in the chapel of the Convent of Jacobins on the western edge of place Ste-Anne.

From a moral perspective, Marbode, Bishop of Rennes in the early twelfth century and also a prolific writer, had little good to say:

> Deserted by good men, it is full of rascals… a town dear to Hell, where fraud is in very air. The unlucky stranger who turns up is soon noted, fleeced and beaten up.

The town changed hands several times during the Wars of Succession, having initially declared for Charles de Blois. During one siege by English supporters of the opposing claimant, Jean de Monfort, a miracle occurred. The bells of Notre-Dame de St-Sauveur suddenly rang unaided and all the candles in the church burst into flame simultaneously. The statue of Our Lady was seen to be pointing to a slab in the floor, and when defenders of the town levered it up, they found a tunnel dug by English sappers and were able to repel the enemy just in time. The same statue was to remain unscathed during the great fire of 1720 and locals believed she herself had put out the blaze: an ex-voto painting in the church shows an apparition of Notre-Dame hovering above the burning city.

The Tour Duchesne and the Portes Mordelaises are the only survivors

The Virgin saves Rennes from fire (Édouard Hue/Wikimedia Commons)

of the medieval fortifications, both renewed in the fifteenth century. The latter, a massive twinned-towered structure, is an important symbol of Rennes' significance, as it marked the entrance of official processions, including dukes on their way to being crowned. The cathedral is just ahead up a narrow cobbled street, the height of its tiered façade accentuated by a pinched perspective. In August 1532 after the union of France and Brittany, François I made his official entry into Rennes here with 500 attendants. He was given the keys to the city, swore an oath to defend Brittany and crowned his son, also François, Duke of Brittany next day in the cathedral.

Steady expansion, including many cloth workers from Normandy, made it necessary to extend the defenses after 1400: a contemporary chronicler Guillaume Gruel says the suburbs were by now "three times the size of the *ville close*," a situation which could hardly offer shelter to such great numbers in times of trouble. A further walled precinct was therefore constructed to the east, including the Abbey of St-Georges. Another enclosure built after 1450 south of the Vilaine protected the rather marshy area heavily populated by artisans and craftsmen where the large church of

Toussaints and the Palais du Commerce, the signature building of Edgar Le Bastard, mayor from 1880–1892, stand now.

Inundations and insanitary conditions were serious problems for Rennes over a long period. Inadequate sewage works led to contaminated water, and the town was notorious for its bad smells. Epidemics, like bubonic plague, were all too frequent.

Before the river was first canalized in 1585, the port of Rennes was of limited access, making use of downstream Redon (see p.246) essential. This also meant that local building materials—schist, wood, cob—were used before that date, and imports like granite and limestone only begin to appear later.

Rennes' political fortunes are reflected in its architecture. The decision of 1561 to site the Parlement de Bretagne here instead of Nantes had profound consequences. Twenty years later it was decided to build a "royal palace" worthy of housing this parliament, but the Wars of Religion soon touched Rennes and building projects of such scale were put on hold. In 1605 the victorious King Henri IV agreed that a tax on wine in the town and cider throughout the diocese should be levied to fund the project. The noted Parisian sculptor Germain Gautier was to take charge of town development, but while he chose a site for the parliament building, local notables asked Louis XIII for his own architect Salomon de Brosse to be involved. De Brosse's design was eagerly accepted and parliament was finally installed in 1655, almost a century into its existence.

The parliament building's grandeur is diminished by its location on one side of a smallish square rendered a touch claustrophobic by the taller surrounding structures. Its tripartite composition of granite, limestone, and dark schist roof has certainly been beautifully restored since the 2004 debacle, and a guided visit offers a glimpse of the interiors, sumptuously decorated by the finest Parisian artists and sculptors. Parliamentarians were quick to employ the talents of these men for their own lavish residences constructed at the same time.

Perhaps the most easily visible legacy of Rennes' status is the largest number of half-timbered houses of any town in Brittany, many of them magnificently restored. These were predominantly the residences (*hôtels particuliers*) of parliamentarians, administrators, and lawyers (hence the epithet *une ville de gens de robe*) rather than commercial barons as elsewhere. By the end of the eighteenth century many were probably of mul-

Gentlemen's residences (Wendy Mewes)

tiple occupancy, from commerce on the ground floor and gracious apartments on the first to humble single-room dwellings at attic level.

The place des Lices, originally just outside the city wall and today the site of the famous food market, contains two of the most memorable. (The name Lices indicates a former jousting site and here in Rennes in 1337 the young Bertrand du Guesclin, already famous for his ugliness and later to become the greatest warrior in medieval France, first made his mark.) The Hôtel de la Noue and Hôtel Racapé de la Feuillée (nos. 26 and 28) were built in 1685. The exquisite façade of the former with its crisscrossed battens was designed to be on show while the neighbor's rough wood-work was originally destined to be covered. Their dimensions indicate the greater space available beyond the confines of the *ville close*, but proximity to a gate into the town was also a factor.

Many other houses of impressive, colorful, late-medieval style remain in the old quarter around the place St-Michel, place Rallier du Baty, and rue Leperdit, but despite these examples of stylish amplitude, the verdict on Rennes remained rather negative. In 1636 Dubuisson-Aubenay wrote, "it is not very attractive," citing dark narrow streets with houses almost touching, bad design resulting in the necessity of going through the main room or kitchen to get to the stables—"like in all the rest of Brittany, the animals take the same route as the men"—and he had never seen so many rats and mice. He even complained that the tables and chairs were too low. As for the people, the workers—*les gars de Rhennes*—were mostly drunk and seditious. At the humbler end of the scale, small houses from the early seventeenth century remain in the rue de la Psalette: no.12, a simple two-story affair, may be the oldest in Rennes, but its neighbors are also listed as historically significant.

During the seventeenth century, religious buildings proliferated as many convents for men and women were established in the town. The Abbey of St-Melaine, which retains transept traces of its Romanesque form, was rebuilt and that of St-Georges enlarged: the name of Abbess Magdeleine de la Fayette who was responsible is still emblazoned along the front. The church here was destroyed in 1820, later replaced by a public swimming pool, still in operation today, with its famous mosaic-decorated entrance porch by Isidore Odorico (who was also president of Rennes soccer club in the 1930s). The huge Jesuit college on the south bank of the river had as many as 3,000 students in its heyday, lodging with inhabitants. Between 1624 and 1649 the chapel of St-Thomas built by this order became the Church of Toussaints. Unusually, it was constructed in Loire Valley limestone with a monumental classical façade.

The Revolt of the *Bonnets rouges* (see p.135), a protest originating in objections to newly imposed taxes on tobacco and stamped paper, brought mayhem to the streets of Rennes in 1675. The rebellion was brutally suppressed here as elsewhere by the Duc de Chaulnes: 5,000 troops were billeted on the inhabitants who suffered cruelly from violence and pillage at their hands. Many were made homeless; Madame de Sevigné described the resulting misery:

> The population of a whole street were forced from their homes and prevented from returning on pain of death. And so one could see all these wretched people—the elderly, pregnant women, children—wandering in tears from the town, not knowing where to go, without food or anywhere to lay their heads.

Further punishment was meted out to Rennes by Louis XIV: parliament was to be exiled to Vannes. It was not allowed back until 1690 when a donation of 500,000 pounds secured the king's favor again. In 1689 the king named an *intendant* to represent royal power in Brittany and keep a more direct eye on events. This was later described by a parliamentarian as "an obstacle to our grandeur." In the Parlement de Bretagne building itself, little curtained boxes above the main debating chamber were to house the King's Eye, or spy. The eighteenth-century political struggles between France and Brittany were to play out largely in Rennes.

The great fire of 1720 radically changed the face of the city. It was started by a "drunken carpenter" in rue Tristin, according to Piganiol de la Force, writing in 1754, who said that 850 houses were destroyed in the blaze. It raged from the 23rd to 29th of December, destroying among much else the town clock tower. A more graphic description survives from the Augustinians who ran the hospital of St-Yves: "our unfortunate city, vomiting out whirlwinds of flames and gobbling up its unfortunate inhabitants." Most public buildings were consumed in the blaze, but by good fortune the Parlement de Bretagne was untouched as surrounding houses were pulled down to create firebreaks. Only heavy rain eventually put an end to the danger and saw the start of urgent attempts to help the displaced population. Temporary shelters were put up to house the homeless, and some of these small houses remain even now: the rue de la Visitation has examples.

The tragic purging of central space nevertheless brought an opportunity for magnificent redevelopment for the elite. The main innovations came in the current place de la Mairie where a veritable official showcase was created with the Présidial and Town Hall on a vast scale joined by a new bell tower with chapel beneath. Under this on the exterior a niche was created to house a statue of Louis XV, ceremoniously installed in 1754 with great festivities. But this turned out to be an unlucky spot for statues. The king's was destroyed during the Revolution and much later replaced by Jean Boucher's depiction of the union of France and Brittany, with Anne de Bretagne kneeling at the feet of Charles VIII, called a "monument of shame" by Breton nationalist Camille Le Mercier d'Erm. This was blown up in 1932 by a like-minded group, the Gwenn ha Du.

The original plan was to give the *intendant* a magnificent house opposite the new Hôtel de Ville, but that was never realized on account of the expense. For a long while there was nothing except trees, but in the nineteenth century a *salle de spectacle* finally saw the light of day, its convex frontage echoing the indent of the Hôtel de Ville opposite, a detail perhaps most evident to birds flying overhead. This was Rennes' theater until the mid-1990s when it became the Opera House. It has a remarkable ceiling painted in 1913 by Jean-Julien Lemordant, a celebration of Breton dance indicating the new sensitivity to native traditions.

The 1736 transfer of the Faculty of Law from Nantes saw the start of Rennes' rise as a university center, an aspect dominant in the wider town today—with 60,000 students—but urban redevelopment overall did little to galvanize the city and stimulate commercial growth. The lack of large-scale industry and vibrant commerce dulled the edges of what had become a worthy but rather stagnant regional capital. The eighteenth century was marked by political bickering and disputes with the king, as the capital of Brittany attempted to stand up to the centralized absolute monarchy, exercising parliament's right of remonstrance against royal impositions and exploitation. The Affaire de Bretagne of 1764 saw Louis-René Caradeuc de La Chalotais, president of parliament, clash with the Governor of Brittany, the Duc d'Aguillon. Louis XV dissolved the recalcitrant institution which backed its leader, and La Chalotais was arrested. He survived a trial without conviction but suffered enforced exile. It was left to the États de Bretagne to carry on the defense of Breton privileges, particularly the right to reject new taxes. Louis XVI was more conciliatory, restoring parliament and La Chalotais in 1774.

When Arthur Young visited Rennes soon after, on the eve of the Revolution, he was surprised by the people's perception of this illustrious body.

> The discontent of the people comes from two causes: the high cost of bread and the exile of Parliament. The first is natural, but what I can't understand is this love for their Parliament, because all its members are nobles, like the États also, and nowhere is the distinction between the nobles and the workers more entrenched, insulting and oppressive than in Brittany.

After union with France, internal attack had no longer been an issue and as early as 1602 the town's fortifications began to be dismantled. The eighteenth-century redevelopment made greater flexibility desirable and in the 1770s officials sought to loosen the straitjacket of the old gates and walls to open up the town and improve movement between center and suburbs. During the following century the emphasis was increasingly on transport and communications, with roads and the railway a priority, and ease of transit around the town. Towers which had survived because of a lack of public buildings for official housing, storage, and prison lock-ups were finally demolished.

Once again in the twentieth century innovation, came from tragedy. Rennes was heavily bombed during the Second World War—once by the Germans in 1940 and then repeatedly by the Allies—and the relief at liberation was to be expressed in expansive new architectural development. For once the beneficiaries were not the upper echelons of society, because despite its position at the helm of Brittany, the city was sadly lagging behind in many practical ways. In 1950 a third of houses had no sewage system or running water. A strong response to the population's housing demands was the priority.

Architect George Maillols came to Rennes in 1947 and his first high-rise appeared on the quai de Richemont in 1950. His influences—Le Corbusier and Bauhaus—are evident in the striking angle windows of the Tour Maillols. Later the insalubrious Quartier Bourg-Eveque across the canal to the west was cleared and redeveloped, a stamp of originality placed on the area by one of the first real skyscrapers in France, the Tours des Horizons, another creation by Maillols. The two connected towers are thirty-five stories high, the units prefabricated and then put together on site. The firm La Rennaise de Préfabrication, founded in 1945 by Georges Travers and Charles Barbé, made these elements for Horizons, as it was to do for many other major projects, including the new university campuses at Villejean and Beaulieu. Built to provide modest accommodation for about a thousand people, the apartments in Horizons were ready in 1970 (and restored mid-1990s). They proved popular with investors who rented out to students and young couples. Maillols was also responsible for the Barre St-Just (rue Jean Guéhenno), an inverted rippling white wave of apartments often likened to an ocean liner, although a more romantic view might perceive a stylized lotus flower.

Another striking block is the Tour de L'Éperon (1975) in the Quartier Columbier south of the river. Its architect Louis Arretche was immensely influential in the development of the modern city, after being called on in 1955 by the mayor Henri Fréville to apply himself to the multifaceted needs of an ever-growing population. In 1946 there were 115,000 inhabitants—a figure which would rise to 198,000 over the next thirty years. Public investment was to be directed to housing, schools, sanitation (still an issue), industrial areas, and transport systems. Arretche's nearby project La Liberté, including apartments, shops, and a huge sports venue, opened in 1961, but was later transformed into a major cultural venue for concerts and spectacles.

In recent years the ugly Champs Libres (2006), with the Planetarium dome and triangular glass bulge contrasting with the flat concrete plinth of the whole center, was created to house the library, Musée de Bretagne—a fine collection—and Espace des Sciences. All these developments south of the river, well-served by the Metro system, have shifted the balance of the city center in recent decades.

Rennes offers much to the casual or devoted observer of architecture but it has nothing of Nantes' seductive charm and soft surprise, of that sense that anything could happen, any sight appear around any corner to delight and captivate. It is more terrestrial, fastidious, and traditional, and, despite the presence of so many young people, far more self-consciously worthy. The fate of one work of art serves to illustrate the prevalent sense of priority.

If only the Alignement du XXI siècle, a stunning sculpture (2005) by Aurélie Nemours in the Parc de Beauregard, had been left alone to dominate its site, it would form a magnificent tribute to the visual and conceptual history of Brittany. The seventy-two monolithic columns (4.5m high x 0.9 wide) set in rows to form an open rectangle, an echo of megalithic structures in Brittany, is designed for the interplay of shadows on the gray granite at different times of day and seasons of the year. The final achievement of this Parisian artist who had many ties with Rennes, the Alignement allows the observer to move inside the work, to become part of its essence and appreciate its relationship to sky and land.

If only. Unfortunately those in charge of FRAC (Fonds Régional d'Art Contemporain) decided in 2012 to construct their new building almost on top of it, reducing the scale and perspective of an impressive monument to a pigmy version. And how seriously *they* take themselves can be seen from the sleek black corrupted pagoda that has seized the space like an alien invasion. It is one of those cases where claims of "enhancing something" really masks a seriously destructive visual impact.

Beauregard is a new quarter just north of the university campus of

Casting an unnatural shadow (Wendy Mewes)

Villejean, an area under development. There is even a suggestion box in the form of a little wooden house on a stick for locals to submit their ideas for their future environment. The park mounts the hill in shallow steps, which must have set the Alignement on its plateau below off to great effect before the heavy black blot of FRAC intervened. The housing development at the summit is a spacious array of colors and styles, with some experimental designs such as the Immeuble Salvatierra by Jean-Yves Barrier in rue Georges Maillols, a low five-story block of forty-three apartments erected in 2001 using wood, hemp, and *bauge*, a material characteristic of the locality (and elsewhere in Haute-Bretagne), with straw incorporated into earth which is then built up in layers to form walls.

The tower blocks and recent housing estates offer a new medium through which to look at Rennes. Tours of such structures are becoming increasingly popular, and the most photographed building, according to post-trip examples sent in to the tourist site, is none other than Les Horizons. I am not surprised, having stood myself for an hour in the rain just looking, absorbed into the sheer beauty of the smiling curves and inquisitive array of glass. Looking at photos is no preparation for the reality. It is a building to fall in love with, a place with personality, emotionally charged architecture that invites connection. Turning attention from grandiosity and *hauteur* to places where ordinary people live could well be the new breath of life for visitor experience. And here Rennes could certainly lead the way.

## PONTIVY: WHAT'S IN A NAME?: SYCOPHANCY, SYMMETRY, AND AN EXPENSIVE PISSPOT

> "…formerly Napoléonville, a curious mixture of the old and new styles."
> *Bradshaw's Railway Handbook to Brittany* (1899)

Pontivy makes much of its central position between north and south coasts, and east and west boundaries of Brittany, lying in the Blavet Valley north of the Landes de Lanvaux. The name comes from the legendary founder-monk Ivy and the first crossing point of the river. It is a natural administrative and commercial center for the surrounding rural region, and was once an important communication junction, with the Blavet taking the form of the Nantes-Brest Canal to the north and the Blavet Canal southward toward Hennebont originally providing a link to the arsenal at Lorient.

Pontivy is a town of contrasts, where even the most casual of visitors can hardly fail to notice that a few steps takes you from the medieval world of half-timbered houses to an orderly grid of streets and squares representing post-Revolutionary development. To the north of the center lies the Château des Rohan, which belonged to one of the most powerful noble families of Brittany, implacably opposed to the Montforts and unusually Protestant. It was one of the few places solemnized for Protestant weddings after the Wars of Religion. The irregular streets around the château mark the medieval layout, with low timber-framed dwellings and even some rare survivals of porch houses, although some have been subject to modernization that almost amounts to vandalism.

Pontivy was already a military center under the *ancien régime*, with a small barracks built in 1768, but a vital military role was in store at the time of the Revolution. Then it became a bastion of the new Republic, while the surrounding countryside was the focus for antirevolutionary activity, a development exacerbated by the decision of the National Assembly in Paris (January 1791) that clergy were to swear an oath of loyalty to the new constitution. This meant that a new order of malleable "civic" clergy, divorced from principles of apostolic faith and the Pope's supreme authority over the Church, was to be established, a shift that mounted to anathema for the devout region of Brittany. In Morbihan eighty-five percent of priests refused to conform and put the state before God: the recusants were subsequently deprived of their office and replaced with more obedient priests. These measures aroused anger in many rural parishes where the *abbé* or *curé* was a figure of great social significance. When persecution of these priests began, armed opposition grew, with the peasants easily roused to defend their faith by more politically motivated leaders. Wide and wooded Morbihan was the most extensive Chouan stronghold in Brittany. These counterrevolutionary Catholic monarchists—with the slogan *Dieu et le roi* (God and the King)—were loosely organized groups, with local leaders like Georges Cadoudal of Auray and Pierre Guillemot, often called the *roi de Bignan*. Priests were hidden in villages, emerging to hold illegal outdoor mass and often to bless the weapons of the counterrevolutionaries. In a letter to the Minister of Police, the Deputy Jean-Pierre Boullé, a lawyer in Pontivy, claimed that Morbihan contained more than 30,000 insurgents, supported by 100,000 of the population who aided them in any way possible.

In the district of Pontivy, sixty-four ecclesiastics asked for passports to go into exile. Julien Guégan the town priest was one of these, having taken the oath but later recanted. The alternative was to go into hiding, although from March 1793 the penalty for avoiding the oath was death. Many priest hunts were organized in Morbihan, with monetary reward for anyone who helped capture a fugitive.

Abbé Le Gouve was one of these courageous men. He hid in a barn, grew his hair long, and dressed in peasant clothes, administering the sacraments in villages around Bieuzy. On the other side, Le Pallec, priest of Guern, wrote to the Bishop of Vannes about "these fanatics transformed into peasants, who preach division, insurrection, anarchy, resistance to the very law… these madmen who have neither faith nor patriotism." He aroused such local hostility by this stance that he himself was forced to abandon his parish and take refuge in Pontivy.

The surrounding countryside was dangerous territory. Many Republicans felt unsafe there and moved into the town, which became a fortified island in a sea of Chouan activity. General Esneval, commander of the troops in Pontivy, was assassinated when he went unescorted to visit estates around Remungol.

Despite the 1795 disaster on the Quiberon Peninsula where English-backed émigrés landed to raise the west of France against the Republican government but were contained then forced to surrender by General Hoche, Chouan activity in Morbihan remained strong. When there was a call for the peasants to turn in their weapons after this debacle, 900 rifles were surrendered in Pontivy. The town remained on the alert as a band of 3,000 Chouans dressed in distinctive red English uniforms (hence the terror of *les Rouges*) took the town of Josselin before being attacked and dispersed by Republican troops in the Forêt de Quénécan.

The English also supplied gunpowder. Chouan leader Pierre Guillemot was a key figure at this time, an able fighter but not so hot on practical details. When the powder was found to be damp, he is said to have had the brilliant idea of drying it out in lighted stoves. The result was double-figure deaths, but he himself survived. Guillemot later escaped to England but returned to try to free another Chouan leader, Georges Cadoudal, from captivity. It was a failure and Guillemot was betrayed and captured soon after. He was executed in Vannes in 1805.

Pontivy provided a focal point for the protection of the new Republican regime, with a thousand soldiers billeted on the town, ready to be employed in flying columns sent out against the Chouan bands. But there was to be a new role for Pontivy when Napoleon Bonaparte came to power. On August 2, 1802 he took the decision to revitalize the town, making it "a great commercial center in peace-time and a significant military base in war." So it was that this small country settlement was singled out to become a political watchdog, and an advertisement for the post-Revolutionary state: it took the name Napoléonville for the first time in 1804. There was to be a physical renaissance to match this grand status, the subprefect Gilbert de Chabrol's plans being chosen the following year for development of public spaces on a monumental scale. A leaflet was issued to celebrate the occasion, printed in French and Latin but certainly not Breton. This was the New France, and unity through language was a key element in the emperor's ambitious plans for his dominion.

A thrill ran through the town when the great man announced a visit for 1808. In an ecstasy of excitement the municipal council decided to erect an Arc de Triomphe and create a special guard of honor to welcome the emperor. It was not to be. At St-Nazaire Napoleon heard that his brother was to abdicate and returned to the political nerve center in Paris.

Pontivy had to wait fifty years for an imperial visit, but it did get the promised impressive new layout.

The central concept of the design was the huge square place Napoléon le Grand, technically place Aristide Briand today but locally known simply as La Plaine. This was large enough to display the skills of up to 10,000 cavalry, from units housed on the opposite side of the river in the new Quartier Clisson (renovated in 1986). This vital element of Napoleon's plan for Pontivy received its first garrison of 660 men and 700 horses in 1811, although it was not finished until 1825. A *magasin à fourrages* to store horses' fodder was built across the river, not too near houses in those days for fear of fire.

Grouped around the main square were functional public buildings, the Palais de Justice, the Town Hall (now also housing the subprefecture), and a prison which no longer exists. Money ran out in 1813 after Napoleon's disastrous Russian campaign. The contractors went into liquidation and most work stopped. The prison was completed but apparently little fit for purpose. Soon after the first inmates arrived, twenty prisoners escaped after making holes in the walls of their cells and forcing an external door.

A new road was to link the old and new halves of the town. The rue Royale from the château was transformed into rue Nationale, a kilometer extension of straight, wide road lined by imposing houses, today mostly containing a bland range of shops. Napoleon's commercial carrot of ten years of tax exemption for new businesses and house construction led to many fine buildings. One or two façades from the period stand out, like no. 29 and no. 83, the former Banque de France building. Green spaces such as the boulevard d'Alsace were also a part of the design and ethos of luxurious leisure. This was all very grandiose, and when Napoleon decreed that there should be a lycée in the town (an honor considering only two others existed, in Rennes and Nantes), there were local worries about the financing: "Pontivy is only grand in the mind of the first magistrate of the Republic..."

When news of the emperor's abdication reached Pontivy the council rejoiced, and immediately planned celebrations for the return of the monarchy. The councillors gave a great feast for the 1,500 Austrian and Hungarian prisoners employed on the building works, but soon after these men left and the construction again ground to a halt. A letter was sent to

Louis XVIII expressing the council's "love and respectful devotion" and asking for the boon of naming their town Bourbonville. No reply was received to this sycophantic drivel but they tried again when the Duc d'Angoulême was visiting Lorient, sending a deputation to plead for Bourbonville. Still no luck, but a document in the town's archives uses the name Bourbon-Bretagne. With Napoleon's return, however, it was back to Napoléonville for a few months in 1815 before reverting to Pontivy.

The final flaunting of Napoléonville came later when Napoleon Bonaparte's nephew became first consul in 1848. The council pleaded for another name change at once, but a note of political caution was sounded from Paris. The council asked again in 1850 and was finally granted the privilege in 1852 by the new Emperor Napoléon III.

This actually had some practical value as he visited in August 1858 with the Empress Eugénie, amid a great furor of municipal enthusiasm. The imperial tour of Brittany was to "faire la gloire" of the emperor and peace after the Crimean War, and Pontivy could pride itself on being a representative of "modern Brittany." An Arc de Triomphe was (again) set up on the Demi-Lune terrace and bigwigs lined up to greet the imperial cortege at the bottom of the rue des Pyramides. The mayor expressed the loyalty of the townsfolk, a thing as "alive and lasting as the flowers of our heath," and referred to the town's special relationship with the emperor's uncle.

The evening banquet produced more speeches: the subprefect spoke of the town's commitment to peace and order; the priest asked for funds for a new church. The emperor, avid advocate of industrial progress, was more interested in the prospect of the new railway (but Pontivy was to wait until 1864 for a station on the Auray/St-Brieuc line). It was left to the Empress Eugénie to take care of the religious aspect, and a promise was made to contribute to the building of the neo-Gothic Église St-Joseph in the Napoleonic quarter. (In a strange compliment, a gargoyle on the main entrance of the church bears the face of the empress.) She spent the night as a guest at the town hospital, where her chamber pot—English porcelain showing Chinese scenes—became a precious possession before passing into local hands and being displayed in a shop window. Much later it became a collector's item, bought by a dealer in Vannes for forty francs and then put on sale in 1915 for ninety.

The imperial couple were a big hit in Pontivy, endearing themselves to the crowd during their visit by asking that the Breton dancers should

Empress meets gargoyle (Wendy Mewes)

perform closer to hand as they wanted to watch them properly. In her memoirs the empress records that "national dances, very lively and animated, were given." On the morning of their departure Eugénie was presented with a suit of Breton clothes for her son and the cortege passed out of the town to shouts of *Kenavo* (goodbye).

The mixture of names in the town today reflects the historic split personality. The rue Royale became rue Nationale after the Revolution. The rue Roi de Rome and rue Marie-Louis disappeared with Napoleon but others still recall his great victories with exotic names like rue Marengo, de Rivoli, and des Pyramides. Old photos show the place Aristide Briand on a festival day with several thousand people making very little impression on the vastness of the square. Today the busyness of car parking fragments the space to the detriment of its scale, but the remaining symbolism of the Napoleonic era and its vanities and ambitions is still well engrained in the profile of Pontivy.

## TRÉGUIER: RELIGION, SECULARISM, AND THE GODDESS ATHENE

"The cathedral is like the town: it doesn't show itself off well and it's very hard to find its true perspective."

Fortuné du Boisgobey

The Revolution was a time when not only people lost their heads. The great Breton thinker Ernest Renan referred to his birthplace Tréguier as a "poor decapitated town" after the bishopric, dating back to the sixth-century foundation by St Tugdual, was suppressed in 1790 when each new *département* could have but one and St-Brieuc was designated capital of Côtes du Nord. The gray buildings and gray men of the Church dominated his memories of a devout childhood and adolescence in preparation for the ultimate goal of priesthood. To the thoughtful child the town was "one big monastery." Renan's positive recollections are of the profound moral rectitude of the priests and the foundation they gave him for contentment in adulthood.

Walking the deserted evening streets the overwhelming sense of enclosure and limits is keenly felt. From every angle the lacy pinnacle of the cathedral is visible and there is a sense of revolving around it, linked by invisible threads, turning this way and that without breaking the contact. The architecture is finely detailed, from the Gothic doorway of the former bishop's house to the ornately carved timber frames, and everywhere are high stone walls, shaping a private solidity. Looking across the town from an upper window, even the lines of houses take on the form of walls. Through chinks and iron gates are gardens, most well-kept, a few paradises of neglect: there is the sense of things happening behind the façades, but in an ordered and measured fashion, closed but not secret. Religion's heart is on its sleeve in Tréguier.

Yves, patron saint of Brittany and lawyers, was born in adjoining Minihy around 1250, probably at the Manoir de Kermartin, now disappeared. A historic figure unlike so many of the earlier Breton holy men, he was to become an ecclesiastical judge with a reputation for championing the poor, traveling on foot all over the countryside to bring justice and the word of God to rural dwellers. His iconography in churches throughout the region shows him between the figures of a rich and poor man, often slightly facing the latter. He died in 1303, was buried in the cathedral—which also contains the relic of his (very small) skull—and was finally officially canonized by Pope Clement VI in 1347 after a long enquiry into the miracles attested at his tomb. These included many illnesses healed, the resurrection of a three-year-old child, saving the life of a blind man who fell down a well, and exorcising a young man of demons after his own mother had cursed him—all from beyond the grave.

His medieval tomb was destroyed at the time of the Revolution, but it was replaced by an elaborate mausoleum, inaugurated in 1890. Anatole Le Braz attended the ceremonies, leaving an account of the intensely reverent celebration:

> Then as the voices faded away, everything went dark again; and the only point of brightness to be seen at the end of the nave was the marble effigy of Saint Yves, watched over by a crowd of poor people.

Each May a huge Pardon still draws visitors, especially lawyers, from all over the world. It begs the question of how many of the robed advocates who pour into the town for this event are in the habit of inclining their heads in favor of the pauper faced with a lawsuit from his rich neighbor.

Ernest Renan (1823–92) regarded himself as something of a split personality. His father drowned when he was five and he grew up close to his half-Gascon, half-Breton mother, and sister Henriette. He had the Celtic instinct for faith, manifested in an early awe of the Breton saints, but it was not to last. In deciding to renege on the priesthood at the final fence in the seminary of St-Sulpice in Paris, he mourned more his mother's broken heart than his own spiritual loss, recognizing an intellectual homecoming in studies of the German rationalists.

He went on to a glorious academic career, pursuing philosophy and linguistic studies in Hebrew, visiting Phoenicia (where his sister died suddenly), the Holy Land to see biblical scenes, and Greece where he conceived one of his most famous works, *"Prayer on the Acropolis,"* a hymn to reason, personified by the goddess Athene. Through such ideas Renan played an important part in the secularization of French culture in the century before the official split between Church and state.

His major work *The Life of Jesus* (1863) provoked profound hostility and controversy. Pope Pius IX was deeply offended, referring to the author's "betrayal" of God. The previous year Renan had been suspended from his teaching post for describing Christ as "an incomparable man," a phrase damning of the divinity of the son of God. Four days later, his course was suspended and it was not until the Second Republic in 1870 that Renan was restored to his post at the Collège de France. Despite all the hoo-ha, Renan's former spiritual advisors remained lifelong admirers of their protégé.

In the last ten years of his life he returned often to Brittany, spending many holidays at Rospamon in Louannec and hosting a "Celtic dinner" in Tréguier, without notably adverse reaction in that devout town. Renan died in 1892, but his influence was still felt and ten years after his death he indirectly again brought controversy, this time onto the streets of Tréguier, when tensions between clerics and secularists in Brittany were running high as the state sought to free itself of the bonds of the Church in the first years of the twentieth century.

The background to this confrontation lies in the acrimonious polarization of social and political values in Brittany during the nineteenth century, a conflict in which the Church was increasingly under attack from Republicanism. The Whites—conservative monarchists originally—and the Blues (progressive Republicans) struggled at the ballot box, the former to retain their social dominance and control of the rural essence of Brittany, and the latter to translate the growing economic significance of the bourgeoisie into political clout. Staunchly conservative were the areas of Léon, Morbihan, Lamballe, and Fougères, while Cornouaille, Trégor, and St-Malo in general supported the Republican movement, which from 1881 had an overall majority in Brittany. A papal declaration of 1892 recognizing the establishment of the Republic in France probably helped many more to take a new political step.

The Church had long exerted enormous influence on a predominantly illiterate population (which in Basse-Bretagne often understood only the Breton language), not only through ecclesiastical services and rituals, but also in education. For adherents of Republicanism, legislation was needed for the emancipation of the people. By 1900 primary education was obligatory and secularized, and the new century soon saw a law resulting in the forced closure of religious training schools with monks, trainee priests,

Renan; thinking not sleeping (Wendy Mewes)

and nuns thrown out of their premises. Demonstrations of support were everywhere but there was little to be done in the face of army and police enforcement.

In Tréguier in 1903 (when formal separation of Church and state was imminent) the Republican intention of placing a statue in Renan's honor outside the cathedral was a severe provocation to the clerics. It was to show Renan seated (actually lolling, as if on the verge of sleep), with a towering statue of the goddess Athene behind him. The political nature of the gesture was underlined by the participation of Émile Combes, President of the Republic and Minister of the Interior (and ecclesiastical affairs), who was to give the first in a long line of speeches scheduled for the inauguration event. Combes himself had already tried to ban Breton in church services, claiming it was a ruse by the priests to keep people in thrall, but such profound lack of concern for Breton culture and heritage rang alarm bells all over the region.

The trouble that broke out in Tréguier encapsulated the bitter grievances between the two parties that had brewed and fizzed all over western Brittany in the latter years of the nineteenth century. Guards with drawn bayonets faced down Christian supporters outside the cathedral on the day of the statue's inauguration. Priests intoned religious service within and opponents prayed fervently, but the bells were silenced by municipal decree for the speeches in honor of Renan. A veritable *parade bleue* of Republican luminaries and defenders of intellectual freedom turned out in the pouring rain to add their thoughts to the huge pot of *libre-pensée*. Many had contributed funds and support to the project. Letters from these donors—including one from John Rhys of New College, Oxford—are presented in the museum now located in Renan's family home. Once the speeches and formal celebrations were over, it all turned into something of a jolly, with visits to the seaside for the guests of honor.

The memory of St Yves and Renan, sons of Tréguier and two great figures, remains a lifeline for this beautiful backwater, stressing the contrast between religion and intellectualism and preserving a schism that seriously shook Breton society. For all the provocative placing of the statue and Renan's high society supporters, one cannot help thinking that the two men themselves would probably have got on rather well. The faded estuary town has certainly had sore need of them. The Swiss traveler Charles Fuster referred to Tréguier in the late nineteenth century as "a town frozen in time," without industrial and commercial development, lacking the communications necessary for active economic interchange with the world outside: "One could say... that even in the total greyness of Brittany, Tréguier is the paroxysm, the absolute of greyness."

It was hardly the place to impress a young man of progressive ideas at that time, but today there is a lot to be said for the town's subtle charms and quiet sense of self-preservation. The cathedral alone is worth the trip.

## QUIMPER: AN ENGLISH PRISONER, THE BOURGEOISIE, A CELEBRATION, AND A QUARREL

"Centre of the true Brittany."

Gustave Flaubert

Quimper, capital of Finistère, is centered around the Odet and Steir rivers—the Breton name Kemper means confluence—its flowery footbridges a legacy of former large houses with access via private bridges to the medieval walled city. Although the earliest settlement (and pottery center) was based on the left bank at Locmaria, the legendary founder King Gradlon began his capital on the opposite side of the river, where the luminously beautiful Gothic cathedral of St-Corentin with its crooked nave now stands. The old walled city preserves short stretches of its fortifications and many colorful half-timbered houses in the narrow streets, today transformed into smart shopping areas.

It is this blend of modernity and history-laden architecture that appeals to the tourist market, but in essence Quimper remains the rural haven of the bourgeoisie that has characterized its development since the Revolution. The town was surprised to find itself the departmental capital in 1791 when it was thought that the choice of the commercial port Landerneau on the River Elorn in Léon was a done deal, and the effect of the political maneuvering that led to this administrative accident has done little ultimately to change a leisurely, affable pace of urban life.

We get an immediate and detailed picture of post-Revolutionary Quimper from Watkin Tench (1758–1833), who served with Admiral Bligh in the British fleet blockading the French Navy at Brest in 1794. They were captured and held first on a prison ship at Brest before being transferred to Quimper in February 1795 under a loose house arrest which permitted Tench to amble at will around the city and surrounding areas. He spoke fluent French (no more use to him "than in Delhi" outside the town where only Breton was spoken) and recorded his observations of the situation in letters to a friend.

He describes how the "stately elms" of a public walk along the river have been cut down to the chagrin of the population, to be sent to Brest for the urgent shipbuilding required by France's post-Revolutionary wars. The streets of Quimper are narrow, winding, and dirty, many with new politically correct names like Street of Voltaire and Liberty Square. Some fine large old houses exist, but all have been shorn of their heraldic emblems in the democratic zeal that prevailed during the Terror. This precaution has been applied in the smallest degree: in Tench's quarters, "I now eat with spoons whence the family marks are carefully expunged."

Things were starting to settle down after the worst excesses, and religion again began to "lift her head": although no national religion would be countenanced, everyone was free by right to practice their own beliefs. He witnessed a service in the cathedral, attended mainly by poor people from the surrounding countryside. More high-ranking citizens would like to participate "but the return of religious worship was yet too young for them to incur the risk." Certainly the officiating clergy had to have sworn the controversial oath of allegiance to the Republic. A man Tench met in the cathedral told him how the altar statues had been pried off and "triumphantly guillotined" in the square outside during the Terror. Tench is disappointed not to have seen the Temple of Reason, France's new religion, erected on Mont Frugy, where the party of Robespierre swore "eternal enmity to kings, and extirpation to aristocrats." Young girls were said to have been forced to process here and swear an oath that they would marry only true Republicans. The temple had already had its day when Tench arrived: "Only a few broken posts and a little thatch now proclaim 'Ilium fuit.'"

Likewise many inscriptions on the Statue of Liberty in the marketplace had already been obliterated with whitewash. He was amused to find shopkeepers recommending their goods to all and sundry as "English," which they indeed were—the spoils of British merchant ships.

Tench's perception of politics was that "royalism, though bent to earth, is not crushed," as he met many with monarchist tendencies, although he thought their hopes for the future were doomed to disappointment. In the town itself the Republicans were in the ascendancy. He lists the occupations of the committee of surveillance as shopkeepers, tailors, barbers, and a butcher among other trades. In the countryside it was a different matter.

Things were on the up for freedom of speech during the months Tench spent in Quimper, as fear of the guillotine receded. In fact he says only four—two priests and two women—lost their heads in Quimper. Others denounced as traitors to the Republic during the Terror were sent to Brest for execution. The prevailing mood was now one of unease and uncertainty, with new announcements of regulations and decrees a regular occurrence, and rumors rife. Before his return to Brest and a Danish boat to take him to Plymouth, Tench summarized the situation:

> This little town is crowded by men and women who, like Athenians, do nothing from morning to night "but tell and hear of some new thing."

Quimper was given something of a makeover in the mid-nineteenth century, with the intention of opening up the straitjacket of the medieval imprint. Little shops and bars which crowded up against the walls of the cathedral were pulled down, as was the large Convent of the Cordeliers to make way for Les Halles, the indoor food market in rue St-François. The hand of departmental architect Joseph Bigot, born in the town in 1807, was everywhere. He added the spires to the cathedral and public *dignitas* to the place St-Corentin with the Musée des Beaux-Arts, which opened in 1872. Sketches and drawings for his numerous works in the area—at least seventy schools and twenty-seven churches, plus glamorous projects like the neo-Gothic Château du Keriolet at Concarneau—are in the diocesan archive.

These improvements together with the tree-lined river walks and green hill of Mont Frugy rising above the town emphasized the rural gentility and bourgeois ambitions of Quimper. It was satirized as such by Max Jacob, Jewish poet, author, and visionary artist who was born here in 1876. His family house on the quay has recently been opened as a restaurant, Chez Max, one of my favourite haunts, but the adult Jacob found his natural milieu in the bohemian quarter of Montmartre in Paris, becoming a close friend of Picasso, Matisse, and Modigliani while still retaining strong links with Brittany. He often spent summers in the region, including that of 1930 at Douarnenez with British artist Kit Wood (see p.114), whose powerful portrait of the poet now hangs in the Musée des Beaux-Arts in Quimper, along with many other exhibits in a special area devoted to Jacob and his circle.

The relationship with his native town remained ambivalent, not least because of his *Le Terrain Bouchaballe*, a novel published in 1923 reflecting real-life events in Quimper after a lawyer, Urbain Couchouren, left land in his will in 1883 for a hospice for the elderly. The mayor, however, wanted a theater, and a long legal and political wrangle ensued over the use of the funds. It took the involvement of the President of the Republic to settle the issue. The theater was built beside the Odet and inaugurated in 1904. Jacob had been against the project, but it was finally given his name in 1998 to become the Théâtre Max Jacob, when the modern Théâtre de Cornouaille was constructed elsewhere in the town.

Bouchaballe, the main character in Jacob's burlesque, is in effect Couchouren, who wants his asylum for needy old people but is opposed by the mayor seeking to exploit oil on the same land. Jacob's opposition to the building of a theater was on principle, rejecting a city transformed by political ambition rather than the wishes of the people. The book was controversially received in the town: "the people of Quimper are mean about me," Jacob wrote.

The wrought-iron *passerelle* over the river opposite the Ouest-France building was added in 1994, the fiftieth anniversary of the death of Max Jacob in the German detention camp at Drancy. Despite his conversion to Catholicism after visions of Christ at the age of forty and a semi-reclusive retirement in the Benedictine abbey at St-Benoît-sur-Loire, he was arrested in February 1944 and died in captivity soon after, before international efforts by eminent figures like Jean Cocteau could get him released. Unless the water is high, a copy of the Modigliani portrait of Jacob engraved beneath on the metal support is visible.

In a poignant irony, the Ouest-France building opposite and the Kodak building further along boulevard Amiral de Kerguélen were designed by the Breton nationalist leader and German collaborator Olivier Mordrel, who came to Quimper as an architect in 1925. In line with his political ethos Mordrel was seeking a new distinctive Breton style, in architecture as in culture generally, a long step forward from the sentimentalized vision of Brittany's peasant past. He became leader of the new PNB (Parti National Breton) in 1931, and, although Mordrel himself was marginalized by the Germans soon after the Occupation, a party conference was held in the Kerfeunten district of Quimper in December 1941.

The bishop at that difficult time, Mgr. Du Parc, was a powerful force, physically impressive in figure and dynamic in word and deed. He was an outspoken opponent of the Germans, threatening Breton nationalists with excommunication, and preaching from the pulpit in July 1940 a reminder of Brittany's inextricable ties and shared fortunes with France: "We will never betray France at the time of her grievous ordeal. No Breton has ever been a traitor."

This call to moral and religious duty contrasts strikingly with Mordrel's mantra that no Breton had the right to die for France, an abusive colonial power with which the Germans contrasted favorably for Brittany's future. Mordrel's cousin Yann Bricler, who owned a *crêpe dentelle* factory in Locmaria, was assassinated by the Resistance on September 4th, 1943. German troops protected the funeral convoy.

In one of those strange coincidences that the muse of history so often enjoys, the rue St-François—a very short street by the food market—contains the house where Max Jacob was actually born, the house where Mordrel lodged during the late 1920s, and the site of a former bookshop owned by Adolphe Le Goaziou, a noted member of the Resistance and hostile to the Breton nationalist movement, who was denounced as a "friend of England" and arrested by the Gestapo, although later freed for lack of evidence.

In 1944 Mordel was in Germany, Max Jacob died in custody at Drancy, and the town of Quimper was liberated by the Forces françaises de l'intérieur who did not wait for the American arrival, but drove out their German overlords with a final battle at Tréqueffelec on the outskirts, where an unobtrusive memorial stands today. The French flag—not the black and white Breton flag, tainted by nationalist connections—was flown from the cathedral spire.

Quimper is on the whole a quiet, orderly place, even in the main tourist season. The exception is a single week at the end of July when the Festival de Cornouaille takes place and the streets are transformed into a backdrop for music, dance, and parades. This event traces its origins back to the Fête des Reines, first held in 1923 when a local cinema owner Louis Le Bourhis organized dancing and other spectacles including the crowning of the "queen" after whom the festival was named. Despite Church opposition to this frivolous activity, it was a great success and continued with elaborations like the performance of Breton bards, including Botrel, until 1937.

After the war Le Bourhis and others, notably Pierre Jakez Hélias (1914–95), revived the idea in the form of Fêtes de Cornouaille, extending the remit to the folklore of Pays Bigouden, a subject to which Hélias was devoted. The net was cast wider still with the first overseas guest performers from Scotland, and the election of the queen began to be less significant with innovations like a march of *sonneurs* or pipers (see p.147). Theirs was an important talent to encourage with the revival of the *fest noz*, as these traditional musicians often played for dancing. This particular event developed into a grand competition, an aspect of the festival which continues to this day.

From 1982 the organization changed and the new Festival de Cornouaille took on a much more international character, with performers from Mexico, Russia, and China, well outside the "Celtic fringe." But the emphasis was still on Breton music, with the highly accomplished

Beating the drum for Breton culture (Wendy Mewes)

Bagad Kemper and young local talent also encouraged. In a controversial event in 1987, Alan Stivell, champion of Celtic music, gave a solo concert in the cathedral, despite clerical opposition.

In the twenty-first century the festival continues in various city venues, attracting up to 250,000 visitors over its six days. Stalls line the quay, talks and food demonstrations are added to the musical mix where top-name international artists as varied as Simple Minds and Joan Baez take to the stage. But unlike the great Celtic festival at Lorient and the Vieilles Charrues rock festival in Carhaix with their vast hordes of devotees, Quimper's celebration remains a more intimate and distinctively Breton affair.

Pays Bigouden, the land south and west of Quimper, is renowned for its dazzling and unique embroidered costumes, such as those on display in the social history museum at Pont l'Abbé. This traditional art, still in use by practitioners like Pascal Jaouen, is celebrated here in the annual Fête des Brodeuses, a sparkling feast of color and movement. The area has attained widespread notoriety through the work of Pierre Jakez Hélias, journalist, author, noted folklorist, pioneer of Breton radio broadcasts, and an important figure in Quimper culture, who was born in Pouldreuzic in 1914. His best-known work is an iconic autobiography *Le Cheval d'orgueil* (Horse of Pride), published in 1975, later translated into eighteen languages and also made into a film in 1980 by Claude Chabrol. This account of his childhood in a poor peasant society made Hélias a celebrity, but the book provoked great controversy and renewed the debate over the nature of Breton identity. Hélias was vilified by the poet and "born-again" Breton Xavier Grall (1930–81) for the perpetuation of a Brittany stagnating in the past and a false glorification of peasantry and Pays Bigouden. This accusation of being a *passéiste* was a much-wielded weapon in the nationalist arsenal, but *Le Cheval d'orgueil* is essentially a childhood memoir recording a former way of life, not a political panegyric.

*Le Cheval couché* (1977) was Grall's virulent response to the content of Hélias' book, but it was also tinged with bitterness and contempt for the admiration the earlier work had achieved. He sneers at the elevation of Hélias as a fount of knowledge about all things Breton—constantly asked his opinion on the Breton language, dancing the gavotte, *crêpe*-making, the *bombarde,* and political autonomy—all carefully chosen stereotypical examples.

Ever effective in written rhetoric, Grall was not so impressive in live argument. A famous TV program of 1977 brought the two authors together on a discussion platform and it was hard to see the coherence and precision of Grall's objection to Hélias' text. Grall claimed that Hélias idealized a peasant past which has little relevance to contemporary Brittany. Hélias' good-humored response to repeated harangues was to defend the integrity of his text and his own devotion to Breton and Brittany: "I defend the people," he said, and insisted that he had simply written about what he knew well. Grall was defensive and dismissive during the confrontation, seemingly ill at ease in the context of debate, his argument poorly articulated. A relaxed Hélias smoked his pipe and smiled.

The counterpositions of these two men and their two texts provide a good nutshell starting point for anyone wanting to wade in to the controversial quagmire of Breton identity.

*Chapter Eight*

# MOOR

## STRUGGLE AND STRIFE

THE MONTS D'ARRÉE: RAG-MEN, NOCTURNAL
WASHERWOMEN, AND WOLVES

> "A land of mist and fighting winds, with place-names as fluid as waves, as resonant as gongs."
>
> Xavier Grall

The Monts d'Arrée is an eerie place. The highest hills in Brittany are hardly mountains—the topmost measures only 385 meters—but they seem to retain an echo of their ancestral imprint, on a par with the Alps when the European landmass was formed, and what they now lack in height is more than made up for in atmosphere. "Though mountains no longer, they remember what they were," says Anatole Le Braz (1859–1926), himself a child of the Argoat in Côtes d'Armor and one of the greatest figures in the conservation of Breton oral tradition.

This swath of central Finistère certainly adds up to more than the sum of its geography, bearing a prodigious weight of legend and specific social history that mirrors the singularity of the landscape. Part of the Armorican massif, a bedrock of sandstone is pierced by jagged peaks of schist and quartzite protruding through a skin of moor. The peaks form almost a ring around the vast bowl of the Yeun Elez, an area of marshes (said to contain the entrance to the Celtic underworld) now largely covered by Lac St-Michel, a reservoir created in the 1930s with a dam at Brennilis controlling the flow of the Elez river.

A series of crests run along the spine of the Monts d'Arrée: Rochers du Cragou (crags), Roch St-Barnabas, Roc'h Trédudon, Roc'h Trévezel, Tuchenn Gador, and Mont St-Michel-de-Brasparts, distinguished by its conic shape and little summit chapel. The most accessible by car remain the most popular viewpoints, even though recent accurate measurements

185

On the wild Monts d'Arrée (Herby/Wikimedia Commons)

make Roc'h Ruz, a little knoll near the communications mast, the pinnacle of the chain. The body of terrain consists of upper moorland (*landes*) of gorse (Le Gall variety here in the west), various heathers depending on the amount of moisture in the earth, broom, and fern, together exhaling the distinctive scent which Le Braz describes as "the perfume of Brittany." Poor soil and strong winds restrict trees to the lower slopes, where some recent evergreen plantations also stand. The low-lying peat bogs (*tourbières*), source of both fuel and legend, are separated from the moor by a belt of scrubby trees—willow and stunted oak. The *sphaigne de la Pylaie*, moss capable of absorbing thirty times its weight in water, and the carnivorous *drosera* are typical plants of this ever expanding and contracting wet kingdom.

Thirty kilometers to the south of the Monts d'Arrée is another hillrange, the Montagnes Noires, to the east green waves of forest undulating around Huelgoat with its famous granite Chaos and the quarries of Berrien. To the north the channel ferry in port at Roscoff is visible on a clear day.

Despite their low stature, the "mountain" area, with its poor routes and harsh weather conditions, has always been both a physical and mental barrier to outsiders, a byword for separation, isolation, and semipoetic desolation. The marsh can still be dangerous, away from the wooden walkways and narrow dykes that provide crossing routes today, much like the methods used thousands of years ago on ancient wetlands.

Exceptional megaliths remain. At Brennilis, a fine *dolmen* in the V-shape that preceded the *allée couverte* retains its earth cover and the development of this later type can be seen at Mougau Bihan near Commana where capstones once removed for road building have been replaced, and carvings of a hafted axe, oars, or implements and raised bumps, imaginatively offered by scholars as goddesses' breasts, can be seen.

The wildlife is tinged with the strange: beavers were introduced on the marshes of Venec near Brennilis in 1968 and the rare short-toed eagle, which feeds on a plentiful snake and lizard population, is occasionally seen around the heights in a long glide on the air currents, where curlews and buzzards are more common. In winter a million starlings perform their evening dance across the wide skies, before coming to roost in conifer plantations where dead trees and the earth beneath bear witness to the weight of mass droppings.

The modern world intrudes harshly on this ancient landscape, in outline almost unchanged in places since Neolithic times when forest clearance helped to denude the hills. On the range to the north of Lac St-Michel stands the TV mast. In 1974 the site was subject to a bomb attack, and one of the two masts of the time, which had been built in 1969 for the transmission of France 3 Ouest, was brought down, resulting in a loss of TV programs over a large area for several months. The deed was claimed as the work of the FLB, part of the L'Armée Révolutionnaire Bretonne, although mystery still surrounds the whole incident, especially as the French army were on maneuvers in the area at the time. Pierre Péron, one of officials responsible for the site, died of a heart attack after seeing the damage.

At the eastern end of the reservoir is the one of the first nuclear power stations established in France, situated here in 1962 for the same reason that the Monts d'Arrée were to form the heart of the Regional Natural Park seven years later: a lack of people and developed land. The park status was by no means uniformly welcomed. Posters issued by the UDB (Union

Démocratique Bretonne) read: "No to the Indian reserve." Some would argue today that the Parc d'Armorique pays scant attention to the local economy and only lip service to Breton culture, preserving an emptiness that serves walkers and camper before the inhabitants.

Despite the appearance of wilderness, man has inevitably had a crucial hand in shaping even this landscape, imposing patterns of piece-meal cultivation, the *landes* providing gorse for bedding and fuel, the *tourbières* a source of peat cutting for fuel. Land patterns changed after a law of 1860 allowing individual parcels suppressed the former communal grazing areas for the many sheep that once adorned the Monts d'Arrée. Today the practice of transhumance has been reintroduced with a flock from Sizun brought each May to graze on the moors during the summer months. Evergreen plantations—especially the Sitka spruce—have become increasingly common and provide timber on a rotational basis, and there are still rough grassy plots on the brown acid soil worked for a hay crop. Around the hunters' training center below Mont St-Michel de Brasparts a large area is now managed for the demands of *la chasse*.

In a densely wooded valley below the eastern crests of the Monts d'Arrée is the Abbaye du Relec, a Cistercian foundation dating back to 1132, daughter house of Bégard in Côtes d'Armor. The site fulfills the order's criterion of a remote setting in a location of natural resources. Here, surrounded by woods, quarries, and water courses, the abbey was able to sustain itself to a large degree with fish-ponds, mills and an extensive vegetable garden. More original was the White Monks' method of clearing and working their extensive landholdings elsewhere in the area, often in less salubrious surroundings than the idyllic environs of the Queffleuth (see p.253).

The *quevaise* (Breton *Kemez*) system was designed to entice workers onto the land with an unusual degree of security and independence. It offered space for a small house, courtyard, and fixed size plot (which could be ploughed in a day) together with access to communal grazing, in a straightforward return for ten percent of produce. General maintenance and a hand at harvest time were the only demands on the landholder, so he could regard himself to some extent as an independent worker. An unusual condition decreed that the land could be passed down through the family, but only to the youngest child, who recompensed the elders. They in their turn moved on to take their own part in clearances elsewhere. If there were no sons, the youngest daughter could inherit, and only if the holding was abandoned for more than a year did it revert to the monastery owners.

Many small fields, roughly half a hectare in size and deriving from this unique system, are still visible on the landscape here today. A walk around the so-called Korrigan Trail at Mougau Bihan, which starts opposite the impressive *dolmen*, gives an up-close encounter with the flora of the *tourbières* and then passes along the edge of such fields. High above Le Relec, the archaeological site of Goënidou preserves medieval remains (twelfth to fourteenth-century) of such a settlement, created from nothing to establish agriculture on lands long fallen into disuse. At least five small farms existed in proximity here, each group of buildings of granite and schist dry stone walls once probably simply thatched with gorse and broom.

The *quevaise* was also practiced by the Hospitaliers of St-Jean, the Knights of St-John (the Red Monks), who had a major base at La Feuillée from the fifteenth to the seventeenth centuries, and whose lands extended well beyond the Monts d'Arrée to cover much of the Trégor. Pierre de Keramborgne, *commandeur* in 1444, established the use of this system on the order's holdings, a practice which continued up to the Revolution.

A letter of 1838 by an engineer named Félix Caron emphasizes the loneliness of the terrain, with not a single house between Brasparts and Plouneour-Menez, a distance of twenty kilometers across the highest points of the Monts d'Arrée. He claimed that travelers had died far from any hope of aid in extreme winter conditions. This unforgiving landscape historically translated into a life of grinding poverty. Xavier Grall in his depressing poem "Les Déments" outlines the grim lives of the deprived inhabitants.

They're fed up with an endless life
In the damp wretchedness of the Monts d'Arrée…

Drunk, deaf, stocky, crimson-faced,
They have refused exile and soulless labour.

Such literary images proliferate. The same profile of excess features in the lurid novel *Clauda Jegou* published in 1936 by Yves Le Febvre. The

189

author was well-known for his *La Terre des prêtres*, a story of the clergy in Léon which led him to be sued by a group of priests. Le Febvre was a staunch Republican, Breton-born but at heart a Frenchman. His take on his homeland is not a romantic or superstitious one, according to Léon Dubreuil in a study of the author's work,

> but a rugged and rough Brittany, that of the Monts d'Arrée where the peasants are as hard as the spine and sharp teeth of the rocks that pierce the high stretches of moor, and whose habits are brutal and sometimes bloody.

Certainly *Clauda Jegou* delineates a tragedy of classical Greek proportions, with ignorance, domestic violence, and alcohol abuse leading to a vengeful murder of son by father. The eponymous figure alienates his upright son and dotes on a daughter as crudely made as himself. He is sent to prison for a vicious assault on his wife and life on the farm settles into a degree of peaceful normality. On the eve of his son's wedding to the daughter of neighbor, Jegou is released from captivity and returns home, feigning humility, but his son turns him away without hesitation. Jegou retires to a cave in the mountains to brood on vengeance. Knowing that his son sleeps in the stables, he bolts the door and then sets fire to the building, watching as all within are burned to death. The next morning, he throws himself under the little train that used to cross the Monts d'Arrée near Roc'h Trédudon.

But there is another side of the coin. This landscape has also bred a strand of independent thought and action, a development that has given the Monts d'Arrée its reputation for radicalism and political activity. The rebellion of the *Bonnets rouges* (see Chapter Six) was well-supported by peasants from this area and their fighting spirit was later transferred to a political context with the significant success of communism in the Monts d'Arrée and a continuing left-wing tradition in elections even today. In the nineteenth century as White and Blue political parties began to crystallize, Monts d'Arrée peasants bucked the trend by tending towards socialism and communism—hence the epithet *la montagne rouge*, the red mountain—rather than following the conservative example set by their priests and landowners, as happened in other rural areas such as nearby Léon. There was little here of that thrall to clerics that predominated social life to the north: in fact, the area was seen as a prime target by seventeenth-century missionary Père Maunoir, a hellfire and brimstone merchant who would have had his work cut out in the Monts d'Arrée where weather gods were more pertinent to life than the demanding rules of Roman Catholicism.

The Huelgoat/Scrignac area was a stronghold of communism in the twentieth century and an area of intense Resistance activity during the Second World War. The arrival in 1930 in Scrignac, a communist bastion, of Abbé Perrot, a staunch Breton nationalist and supporter of militant opposition to the French government, was a misguided ecclesiastical bid to induce some balance into the priest's political activism. One of his projects was the building of the Chapelle de Koat-Keo, an attempt in conjunction with the nationalist architect James Bouillé to establish a distinct neo-Breton religious style, just as Mordrel had done with civic buildings in Quimper. Perrot's association with Breton collaborators like François Debeauvais and Célestin Lainé, and his alleged hoarding of weapons in the presbytery, set him in political and patriotic opposition to the majority of his parishioners who considered Germans the enemy and not the French. Conflicting stories still abound: he sheltered Allied airmen, he denounced some of his own flock. He was eventually assassinated by a member of the Resistance in 1943, and although most locals avoided the funeral service, it was well-attended by Breton nationalist luminaries for whom Perrot was a martyr and a hero. A militia group that was subsequently formed to attack the Resistance was named Bezen Perrot in his honor. He is buried in the graveyard at Koat-Keo, and remains a controversial figure to this day. Scrignac retained its leftist bent: in cantonal elections in 2008 the communist candidate took the majority of first round votes in the *commune*.

It is the evolution of the area in its own discrete mode that gives the Monts d'Arrée its particular flavor, quite unlike any other part of Brittany. Bretons from the coastal areas speak of it as a hostile other world, not a place to live and work. A resident of Fouesnant on the south coast recently told me it gives her shivers just to cross on the main road to Morlaix. But it is no coincidence that the grim reality of the *montagne* produces the richest scope of the imagination, as varied as the shape of mist.

*PILHAOUERIEN*: LIFE ON THE ROAD, RAGS TO PAPER, AND AN
INDEPENDENT ATTITUDE

The Monts d'Arrée were seen as a physical and even psychological barrier
to trade and travel by those who lived to the north in Léon or further
south beyond the Montagnes Noires. Notorious for the wild inhos-
pitability of the terrain, subject to fearsome blasts of weather, so often
wrapped in thick fog and home to legendary horrors, the area would have
been a virtual no-go zone commercially were it not for the activities of
local *colporteurs* (peddlers) and *pilhaouerien* (rag-and-bone men) who un-
dertook the movement of goods.

Exceptional circumstances produced uncommon responses to the
poverty of the land in certain *communes* where a family could not be sus-
tained by a tiny plot of less than five hectares of poor soil. In Brennilis and
Botmeur, Loqueffret and La Feuillée (the highest village in Brittany), up
to two-thirds of the population were involved in itinerant trade, at least at
times of the year outside the labor-intensive moments of the farming calendar. Journeys in the extremes of winter were routinely a harsh necessity.
Émile Souvestre comments that Breton peasants are not natural businessmen, but cites the *pillawer* ("a kind of modified bohemian") as an

Scraping a living (Wendy Mewes)

exception. He contrasts their "emancipation" with the stationary and superstitious lives of traditional agricultural workers.

The correlation between thin acidic soil and individual enterprise is
made clear at Loqueffret, standing "amidst lands so uncultivated, it seems
no man has ever passed this way." It is fitting that today the village houses
a museum, La Maison du Recteur, devoted not only to the religious life of
the area but also the *pilhaouerien*.

The profession of *pilhaouer* was hereditary, with sons or nephews
trained up from an early age after schooling was done. Given the lonely
voyaging far from the native *commune* it was thought suitable only for
men, although wives did sometimes accompany their husbands on a trip
if not needed to work the land, and in at least one case a widow was
allowed to continue the family business in order to survive. In the early
twentieth century Marianna Hamon went around collecting rags in a
basket on her back after her husband Louis Nicolas was killed when his
cart overturned on a bend on the outskirts of Brasparts.

This itinerant lifestyle was not eased by the treacherous terrain and
long distances involved. Each *pilhaouer* had his own traditional territory
which remained unchallenged by rival enterprise, but the area may have
been surprisingly far from home considering the lack of decent roads and
a journey on foot. Some from Botmeur went west to the Crozon Peninsula or Loquirec on the north coast. A rag-man from Brennilis went as far
as the Gulf of Morbihan, while the Tosser family from the same village
were lucky to have a patch at relatively nearby Pleyben. Lili Tosser remembered going out with his father after the Second World War to learn
the trade, describing the network of villages they visited: Gouezec, Briec,
Brasparts, Loperec. Total trips took days or months according to the location.

Before the First World War the *pilhaouerien* walked, using their horse
to carry the goods before the use of carts with two high wheels. They would
herald their arrival with a cry, *tamm pilhou tamm* (any rags?), or blow on
a horn. If they were in luck there would be a funeral in the village and
everyone attending would know to get home and organize their offerings.
Lili Tosser described the women's chatter:

*Gast! Ar pilhaouer 'zo ase! Daw eo din klask un dra bennag dehan!*
Damn, the rag-man is here. I must go and fetch something for him!

After the Second World War motor vehicles were increasingly used. Bretons who were children in the 1950s and 1960s remember the ragman arriving in a van and knocking at the door rather than shouting his presence as in the old days. But by then the whole context of the profession had changed and scrap metal was the prime commodity.

The history of these itinerant tradesmen men goes back centuries to the primitive peddlers observed by Jacques Cambry on his travels in 1794. He equated the nature of the landscape with their practice:

> La Feuillée is on a hill… this poor, abandoned, isolated commune in the middle of a deserted area has infertile lands, inadequate for the nurture of the inhabitants: their industry must make up for the aridity of the soil… an area that long-standing preconceived opinion still presents as savage, inhabited by a type of brute in human form, given the epithet "wolf of the mountains."

Although Cambry stresses their separation from others, he is surprised to find "a certain vivacity, ideas, and a better ability to speak French than Breton peasants elsewhere," an asset easily explained by the wide context of their working life. He describes peddlers with their packhorses carrying clogs, coal, and salt, or apples and chestnuts from Carhaix, Langonnet, and Brasparts.

These basic commodities seemed to have formed the basis of transient trade in the eighteenth century, but the emphasis was to change later to the important work of *pilhaouerien* (French *chiffoniers*), whose main target was rags although they also collected horse hair, fox pelts, rabbit skins (for fur or used in glue by furniture makers), pig and boar bristles for hairbrushes and paintbrushes, and bone for buttons or more glue. Coastal searches often yielded the best haul of quality rags given the greater prosperity of the littoral and the access to old nets and sailcloth used in maritime activities. As fish and vegetable canning were important coastal industries there was also potential for scrap-metal collection there in the twentieth century.

The main use for rags was paper making from the first half of the seventeenth century, when many abandoned corn mills were taken over by this new industry, up to the end of the nineteenth. With the proliferation of printing as demand for books and administrative documents grew, more and more paper factories sprang up in river valleys, especially just north of the Monts d'Arrée, and the supply of cotton rags was crucial for this burgeoning industry, which exported its products to Portugal, Holland, and England.

The *pilhaouer* would either sell direct to the mill owners on a regular basis, or use a wholesale merchant. These enterprises, located in most sizeable towns in Brittany, both took rags and supplied the rag-men with items for exchange with their rural customers, possibly offering a small advance against returns to help cover the cost of the rag-man's board and lodging, an important factor in the budget of any itinerant trader. Sometimes he would stay on a farm, using an outhouse to store and sort his produce, but some preferred a basic hotel with meals included in the modest price. If the man's wife and family traveled with him, cheap rentals were more practical. The Lagadec brothers from Botmeur actually bought a two-room house in Camaret so they had somewhere to sleep and store goods while they were on their patch.

The mechanics of the trade consisted of barter rather than a financial transaction, and before each journey the *pilhaouer* stocked up with wares. He then traveled well-loaded with goods to offer in return for rags and skins, which were weighed on a balance (not the most accurate of methods, regardless of whether a discreetly placed foot held up the load). The main items on offer were crockery, usually plates and bowls, and glasses, but household utensils, handkerchiefs, or even fruit in season were also useful bartering tools at remote dwellings. The most prized object was a soup tureen, but it might take several visits before such a reward was earned and the rag-men were trusted to accumulate value fairly.

Examples of the blue and white Quimper pottery often used for exchange can be seen in the museum at Loqueffret, in addition to a plate with a painted cockerel motif, an import from Rouen. It is an irony that the *pilhaouer* himself later formed the subject of decoration on some plates. An example from Quimper in the 1920s depicts him on horseback, gaunt-faced beneath a large black hat. His *commune* is given below: La Feuillée.

In the 1850s the rise of the more highly mechanized English paper market became a serious threat, to the extent that Breton operations urged the government to adopt protectionist measures. Those hopes came to nothing as Napoleon III's recognition of the need for France to industrialize as quickly as possible led to a free trade agreement with Britain in

1860. Rags continued to form the basis of Breton paper production until about 1890 when the discovery of wood pulp extraction led to changes in technique. There was also an increase in the use of synthetic fabrics, although some demand for rags remained in the twentieth century, particularly for polishing cars, with garage owners buying direct from the *pilhaouerien* after the Second World War. But diversification became crucial as the paper market declined, and scrap metal was soon a more sought-after commodity. With the modernization of agriculture and increasing use of tractors, many metal implements became superfluous for farmers and a source of good revenue for the rag-man.

The *pilhaouerien* had a curiously ambivalent social status, set apart from the traditional peasantry which remained firmly wedded to the local land yet welcomed in isolated farms and rural communities as harbingers of news and connection with the world outside. Their representation in oral tradition is similarly mixed. A song composed by the Recteur of Loqueffret in 1860 presents one from that village in rather an unflattering light. It purports to be the complaint of Maryvonne, married to a "stinking" rag-man who sets off from the village for Sizun with his weighing scale and his pipe, but is more interested in imbibing with his mates than living a Christian life. The *pilhaouer* is a drunken sot who will come to a bad end and his wife will readily call on Ankou (the Breton Grim Reaper) to take him away.

Émile Souvestre recorded the text of another song, likening the rag-man to a Wandering Jew, in an evocative rendering of the poverty of his material and spiritual life: "*le pillawer n'a ni foi ni paroisse*" (the rag-man has neither faith nor parish). On the road he slept in ditches with nothing to eat but black bread and water from a pond. He worked instead of going to mass or confession, and he was a stranger to his own village, not knowing if he would find a coffin or a cradle on return. He took his son into the trade at the tender age of twelve, exhorting him to pray to God for warmth from the sun and sweet grass for a bed for a "child of the mountains." But there is hope even for these outsiders, according to the song: Christ does not judge as men do and will accept any honest, Christian soul:

> Just as the rags you collect get filthy on the route but are washed and pounded into the finest white paper at the mill, so will it be for you,

pillawer. When your soul leaves your poor body covered in rags in some ditch, it will rise white and beautiful, and angels will escort you to paradise.

Pontus, a character in the novel *L'Erreur de Florence* (1903) by Charles Le Goffic, explains the life of the *pilhaouer* to Florence Trelawney, a Cornish guest of his family. Despite the privations of home life for itinerant merchants, the rag-man makes it a point of honor to return to his village each year for the day of the Pardon to participate in the festivities by offering prayers and a candle to the patron saint like everyone else, a mark of belonging, of social and religious identity. The moral of Pontus' description is that spiritual nourishment is more important to the Bretons than physical well-being.

The *pilhaouerien* were familiar figures up until the 1950s. Journalist and author Louis Ogès relived his childhood memories of the *pilhaouer* in an article, describing how the almost exotic appearance of one "come down from the mountain" attracted something like celebrity status among the children of the village who watched in wonder as parcels of pottery were unwrapped, and who were sometimes allowed to help with the weighing of rags.

The *pilhaouer* existed in other parts of Brittany, especially the Trégor, but they seem a natural product of the peculiar character of the Monts d'Arrée. Villages like Commana and Plouneour-Menez on the northern slopes of the same hills did not follow the same pattern, with occupations like quarrying, carpentry, horse-dealing, and clog-making to sustain their communities, which had closer access to the more prosperous region of Léon. Whilst *pilhaouerien* performed an important economic role in moving and recycling goods over a large geographical area, they remained separate from conventional society, their independence of attitude serving as a paradigm for their territory and the rich distinction born of infertile soil. They also did much to create a widespread image of the people of the Monts d'Arrée as unconventional individuals, bound by their own rules, driven by their impoverished background to gain a meager living in such an outlandish way, so strikingly different from the traditional home-focused lifestyle of most rural Bretons.

## LEGEND: DEATH AT LARGE, FATAL DANCING, AND A BLACK DOG IN THE BOG

"In Brittany, the imagination has little effort to make in transforming banal realities distorted by nocturnal uncertainty into something supernatural."

Paul Sébillot

Landscape determines legend, and the stark wasteland of the Monts d'Arrée, so often shrouded in mist and murk, throws up an appropriately somber and menacing cast in tales ringing with danger and death: what the area lacks in produce of the soil is more than made up for in fertility of imagination. The forceful weather patterns ebbing and flowing across the landscape at speed contribute to a shifting sense of reality that enhances the awareness of extreme possibilities. It is said that sightings of a large man all in black accompanied by a huge black dog roaming the marsh and moor prefigure terrible storms and the release of evil spirits from the underworld.

It is yet another context for the Breton discrepancy between appearance and actuality. Distorted vision and hearing are common contributors to the atmosphere of mystery and fear: are the unnerving flickering lights *feux follets*, harbingers of evil which lure men onto the quagmire, or merely the blinking remains of smoldering peat fires? And those plangent cries reverberating in the shapeless mist—lost souls moaning out their agony or just the muffled cry of a marsh bird?

The Monts d'Arrée are elemental, ruled by geography and climatic conditions, a place where the presence of death broods as large as life. Dangerous enough places to cross even in daylight, but in gloomy weather or black night all manner of bizarre threats awaited the hapless traveler.

The Washerwomen of the Night are a case in point. It is hardly the sort of hazard one could anticipate. This group does their washing in the darkness at the edge of the marsh, on the look out for any sign of human presence. Then the poor wanderer is summoned enticingly to help with folding the laundry and seals his own doom, crushed remorselessly in the twisted fabric that becomes a shroud. Advice offered to avoid such a gruesome fate is to wring the material only in the same direction as the washerwoman, who will soon get fed up as her work fails to advance in this fashion. An endearingly bathetic painting by Yan Dargent (1861) in

Quimper's Musée des Beaux-Arts portrays the scene on a wild moor peopled by dead tree trunks and what looks like a herd of madwomen and flying sheets.

The origin of the story is impossible to get at. It is not particular to the Monts d'Arrée but fittingly placed here in a lonely and desolate terrain. In other parts of Brittany the story attaches to a rural *lavoir* (washing place) and often figures a single washerwoman. There are similar tales in Ireland and Scotland and other parts of Europe. Some say these ghostly *femmes fatales* are manifestations of the doomed souls of women who killed their own children and so are condemned to endless punishment or until they have paid for their sins through this hard labor. Other explanations include women who died in childbirth or otherwise prematurely who "live out" a normal lifespan in this everyday occupation but with highly unsociable hours. The most mundane suggestion is that they were washerwomen in life who cheated the poor by scouring their clothes with pebbles to save on the cost of soap, so eternal scrubbing is a simple post-death punishment.

Certainly they belong to a less than benign version of the traditional White Lady ghost story, a European folk motif, but rather than sheer malignancy their appearance is often interpreted in legend as a presage of death for a relation of the person they encounter. Anatole Le Braz records an account where young Jozik, in search of her drunken father, has such a meeting. The washerwoman addresses her by name and shakes out a shroud that gets bigger and bigger until it covers the whole lake. Jozik runs home frightened, until she finds her father is there and all seems well. But he is dead by morning.

In the Monts d'Arrée they are not always menacing. François Cadic (1864–1929) wrote that the penitent washerwomen from Brennilis seemed to accept their punishment cheerfully enough, for they used to sing:

> On misty nights one could hear their voices rising from the banks of the Elez, in a religious song so sweet and mellifluous that one might think it was performed by a choir of angels.

Wasteland is natural territory for Ankou, Death's skeletal henchman clad in cloak and wide-brimmed black hat, driving his clanking cart over the rough tracks in search of victims. René Trellu preserved a story of the origin of Ankou in the Monts d'Arrée. Veig Richou, an old *pilhaouer* from Loqueffret well-known throughout the area for his big black hat, long white beard, and drinking habits, was returning home from a working trip, knowing the end was near but wanting to reach his own village before expiring. But the crossing of the mountains proved a challenge too far for his aging physique and dwindling spirit. With the cart broken by the side of the rough path, Veig Richou sank down at the foot of Roc'h Trévezel.

Meanwhile both the Devil (or Red Man, *Potr Ru*, as he was known in Basse-Bretagne) and St Peter were concerned at the lack of recent re-cruits from the Monts d'Arrée and each petitioned God to be allowed to come down to earth and claim the soul of Veig Richou. The Devil was confident of winning this one, as the old man's bad habits and lack of attention to religious duties were notorious, but St Peter insisted on a formal weighing in the balance and to their great surprise they found that Veig Richou was neither good enough for Heaven nor bad enough for Hell. So what was to be done with him? They decided there was nothing for it but to revive him and send him back to his old profession. But Veig Richou refused.

Next each demanded that he work for them on earth, but he asked what it was he could do, he was old and worn out and unfit for any more hard physical labor, nor did he have tools with which to work at another trade. The Devil and St Peter rummaged on the laden cart and came up with a hammer, which he rejected. Then a bent ploughshare—same result. Finally they unearthed an old scythe, rusted but still sharp, and finally Veig Richou agreed. He would keep his old horse and his old cart, but he would work mostly at night, harvesting souls, one for the Devil, one for St-Peter. He became Ankou of the Monts d'Arrée, and people soon un-derstood that though the rag-man from Loqueffret was seen no more, he still worked his patch, turning up as he always did at unexpected times in the hamlets of Kerbruc and Mougau and Kergreac'h, but in a new guise, his approach heralded by the ominous clanging of his cart and ready to take without discrimination young and old, rich and poor…

The entrance to the Celtic underworld was said to lie in the Yeun Elez, the deep morass that predated the reservoir. At a spot called Youdig—the name echoes the belches in a bubbling bowl of porridge—when the water boils up, beware, for he who goes too close in curiosity will be sucked down into the bottomless bog and never seen again. It became a venue of exorcism, most famously in the tale recorded by Anatole Le Braz in *La Légende de la mort* (1893), a work of collected traditions which preserves the distinctive flavor of death in Basse-Bretagne.

The story of the priest Tadic-Coz (little old father) and the black dog has many versions. Jobic, a young soldier from Côtes d'Armor returning home from war, is persuaded by the elderly cleric to take a black dog on a lead to a nearby presbytery. He is willing to put off his homecoming for an hour or two to do a good turn and sets off with his wild-looking charge. But on reaching his destination, the priest in residence refuses to take the dog and sends Jobic on to another presbytery. Here the pantomime is repeated, and, as Jobic becomes more and more infuriated at his enforced guardianship of the beast, each stage of the unexpected journey leads closer and closer to the Monts d'Arrée.

Finally they come to Commana and this time the priest does not turn Jobic away, but sets off with him and the dog over the hills to the heart of the Yeun Elez where they come to a stop in the dark of night at the bleakest spot of black water. Jobic is told to lie flat on the ground and avert his eyes. The priest slips his stole round the dog's neck and then Jobic hears a huge splash and a terrible howl before a furor of noise and movement arises all around them, causing the young man to tremble in fear of his life. After what seems an age, silence falls again and the men are able to retrace their steps. Jobic is told to call at each presbytery on the way back and relate what has happened. When he finally gets home he is minded to reproach Tadic-Coz, but the old man explains that the dog was implanted with an evil spirit exorcised from Jobic's own dead grandfather and plaguing the rest of the family. Now it had been sucked down to hell where it belonged, so the family—and the grandfather's soul—could be at peace at last.

As so often in Basse-Bretagne, where the Church was anxious to stamp its mark on locations with strong pagan associations, local legends are a mesh of diverse strands in a place where the worlds of Celtic imagination and Christian doctrine collide. The Monts d'Arrée were regarded as an important target for seventeenth-century missionaries, steeped as they were in the tales and superstitions of an earlier civilization whose legacy was passed down in songs and stories that exercised a stronger hold on the mind of the population than that of religious rules and tracts.

The struggle between priests and the irreligious inhabitants of the Monts d'Arrée was also translated into the language of legend. The Stone Wedding Party (An Eured Vein) is actually a Neolithic alignment of more than seventy stones stretching across a plateau of scrubby moor south of the reservoir basin. Its etymological tale tells of a group of revelers winding their way home merrily after a marriage, still singing and dancing to prolong their celebration. In their path came a priest, who was taking the last sacrament to a dying man. They refused to make way for him, joking and laughing at his somber mission, until his curse left them petrified, each on the exact spot where he was standing.

An invitation to join the *korrigans' ronde* may seem a safer bet, but once the traveler joins the circle he may find himself literally danced to death. These imps of Basse-Bretagne are a special breed of little people, cantankerous, mischievous, and unpredictable. Today the *korrigans* have been relentlessly trivialized by the tourist trade and exploited as an amusing oddity—part of "quaint old Brittany"—which does scant favor to the oral tradition where they seem more representative of a side of the Breton character. They also symbolize a resistance to the Christianization of the peninsula, pushed by orthodoxy into the extremities of underground living or among the megalithic stones on the remote moors. Le Men, writing in 1872, indicates that the Church set out to undermine the *korrigans* with the story of their exile in the face of the reading of the gospel.

The Neolithic *dolmen* at Brennilis has the local name Ti-ar-Boudiged (*boudik* being a type of little person), so it is the "house of the *korrigans*," the remaining roof mound creating an effect not dissimilar to a hobbit's house in Tolkien. But it is on the *landes* that they love to dance in a circle as night falls and where anyone disturbing their sport may pay a terrible price for the presumption. On the other hand, goodness is often rewarded as in the tale of the hunchback who finishes the words of a song to their satisfaction and so is granted a wish and has his hump magically removed. Another who rudely interrupted and gave them a harsh-sounding rhyme had his load doubled.

The *korrigans* have retained their hold on the modern-day Monts d'Arrée in the context of tourism. A guided walk with lanterns might bring visitors face to face with a little gnome up a tree who—surprisingly for such private characters—can be persuaded to come down and give a humorous talk in front of a blazing fire. *Conteurs* tell their stories, there are *korrigan* puppet shows, numerous books of cartoons and much other artwork of variable quality. The grotesque face and image of the *korrigan* has become a kind of badge of honor in the Monts d'Arrée, ironically a password for pseudoauthenticity of Breton-ness, but perhaps appropriately for the concept of separateness that still reigns in the *communes* of the moors.

All the legends with their emphasis on blackness, gloom, fatality, and malice fit the perceived physical dangers of the landscape, and the underlying sense of hardship and suffering encased in the reality of life in such surroundings. The solitary characters, those set apart from society, little people who keep themselves to themselves, all echo the peculiar nature of the mountain people and their self-contained environment, cut off from easy connection to the world outside.

## Wolves: tamed by saints and hunted by an enthusiastic Welshman

The wolf (*ar bleiz*), that archetypal symbol of wildness, once roamed the lonely reaches of the Monts d'Arrée. The Dartmoor ponies and Nantaise cattle that today are part of the management system of the Landes du Cragou would not have lasted long in the nineteenth century. This extension of crag, moor, and wetland with a whispery echo of prehistoric oak forest near its summit looms above the village of Le Cloître-St-Thégonnec, home of the Musée du Loup, devoted to the history of the wolf in Brittany, a story lasting up until the last sightings in the early twentieth century.

The taming of wolves was a recurrent motif of Breton religious traditions from the Age of Saints, emphasizing the power of Christianity over paganism. Even wild ravening beasts recognized a saint when they saw one. St Thégonnec himself ordered a wolf which had killed the donkey pulling his cart full of building materials to take its place. The same story is told of St Hervé, although in his case the wolf remained a constant companion, like a tame dog, for the rest of his life, an instance of fidelity exploited in the saint's iconography. St Brieuc was once attacked by a pack of wolves which all fell down before him when he made the sign of the cross.

It was good propaganda in rural communities to present agents of the Christian God as a triumphal force over a major predator whose activities could mar a livelihood.

In 1789 there were as many as 5,000 wolves in France, with about a tenth of those in thickly forested Brittany, a well-established threat. They particularly liked the combination of remote *landes* and scrubby *bocage*, as forests with their wealth of trades were considerably less peaceful places than they are today. On the lonely routes of the Monts d'Arrée travelers might be the object of attack by wolves. The legend of Veig Richou given above reveals that this was the only fear felt by the old rag-man during his work. A treatise (1963) by Louis Durand-Vaugaron on the wolf in Brittany during the years 1773–1872 includes various oral testimonies of incidents where wolves attacked men as well as animals. In Plouneour-Menez, the neighboring parish to Le Cloître-St-Thégonnec, a wolf is said to have bitten eight people before attacking a flock of sheep near Commana. When Jean Quemener ran to the scene to drive the wolf off, it seized hold of him and only a grim struggle by his servants forced the beast to release him. The wolf was finally knocked senseless by blows with a pitchfork.

Appeals were made to saints for protection, especially St Hervé for his

Wolf leading the blind: St Hervé and an unlikely pet (Wendy Mewes)

close connection with wolves, although it was advised never to call a wolf by its name but to use Gray Foot, Dog of the Night, or—humanizing touch—Yann or Guillou (Willy).

> Go away in the name of St Hervé if you are a wolf
> And in the name of God if you are Satan!

> *Sant Mikel braz a oar an tu*
> *D'ampich youhal ar bleizi du*

> Great St Michael knows the way
> To stop the black wolves howling!

*La danse du loup*, today revived after falling into abeyance when it became irrelevant with the disappearance of wolves, derives from a shepherds' ploy to keep their flocks safe. They would dance on a flat rock, their wooden clogs striking the hard surface with the insistent rhythm of a drum. The loud noise thus created would keep the predators at bay. A story from 1862 in Poullaouen tells how people gathered after the sighting of wolves in their vicinity and performed this dance together as a precautionary measure. Old people who could remember the distinctive dance used as entertainment in their childhood years told how it could be done by a single dancer using the hearth stone to produce a loud beat or by a group in the round, attaining an impressive volume of sound. It would have been accompanied by vocals. The text of a song about the conversation between a wolf and a donkey (very much like La Fontaine's fable of the Horse and the Wolf) is given in the museum.

Here are also some graphic reminders of popular attitudes: the engraving of a wolf hung from a tree like a man, the wolf's feet nailed to a door as protection from evil and local legends of werewolves. An extract from the *Gazette de France* in 1781 describes an unusual pack of wolves found in Brittany "of a strange type and eager for human blood," with long muzzles, larger paws, and very sharp nails. Because there was a strong—and erroneous—popular belief that wolves did not touch men, evidence to the contrary suggested some special type of evolution in the animal producing werewolves.

Another gruesome exhibit is the metal wolf traps, like those found recently still in situ on the land of an agricultural school at Nivot near St-Rivoal. The last wolf seen in the area near Loqueffret in 1906 was said only to have three legs, probably the result of gnawing itself free from such a trap. In the latter days of wolves in Brittany, a quicker fate was sealed by the use of strychnine-dosed meat.

Toponymy in Brittany recalls so much of the vanished rural world and many place names retain the echo of days when wolves roamed the area. Near Le Cloître-St-Thégonnec is Poul ar Bleiz (Wolf Pool) and elsewhere Ty-Blaise/Bleiz (Wolf House, but other interpretations are possible), Roc'h ar Bleiz (Wolf Rock), Kerambleiz (Wolf Village), and Toul Blei (Wolf Hole). In Haute-Bretagne there are over a hundred place-names related to the wolf.

An important text on wolf hunting in Brittany by Edward William Lewis Davies was published in 1875 after two seasons of sport in central Brittany where he was based mostly in the Carhaix area. He described the "interminable forests bristling over the backbone of Brittany" as ideal wolf territory, it being impossible to cover such dense terrain systematically. It was a very real problem for the peasants, who faced

> …the impossibility of defending their unhoused beasts from the attacks of wolves, which sometimes in pairs and sometimes in packs, according to the severity of the weather, are a scourge to the whole country.

A child guarding flocks was safe enough by day, but as soon as night fell, the wolf became "a daring and destructive enemy: the very houses of the peasantry are not then secure from his attack." Drawings in the museum illustrate this—including incursions via the roof—and Davies confirms that "this is no imaginary danger; the thing has occurred over and over again to the clog makers of Duault and Huelgoat."

He recommended the wolf hunt as a perfect way to see the "Celtic population of lower Brittany in its rude simplicity—natural, wild and unchanged as it is by the varnish of modern civilization"—and described their cries when the hunt was on of "Harz ar bleiz, Harz ar bleiz" as unearthly, ringing through the woods to terrify the stoutest wolf and remain seared on a stranger's memory.

He rode with the Comte de St-Prix, the official called a *louvetier* in charge of responding to the worst threats by wolves and wild boars, and recorded how peasants from a certain area would send word, asking St-Prix to bring his hounds and have a day of hunting to oust the beasts that were savaging their animals and homesteads. The book describes the hunting—not only for wolves—in exhaustive and unappetizing detail that make it a difficult text for animal lovers but an intelligent and positive assessment of many non-material aspects of life in late nineteenth-century Basse-Bretagne. Davies spoke Breton, commenting on the closeness to Welsh and the special welcome for such Celtic cousins here, and mixed with Bretons of all social classes during his long stays. "This community of blood and language," he wrote, "is a key to the Breton's heart."

The book has proved popular on both sides of the Channel. A re-edition in French in the 1990s created funds to be donated for the preservation of wild spaces, and the new reserve on the Landes du Cragou was one to benefit.

Wolves became gradually extinct as farming practices changed and great reaches of thick cover disappeared. In the second half of the nineteenth century many areas of moorland were reclaimed for cultivation by new techniques. Now the buzzard is the largest predator to haunt the misty heights of the Landes du Cragou. The last prime, or price, on a wolf's head was paid to Pierre Berréhar in Le Cloître-St-Thégonnec on 6 October 1884, although sightings continued for another twenty years elsewhere in the remaining wilds of the Monts d'Arrée.

The millennium-old Chêne à Guillotin, priest's hiding place (Wendy Mewes)

*Chapter Nine*

# FOREST

## LIFE AND LEGEND IN THE GREENWOOD

Although rumors of a dense forest cover for the Armorican Peninsula in comparatively recent times may be greatly exaggerated, the woodlands that remain encapsulate many aspects of Brittany's social and imaginative history. Nowhere is landscape more a matter of practicality, home of a raft of sylvan skills like clog- or charcoal-making, source of all-important material for ship-building and an arena of opportunity for aristocratic hunters and poachers alike. By their secretive and enclosed nature, forests also gave rise to legends galore and offered concealment to salt-smugglers, robber bands, and priests on the run. These diverse activities have been replaced today by quiet green spaces still teeming with animal life—deer, wild boar, red squirrels, pine marten—and managed for timber and outdoor leisure use, but each forest retains a distinct personality, fashioned by its past.

FORÊT DE FOUGÈRES: LEARNED OAK TREES, SPILLED SALT, AND NASTY INSECT BITES

> "…the strong scent of the forested land rose like a cloud of incense, intoxicating those who admired the beauty of the area."
>
> Honoré de Balzac, *Les Chouans*

It is quite an experience to leave the town of Fougères heading northeast and immediately plunge into this dense forest—"powerful ramparts of verdure" as Flaubert's traveling companion Maxime du Camp describes it—full of secret places and hidden corners of history. Its special quality comes from the high percentage of beech trees: as many as three-quarters of the 1,600 hectares are composed of these slim, stately specimens, rounded out by oak, chestnut, and a few conifers. Three hundred hectares were lost in the storm of December 26, 1999, so there is plenty of young growth to support the majestic giants. The height of the land on which the forest rests is apparent from the rises and falls of the main road to Landéan passing like an arrow through the center. Scant remains of a Gallo-Roman camp mark one of the highest points, and various lakes the lowest levels. It has been very much a border forest of the Marches, "barring the passage between Dol and Avranches," as Victor Hugo put it, a place of strife and confrontation.

Occupation from prehistoric times is attested by the presence of megaliths, like the striking Cordon des Druides, an alignment of more than fifty quartz stones of varied size near the Carrefour de Chênedet. Two granite *dolmens* can also be seen: La Pierre Courcoulée (or Pierre des Huguenots) and, less well-preserved, the Pierre du Trésor, which lies on a beautiful path sadly disturbed by traffic noise. These monuments would not have been constructed originally to be concealed in thick forest as they are today, and the burial sites would more likely have been covered by mounds of earth in the center of well-cleared ground. Maxime du Camp, describing his visit to Fougères with Flaubert, said that "the forest is celebrated for its Druidic monuments," a typical false association of the nineteenth century.

A walk up past the Croix du Fouteau, or "Beech Cross" (which may represent Christianization of a former Celtic cult center), leads to the Iron

Forest burial: Pierre Courcoulée (Wendy Mewes)

Age fortified camp called locally Oppidum du Poulailler, which offers little sense of its lofty position today because of the close-packed trees, and no view to spy out approaching danger which must have been its advantage originally, but the banks and ditches are still in evidence, and tramping about the perimeter gives a sense of the size and defensive arrangement. The Roman road from Rennes to Bayeux led through the forest, to the west of the current D177, continuing the line of the Chemin Mélouin north past the lake at Chênedet. The camp covers twenty-five hectares, with two escarpments above the River Nançon to the west and Grande Rivière to the east offering natural protection. The quantity of stone found in the embankments may indicate an original *murus Gallicus* construction, as described by Julius Caesar. It is possible that before the Romans arrived the whole surrounding area was cleared and farmed by the Celtic tribe of the Riedones whose territory covered northeast Brittany.

This part of Brittany retains many fragments of old woodland. According to the writer Chateaubriand, "in the twelfth century, the cantons of Fougères, Rennes, Bécherel, Dinan, St-Malo and Dol were covered by the forest of Brécheliant," the model of Arthurian Brocéliande, and there is good reason for seeking to site that fabled woodland here (see p.219). Evidence of medieval clearances for cultivation and animal-rearing can be seen in many place-names around the forest—La Vigne, Touche-Cochonnais (Pig Farm), Villeboeuf—and the boundary has not changed much for the last 800 years.

Forest was commonly a place of retreat for religious figures in the eleventh and twelfth centuries, a pure and secret environment for devotion to worship and contemplation. L'Ermitage on the road to Parigné, now private property with a balconied house and hidden lake, was said to be the favored meditation spot of Vital de Savigny, a noted religious figure born around 1050 near Bayeux, after Raoul de Fougères gave him land to establish a monastery. One of Vital's companions, Bernard de Tiron, renowned for his hermitic tendencies, spent an inordinate amount of time in an oak tree in the forest, which itself acquired the epithet *quercus docta*, "learned oak," by association. Chênedet, the hamlet name of what is now the outdoor leisure center of the forest, may also have got its name by the same token (*chêne* meaning oak, *doctus* becoming *det* in Gallo). The lake here is as popular today as it was in 1849 when a local report mentions this rendezvous of young people with the caveat that they take a risk in bathing regardless of the potentially harmful quality of the water—not an issue now.

A vanished monastery of St-François on the eastern edge of the forest has left nothing much visible but the name of a farming hamlet. It started as a hermitage, the land for a chapel granted by Duke François I in 1440, but became a Convent of the Cordeliers, as Franciscans were called, with the permission of Charles VIII, King of France, husband of Anne de Bretagne. The small community lasted until the Revolution when only three monks remained. It was common in popular tradition to imagine the vast wealth of churches and abbeys, which perhaps accounts for the unlikely story that the monks here hid a large solid gold statue of their saint—himself a shining example of the vow of poverty!—somewhere near L'Ermitage, either buried under a tree or thrown into the lake there.

The forest now is neatly segmented by roads and many internal forest routes open only to walkers or horseback riders. Circuits for exploration weaving through the trees between these straight avenues start from named crossroads (*carrefours*). It is a focal point for weekend outings today as it was in the early years of the twentieth century:

> On Sunday afternoons we used to go as far as the forest to drink a cup of cider and eat a pancake with the clog-makers…

This is from an account by Jean Guéhenno, a cobbler's son from Fougères who was to become a famous writer and literary critic. It was not only shoemakers who labored in the forest here: Flaubert's fleeting visit leaves a graphic description of the glassmakers and their hot work, situated at the edge of an ample supply of fuel for their furnaces:

> We saw men, half-naked, covered in sweat, passing like ghosts with their twirling arms at work. From the hut came a singular noise: the snorting of the bellows of the forge, the fire crackling and sounding like the murmur of human voices.

A stone cross marks each end of the main road. One story makes them offerings of a father's thanks for finding his lost daughter in the forest, hence the title "Recovery" given to both. In the north before the entrance to Landéan the best-known Croix de Recouvrance (today moved a little from its original position) was the focal point for protests against conscription in 1793. The Revolutionary government had done away with Bretons' special dispensation from call-up outside their own territory and many hundreds gathered to refuse the newly imposed duty.

The forest's capacity for cover and camouflage makes it historically a place for violent clashes and the menace of ambush. The location of Fougères on the borders of Brittany near Mayenne and the birth of Chouannerie led to much anti-Revolutionary activity in the area, dramatized by Balzac and Victor Hugo in their novels on that topic. A saying that the Moulin d'Avion (or Avillon) is cursed, as its stream ran red with Breton blood, is another reminder of the Revolutionary struggle in which both sides saw heavy losses. The miller abandoned his home and business to avoid the fate of others, assassinated or even driven to suicide in those desperate times.

But the forest of Fougères was also the scene of another often bloody conflict, the illicit traffic of salt, or "white gold" as it was called. Brittany enjoyed an exemption from the *gabelle,* or salt tax, as part of its special privileges granted on union with France in 1532, a concession of enormous value. The region was a major producer of this basic and essential commodity on north and south coasts, especially in the area of the Brière around Guérande, still famous for its salt today. This kept the price in Brittany low, sometimes as much as thirty times cheaper than across the border—hence the attraction of smuggling, with high profits making the risks of capture worth taking. Fougères held a regular salt market and here the *faux-saulniers*, as they were called, sourced their merchandise and stored it ready to load up for daring journeys through the forest, taking smaller paths to try to avoid detection by the customs officials often lying in wait in the plentiful cover. Both sides were armed in anticipation of the frequent nocturnal clashes.

One of their routes, the Chemin Mélouin, is today a rough surfaced track with a wide verge kept sharply trimmed on the old Roman principle of preventing easy ambush with no cover near the road. But step off into the wood on a narrow, winding path through a surprisingly dense legion of spindly trunks and you do not have to go far for the somber atmosphere to conjure up a very different story of stealth, risk, and fear. A night journey leading a laden horse along the dark and twisting narrows, straining at every step for the tell-tale rustle of men lying in wait in the ditches. Once they had intercepted the smugglers, the customs officers would slash the salt bags with their swords and stamp the salt into the ground to ruin the content. This gives the name *Gâte sel* (place that spoils the salt) for another route, a track leading north from the Carrefour des Chevrettes, this time a thin path edged with fir trees which keeps fairly straight until finally dropping down to the road by the Moulin d'Avion. A safe journey across the border into Maine, Anjou, or Normandy would see enormous profits for successful smugglers. Arrest and conviction could lead to years of forced labor in the galleys of the French Navy.

A final curiosity of this historically rich forest can be found near the main road at the northern edge of the forest. The Celliers de Landéan date back to the twelfth century, and although their purpose is still a matter of speculation, the fifteen-meter, underground, brick-vaulted room reinforced by eleven granite arches is impressive. It may have been a storeroom of the lord of Fougères' former hunting lodge, the Château de la Forêterie, now disappeared, or built with the specific purpose of concealing Raoul II's treasures from marauding English soldiers of Henry II's army. In 1841 Prosper Mérimée, the Inspector of Monuments, visited and gave an amusingly ironic account of his experience:

> …in the middle of a wood is a big hole, and in this hole an arcade and large pieces of masonry, and under the arcade a black hole with a lot of water and frogs in it.

He bought three candles for the descent and "made my will and sent my last words to the commission" before entering. He had no idea what the structure was, recording local ideas that it concealed the entrance to a ten-kilometer tunnel between Fougères and Landéan or once housed Roman baths, but he did recognize its merit as a piece of Romanesque architecture and the Celliers were classified as an historic monument in 1862. Mérimée survived his watery exploration without even a cold, but he did get an enormous swelling "the size of a Doric column" from an insect bite.

## FORÊT DE PAIMPONT: MERLIN'S TOMB, THE VALLEY OF NO RETURN, AND THE EMPEROR'S NEW CLOTHES

To the west of Rennes, this lush, mainly oak and beech forest extends over 9,000 hectares of hilly landscape. It remains mostly in private ownership, with only a small section in the control of the Office National des Forêts, and is still prime hunting territory, with walking restricted in theory to waymarked paths covering the major sights. From the mid-seventeenth century the owners were keen to develop the use of natural resources beyond the basics of timber and fuel. Over centuries there were long-running disputes between local inhabitants who depended on the forest for their livelihood and the proprietors who looked to exploit the territory for profit. Open-face mines to extract iron ore were worked from the 1650s and the attached forges became major consumers of wood. In the eighteenth century there was burgeoning business in bleaching work for the cloth industry, another activity extravagant with heating fuel.

An enquiry of 1783 pronounced the forest almost exhausted, with wild moorland and scrub replacing the trees, and the Revolutionary period made even greater demands on the supply of wood. Pine was introduced in 1813 as a quicker fix to the shortage, supplying the forges which were at their height of production up to the 1850s. Purchased in 1875 by Louis Levesque, an industrial magnate from Nantes, and developed by his son later on, the forest became a hunting mecca, attracting many distinguished visitors, like the Duke of Westminster in the 1930s, for sport.

Today the Forêt de Paimpont is a most beautiful land of dense woodland cover, secret valleys, limpid lakes, striking châteaux (like Trécesson, built in the local purple schist), extraordinary individual trees, and strange megalithic remains. The lakeside village of Paimpont centers on an impressive abbey, a later foundation on the site of the original priory established by Judicaël, King of Domnonée, in 645. To the west, the small settlement of Tréhorenteuc has a pretty seventeenth-century church, unusual for its 1950s repackaging by the Abbé Gillard, who devised the elaborate Arthurian-themed decorations. This brings us to the crux of the matter concerning the Forêt de Paimpont.

The forest is heavily promoted for tourism under the name Brocéliande, fabled forest of Arthurian legend. The marketing is bold, coherent, and ubiquitous, everything fitted to the well-known theme, giving the forest a legendary identity which has been effectively reinforced by constant repetition. It is rather like the emperor's new clothes. The visitor may have many questions about the Arthurian legends and their context but "what's the evidence that this is actually Brocéliande?" is unlikely to be one of them, so assumed and confident is the presentation. The Château de Comper contains an interesting permanent exhibition devoted to the "Arthurian imagination," and claims its lake as the scene of Lancelot's upbringing in an underwater castle after he was snatched by the fairy Vivianne from his parents, Ban and Helen, who lived in the Marches of Brittany (an important detail, as we shall see).

According to Geoffrey of Monmouth, who almost single-handedly created the Arthurian story in his *History of the Kings of Britain*, Arthur was often in Gaul, had aid from Breton lords in battle and came specifically to Mont St-Michel to tackle a notorious giant. (A once prolific forest just to the south of the Mont is another claimant for the title of Brocéliande.) Other tales associate Arthur with places along the north coast of Brittany, but Arthurian tradition in Armorica centers primarily on Merlin and Lancelot. The *Roman de Lancelot du Lac* (c. 1220) makes the birthplace of the latter the Marches of Brittany, and the distinctive red and white coat-of-arms of Lancelot appear later in history as those of the Coëtquen family, once lords of Dol and Combourg. The same text describes the snatching of baby Lancelot by the fairy Vivianne, and her later ensnarement of Merlin, who fell in love with her, in a cave—and this living tomb is placed in Brocéliande.

There is no denying that the forest of Paimpont is deeply atmospheric and thoroughly convincing as the setting for the Arthurian stories if one is predisposed to enter into the spirit. And who would not want to be strolling in the footsteps of Merlin or Lancelot? It is a marketing dream. The Val-sans-Retour (Valley of No Return) has a glassy lake, the Miroir aux Fées, apt for a fairies' mirror, and high rocky perches on which Morgane— half-sister of Arthur—may have viewed with satisfaction the trapped false lovers she decreed should be imprisoned here by invisible walls after being betrayed herself by her own lover, Guyomarc'h. Further up the valley, the streams run red, tell-tale sign of iron ore, but a graphic extra for searchers of mystery. The silence is palpable and rich, as is often the case with places of historical significance, but… until recently a notice-board at the entrance to this valley stated baldly that another valley had been designated that of No Return, but when a factory was built there it seemed politic to move it here. I have seen this board many times and was surprised it was allowed to remain so long. On my last visit it was gone and now nothing casts doubt or provides fuel for cynics to spoil one of the best walks in Brittany.

Merlin's tomb is another story. Because of the tactical geographical changes, it is now a long way off at the other end of the forest, and it must be one of the most anticlimatic sights on offer in the region. Two stones wedged together are all that is left of a Neolithic *dolmen*. The stones are small and unremarkable. No amount of hanging ribbons, messages inserted in the cracks in the rock, or spiral paths can make this a place of any significance whatsoever. And was not Merlin supposed to be trapped in a cave in the legend? How can he be held fast within something that has no inside?

Beautiful place this forest certainly is, but Brocéliande? Many would disagree.

Brocéliande is of course a literary creation, fashioned from the imagination of various authors, but this process is rarely pure invention, with threads plucked from personal experience, visual memory, cultural consciousness, and social connection. The first person to mention the forest—not in an Arthurian context—is Wace in *Le Roman de Rou*, a chronicle of the Kings of Normandy written around 1170. At an earlier point in his life Wace enjoyed the patronage of Henry II, becoming a canon in Bayeux through his favor. Here he calls the forest of Brecheliant vast, well-known in Brittany and the subject of many stories:

> …*Brecheliant*
> *Donc Breton vont sovent fablant*
> *Une forest mult longue e lee*
> *Qui en Bretagne est mult loee*

He also mentions the marvelous spring of Barenton, where storms can be summoned by splashing water on a large stone at the head. This scene figures in the work of his contemporary Chrétien de Troyes, *Yvain, le Chevalier au Lion*. It is this author's work which introduces the whole romantic tradition of Arthur's court, Lancelot's exploits, and the quest for the Holy Grail. He uses the form Brocéliande to describe the forest where the spring is situated. In another text of Welsh origin (c. 1200), *Owein, ou le conte de la dame à la fontaine,* the locale specifies proximity to the sea. It is also the fateful meeting place of Merlin and Vivianne.

The Forêt de Paimpont's claim to be Brocéliande seems to have sprung originally from its old name Brécilien. In a document of 1467, the *Usemens et coustumes de la foret de Brecilien,* created for Guy de Laval, a sidekick of Joan of Arc and lord of Comper, by his chaplain, a spring in the forest is designated the Fontaine de Bellenton (Barenton). (Today it is certainly a romantic spot, requiring a long walk from the nearest parking. The large flat stone, or *perron,* is usually covered with offerings from modern pagans or Merlin enthusiasts.)

This was the extent of the association until the nineteenth century, when Celtic interest and thirsty Romanticism were actively seeking locations for the stories of oral and written tradition. Once places in the forest were given specific associations with Arthurian tales, it was a done deal and with a sleight of hand worthy of Merlin himself, the great marketing triumph that is today's Pays de Brocéliande was underway.

The influential *La table ronde,* a mammoth verse reworking of the Arthurian tales by Auguste Creuzé de Lesser, was published in Paris in 1812. This contained the first placing of the Valley of No Return in the mythical forest of Brocéliande. The missing link was supplied in 1824 when Blanchard de la Musse, judge by profession and enthusiastic polymath researcher by passion, fixed this location in the Forêt de Paimpont. He believed that the Arthurian legend was actually history but presented in epic style like Voltaire's *La Henriade,* in honor of Henri IV.

His close friendship with Jean Côme Damien Poignand of Montfort, an antiquarian who claimed to have excavated the tombs of Merlin "and his wife" Vivianne in the forest near the source of the stream "Mel" at the end of the Valley of No Return, encouraged his determination. He duly located these Arthurian sites in the east, around the stream of Mell-aon and Pont Dom Jean. When questioned on these claims he replied that no one who knew the local geography and Celtic language could fail to be convinced of the veracity of the association.

The Forêt de Paimpont has its own drama of sweeping hillsides, tumbling waters, and exposed vantage points offering expansive views over the treetops which intensify the sense of containment within a vast sylvan entity. Natural beauty here lies untouched by development, peopled only by infrequent hamlets lying low in the landscape. Apparently these days such simple natural advantages are not enough to build a major tourist destination, and under the "Brocéliande brand" the economy of an entire region now rests on what may well be a spurious claim. Certainly not everyone is under the spell. Before all the hype, Chateaubriand, a man of the Marches of Brittany, described the twelfth-century forest of Brecheliant as located between Rennes and Fougères. Increasingly rigorous contemporary studies are challenging the basic premise of equating Paimpont and Brocéliande. If twelfth-century sources place the magical forest near the sea and in the Marches of Brittany, then Paimpont is a pretty poor candidate, geographically speaking.

Christophe Déceneux, a local historian of Combourg, has been researching the issue of Brocéliande for many years, amassing a wealth of evidence to support his theory that the forest of Arthurian romances was that which once extended from Mont St-Michel to Combourg. I raised the question of Merlin's disappointing tomb and he pointed out that such is the geology of the Paimpont forest area—primarily schist—that caves are not found there. The Marches are a better candidate. He showed me a photo of another candidate for the magician's prison, a grotto on the sheer lip of Mont Dol, just below the chapel and Rocher du diable (Devil's Rock). When I made a trip to see for myself, the connection is at once compelling. It is a superb cave, a perfect secret trap for that most tricky of customers, Merlin. Mont Dol itself, sticking up from the plain north of Dol-de-Bretagne, may also have been the inspiration for the Mont Douloureux of the legends—not for an etymological connection, as Christophe is quick to point out, but because the location and the *jeu de mot* combined may have proved irresistible. He proposes the place name Broualan—Alan's Hill—a high point in the original forest, near Combourg, as the original linguistic link with Brocéliande.

So ingrained is the Arthurian brand now that it is hard to escape its heavy hand in shops and services of the Forêt de Paimpont, but it must be said that the sites themselves remain free of tacky notice boards, waymarking is unobtrusive, and the power of the scenery soon takes over from superficial interpretation under the verdant canopy. Perhaps we should be grateful for private ownership after all.

The true, natural identity of this forest is encapsulated in the presence and personality of various exceptional trees. The Chêne à Guillotin, a gnarled oak over a thousand years old, is apparently named after a local priest, Abbé Guillotin, who is said to have hidden in its massive hollow trunk to escape from Republican soldiers during the Revolution. When his pursuers arrived, they checked the entrance to the interior but found it covered by a massive and dense spider's web, proof that no one had recently entered. Thus saved, he later attributed the miracle to Notre-Dame de Paimpont, whose cult statue can be seen in the nave of the abbey church there. Unfortunately it seems this story may be merely a product of 1970s hype.

The Hêtre de Ponthus, with its rampant branches standing out from the surrounding fir plantation, lies not far from the Fontaine de Barenton, although its location remains unadvertised thanks to abusive behavior of some previous visitors. This beech is over 300 years old, and has been named after the hero of an early fifteenth-century romance concerning Ponthus, a Prince of Galicia, who marries Sidonie, daughter of a King of Brittany. It was again Guy de Laval in the document of 1467 who brought this literary figure to his forest, giving him a court where he held jousting tournaments at the spot the tree stands today, and where local tradition says a château once stood.

A more overtly symbolic forest specimen is the Arbre d'Or, the Golden Tree. This gilded sculpture formed from a chestnut tree by François Davin is a modern statement of regeneration and the triumph of nature's irrepressible spirit after the terrible destruction wrought by fires in 1990. It stands by the Miroir aux Fées at the entrance to the Valley of No Return, and its staunch reality will doubtless in future centuries be transformed in legend to a miracle growth of solid gold.

There is plenty in the forest for those who prefer to be on more solid historical ground, and reality is of course often more thought-provoking than legend. Various megaliths include the Jardin aux Moines, the name as mysterious as the Neolithic monument, a rectangular outline of stones divided into "rooms." The contrast of white quartz and purple schist is noticeable, but whether this is artistic intention or simple practicality is impossible to say. The site is called the Monks' Garden from later stories of badly behaved clerics turned to stone. The name of the Tombeau des Anglais, a rather battered *dolmen* not far from Merlin's sad tomb, has a more prosaic origin, reflecting local memories of clashes in the Hundred Years' War in this locality, particularly the Battle of Mauron in 1352.

It is a pity that Merlin and Lancelot overshadow the strange but true tale of Éon de l'Étoile. From a noble family, Éon became a hermit in the

Forest of Paimpont, based near the hamlet today called Folle Pensée or "Mad Thoughts." The isolated life seems to have taken its toll on his mental state as he became delusional, believing himself to be the reincarnation of Christ. When he heard the Latin word *eum* in the mass (*per eum qui venturus est judicare vivos et mortuus*—through he who will come to judge the living and the dead) he thought it was his own name, Éon. Such was the beginning of a cult, as many followers came to join this new Jesus, the crowd soon turning into a thieving gang, carrying out raids even on churches and châteaux. Wild parties took place in the forest hideout, with Éon dressing up in rich robes looted from abbeys. He was accused of black magic rites, summoning evil spirits, and being the Devil himself. As branches of the cult began to spring up elsewhere, the Church took decisive action. Éon was arrested in 1148 and charged with sorcery and heresy, and he continued to claim he was the son of God during his trial. The court's decision was that as his mind was deranged, he should be held securely in a monastery rather than put to death, but he died in his holy prison soon after. It is said that his spirit still haunts that part of forest: something other than Merlin for walkers to think about on those lonely trails…

## Forêt de Coatloc'h: clogs, miserable Margot, and a nursery rhyme

"…this superb forest… provides wood of great beauty."

Jacques Cambry, 1799

The two biggest changes in forests over history are population and noise level. Once busy working and inhabited places, they are often silent now, especially outside the hunting season. The Forêt de Coatloc'h (Wood of the Lake) near Scaër in southern Finistère may have begun life as a ducal hunting and fishing reserve, but like many others it became a hive of economic activity in the nineteenth and early twentieth centuries. Today it has reverted to a managed domain of rectilinear parcels covering 300 hectares and providing walking and cycling trails which link up with the Green Way to Rosporden.

Traces of a "château" in the heart of the wood—on a high point north of the Maison du Garde where the forest manager once had his base—

doubtless fueled the legend of ducal interest, although the remains dating back to the early Middle Ages are more of a feudal *motte* than a castle. The Manoir des Salles to the north of the forest later replaced this, and the lake indicated in the name Coatloc'h, long disappeared, was also in this location as remains of a raised retaining bank show. An old story has it that nobles from the manor house used to take a boat to the chapel of St-Michel for mass.

The area around Scaër was renowned for its tradition of clog-making. The Chauvel family are still nearby in the business their ancestors practiced in various places at least from 1720. Although mechanical production gradually became more widespread than the handmade version in the twentieth century, demand was still great. Even many photos of Resistance fighters during the Second World War illustrate the incongruous combination of clogs and deadly weapons. Today the Forest of Coatloc'h is strongly associated with the production of wooden shoes (*Bo(u)tou Koad* in Breton), although a reconstructed clog-maker's hut is the only obvious legacy of an occupation of great importance in Brittany, where such footwear was used by all the ordinary population. A worker would get through up to six pairs a year and the clogs were often sold at markets by the dozen. There would be plain ones for everyday wear and degrees of incised, painted decoration for other occasions like fêtes and weddings, where elaborately adorned versions would be tied onto the bride's feet with colored ribbons.

Beech, birch, and alder were commonly used for making the footwear. The Forest of Coatloc'h retains a few stands of ancient oak and beech, some more than a hundred years old. In Jacques Cambry's time there was a lower layer of alder buckthorn filling in all the gaps between the "noble" trees. Parcels of forest were allocated to each clog-maker, who then exploited the patch for about two years before moving on elsewhere either in the same forest or further afield. They lived in simple, makeshift dwellings of wooden frames covered with branches with a central hearth and smoke-hole, called a *loge* (French) or *loj* (Breton), a word retained in place-names like Loj Stang and Loj Gaor around the forest today.

The clog-maker's hut at Coatloc'h has recently been restored to give a visual impression of working conditions, and each July a Fête du Sabot held there celebrates the old skill with demonstrations of handmade and mechanical methods. The art of the *sabotier* still lives to a limited extent

Coatloc'h : simple life of sabotiers (Wendy Mewes)

today as demand continues for these traditional Breton shoes for practical use or as decorative souvenirs. Any museum of rural traditions—of which not surprisingly there are many in Brittany—will have numerous examples of different types of clogs, including the poachers' special with the heel at the front to give a misleading idea of direction taken!

Old postcards and *chansons de métiers* provide vivid reminders of the harsh forest life, although it was not immune to romanticization. One card showing a clog-maker cutting his wood has a few scribbled lines on the picture by our old friend Botrel:

Ah! How happy we are,
So free beneath the blue sky:
Being far, so far from men,
We are near, much nearer to God.

In fact, the rude, itinerant life of the clog-maker often gave him the same sort of bad reputation as the *pilhaouer* (see p.192). *La Chanson du sabotier* (The Song of the Clog-maker) recorded by Luzel tells the sorry tale of a girl who goes off into the forest with a *sabotier* and thus ruins her prospects. The man is not at all sympathetic to her plight—he says she'll always have fuel at least, and he is prepared to fetch water, but when the food is finished, he will be off. Miserable Margot regrets the life she might have had, marrying a farming man with a dozen bulls in his stable and a plump horse:

> The clog-maker cares nothing for that
> As long as he has his hut full of children,
> And when he works
> He cares little for water
> But is always full of wine,
> White and red, or brandy.

Anatole Le Braz records the story of Jean Pentecôte, a mysterious old man who dies when visiting a group of *sabotiers*. The doctor called upon to give a death certificate questions them about the deceased's origins and gets this reply:

> People of our trade are from everywhere and nowhere. We have no house. Because of all the coming and going, like the winds or the seasons, we even forget where we were born… We are from where there are beeches to shape into clogs, that's all.

In fact, the old man turns out to have been a noble who gave up everything for love of a clog-maker's daughter and devoted himself to her traditional lifestyle.

Coatloc'h was once a ducal hunting forest and local tradition attributes its creation to Duchess Anne. She is said to have come across a dead magpie near Roz ar Bic (to explain the name Magpie's Hill) and decreed that the spot should form the boundary of her new plantation, a superstitious ploy to keep death at bay. Evidence can still be seen of the banked wall which once enclosed the entire area—noted by Cambry on his visit—designed to keep animals inside the hunting zone. Another more general connection is that popular tradition calls Anne the "Duchess in Sabots," although it is hard to imagine that great image-conscious lady in rough clogs. The nursery rhyme is known throughout Brittany:

> There was Anne de Bretagne, a duchess in sabots
> Returning to her lands
> In sabots, fa la la.
> Ah ! Ah ! Ah !
> The wooden clogs live on.
> Anne became queen, with her sabots,
> The Bretons were in misery, in sabots, fa la la.
> Ah ! Ah ! Ah !
> The wooden clogs live on.
> The Bretons were in misery, with their sabots,
> They no longer had a ruler, in sabots, fa la la,
> Ah ! Ah ! Ah !
> The wooden clogs live on.

## FORÊT DU CRANOU: TRAVELING TREES, BLOOD SACRIFICE, AND IMBECILE TOURISTS

> "Dense in nature and resonant in name, the forest of Cranou, bringing together mineral and plant in all its sonority, a dark fragment of the Breton mystery…"
>
> Philippe Le Guillou

This is the largest forest in Finistère, extending for more than 1,300 hectares over the southern slopes of the Monts d'Arrée, spread between the *communes* of Hanvec, Loperec, and Le Faou (beech in Breton), and touching on the village of Rumengol, which has one of the best churches in the area. On the northeast edge is the domain of Menez Meur, part of the regional Parc d'Armorique, where the forest setting houses a nature reserve of Breton breeds and wild boar.

In 1987 Cranou suffered widespread destruction in the great storm, which brought down about a sixth of the trees. Today it is managed by the state and includes an arboretum designed to monitor the effects of climate change. It is popular for all the normal forest pursuits: hunting, walking, riding, and—in the autumn season—mushroom picking, when *cèpes* and many others are abundant. Each October a Fête des

Champignons is held a few kilometers away in Brasparts, presenting several hundred types with details of their properties and uses or poisonous potential.

The trees of Cranou have made their way all over the world and witnessed some real adventures, carrying corsairs like René Duguay-Trouin (see p.97) on his travels in the early eighteenth century and keeping the French Royal and then Republican Navy afloat for hundreds of years. The humid west coast climate, schist and quartzite bedrock, and acidic soil combined to make an ideal location for oak and beech. Their timber was in constant demand for shipbuilding in Brest, tons of long, straight logs being transported on rafts to the yards across the inland sea of the Rade de Brest via the estuary port of Le Faou.

An old saying recorded by Anatole Le Braz has one of those multiple origins so characteristic of oral tradition: "In the forest of Cranou, there'll never be a shortage of wood."

Some say it was St Conval who gave this benediction during the Age of Saints. He cut down wood for his oratory in the nearby Forêt du Gars at Daoulas and was chased away by the furious local lord. Conval put a curse on that forest and a blessing on Cranou, where he was welcomed and encouraged to settle. His hermitage later became the site of a chapel which remained in service in the forest until the mid-twentieth century, before being considered too far removed from civilization by the clergy and "moved" to Toulboën. (In fact only the original bell tower and some statuary were retained.) One lone remaining half-column of the chapel's calvary can still be seen in the forest: it bears the inscription R.DORE MA FAICT and the date 1627. The man responsible, Roland Doré, a sculptor from Landerneau, was to become the most celebrated craftsman of his age in western Brittany, as exquisite work in the area shows (see p.49). The *fontaine* of St-Conval, with a replica statue of the saint, still presides over its spring water in a little-known location amid the forest undergrowth.

Another version of the blessing of prolific growth recounts how a blacksmith became jealous of his wife's frequent visits to the Abbey of Landévennec, believing the monks to be the attraction rather than the religious services. When she gave birth to seven sons, her husband carried them off in a kneading trough to the shore (where the ships' cemetery is today in the Aulne estuary) and launched them into the water. The infants were rejected at Daoulas but received kindly at Le Faou, hence the recrimination and reward.

Conval was not the only holy inhabitant of Cranou. Pezrec, said to have been a Cornish or Welsh prince by origin, came to Armorica to evangelize but found the solitary life more appealing, becoming a hermit in the forest and living alongside the wild animals. Local names like nearby Loperec are derivations. He may be the St Petroc of Welsh origin and Cornish fame, who landed with his companions in the Camel estuary and established a monastery at Padstow. During the next thirty years he traveled widely—including his time in Brittany—before retiring to a hermitage on Bodmin Moor where a priory later housed his relics. In 1177 these were stolen by a rogue monk who carried them off to the Abbey of St-Méen in Brittany. Henry II had to throw his weight around to get them returned, an event which still has a ritual celebration in Bodmin each year.

The Forest of Cranou originally belonged to the Vicomté du Faou. During the time Cardinal Richelieu held that title the forest was devoted to supplying the arsenal in Brest and Louis XIV continued this practice in the early eighteenth century. Richelieu had been the instigator of Brest's development as the Atlantic port of the French Navy in 1631: fifty years later the city took the role of regional capital from St-Renan. The Navy needed wood not only for shipbuilding—particularly long straight oaks for masts—but also for fuel, and structural work around the port.

The demands of the Revolutionary years almost exhausted the forest here as elsewhere and a period of recuperation from 1818 was essential. Control of the forest passed to the state administrative structure Eaux et Forêts in 1829. In the mid-nineteenth century wood from the forest was used for barrels, clogs, fuel, and fortification as well as shipbuilding, and Le Faou's industrial success was based on the timber trade. By 1886, however, imports of wood—oak from America and pine from northern Europe—and fuel (coal from England) meant that demand for local supplies was lessening. Even in the important Breton conservation industries, tin was beginning to replace wooden barrels for containers. There was, however, still business in building fishing boats. The Morvan enterprise in Le Faou dealt with 3,000 tons of wood annually, most of which came from Cranou.

The close links between the forest and the Navy are evident in the work of naval sculptors in the church of Rumengol, where they were

A dolmen, a Druid, and assorted saints (Wendy Mewes)

responsible for the two transept altars of astonishingly lavish gilding. No one is sure of the origin of the name Rumengol, but one nineteenth-century interpretation has given birth to a colorful tale that brings the Druids into play. (It is worth noting that these priests and bards of Celtic society are still present today in Brittany in a neo-Druid form active for more than a hundred years. The renowned former Grand-Druide and influential writer, Gwenc'hlan Le Scouëzec, died in 2008 in nearby Bras-parts.)

The stained-glass window, dating from 1884, behind the high altar has an unusual subject: a statue of Mary and child sits on a huge *dolmen*, while a couple of saints pontificate, a kneeling king holds the model of a church and a Druid sits quietly in a corner, robe drawn across his face, arm around his harp.

Le Chévalier de Freminville, a non-Breton, otherwise known as La Chévalière for his love of dressing up in women's clothing, in his *Antiquités de la Bretagne* (1829) interpreted the name Rumengol as *ru* (red), *men* (stone), and *gol* (light) and therefore linked this glowing stone with a former "men-hir" and Druidic practice, as at that time most people still associated Neolithic monuments with the Celts. From there it is a short step to the blood and human sacrifice, as indicated in a local canticle (with reference to the Roman poet Lucan):

> On the red rock, the blood is shed
> In Cranou, at the heart of the forest,
> Under the oak of Teutatès
> Men slain without pity.

In 1859 Edouard Vallin in his *Voyage en Bretagne* describes the forest of Cranou as a "sombre retreat, where the Druids came to carry out their mysterious sacrifices."

Inevitably a legend developed to back all this up: King Gradlon and St Guénolé were walking on Menez Hom after the destruction of Ys when they saw flames from a neighboring hill. When the king told the saint they came from a Druidic sacrificial ritual, the horrified Guénolé insisted they ran all the way to put a stop to such outrage and convert the Druids to Christianity. Apparently this was an easy task and a statue of the Virgin (an anachronistic reference to the Age of Saints, but very nineteenth-century) was erected on the sacrificial stone itself. Gradlon vowed to build a church on the spot: Rumengol. So the stained glass window mentioned above records the Christian triumph over dastardly pagans.

A much more down to earth translation of Rumengol gives us *Remed-oll*, or cure-all, a version paying tribute to the miraculous healing powers of the *fontaine* on the main road near the church. In 1833 Émile Souvestre rejected the Chévalier's recent theory, asserting that the priest at the church had assured him the archives showed clearly that the prosaic explanation was correct. Regardless of the name, the site did indeed become an eminent place of pilgrimage, bringing fame and fortune to the shrine of Notre-Dame de Rumengol. Her cult is one of the most celebrated in Finistère, with the two Pardons attended by thousands even today. In 1899 the constant procession of devotees made an impression on Jean Guillou, whose account derives from that published five years earlier by Anatole Le Braz in *Au Pays des Pardons*:

> They pass, bare-footed, staff in hand,
> Holding their wreaths and singing canticles:
> At dawn they take their route to Rumengol
> Those mystical Breton pilgrims.

In 1901 as many as 30,000 attended the Fête de la Sainte Trinité. Two years later we have the account of observer Laurent Tailhide, a Gascon from Tarbes and never one to mince his words. He seems most concerned with the tourists—"imbeciles on wheels"—who pass the great procession in their cars raising clouds of dust and filling the air with gas fumes.

## Chapter Ten

# RIVER

## FLUENT LINKS

Waterways are one of the great glories of Brittany, never far away in stages of either infancy or adulthood. *Abers* (river mouths) and *rias* (inlets) are characteristic features of the jagged coastline, and rivers of the hinterland, swollen by Brittany's rainy climate, have served many a mill and tannery, or provided hydroelectricity. As the river's task is to provide a two-way connection between land and sea, so Brittany's tidal estuaries have enabled inland towns like Landerneau, Quimper, Morlaix, and Redon to thrive commercially in an exchange of goods with the outside world. Harnessing water power through the development of an extensive canal system was an important boost to transport and communication in the heart of the region in the nineteenth century before the railways came along and spoiled it all. But the river is also an invitation to the interior which may be unwelcome, as in the case of Viking raids which penetrated as far inland as Rennes, made vulnerable by the powerful Vilaine.

THE LOIRE: NANTES THE SIREN CITY AND A HOUSE IN THE WATER

> "…this beautiful river with boats and ships that come and go all over Europe. Little wonder we see it so flourishing."
>
> Jouvin de Rochefort, 1672

> "Nantes—neither completely inland nor completely attached to the sea—neither cat nor fish—just what it takes to create a siren."
>
> Julien Gracq, *La forme d'une ville*, 1995

Nantes' fame as a port has somehow coined the popular notion that it is by the sea, skipping over the fifty-six kilometers of the Loire to the west that separate the beaches of the Côte d'Amour or the industrial

231

center of St-Nazaire from the settlement that was once the main city of Brittany. In the other direction, the sumptuous châteaux that have become synonymous with the word Loire are but a distant whisper. What we might call the Breton Loire is a functional, workaday wide gray streak of shallow water, lined by marshy emptiness or brutal refineries, even if the river has become a showcase for contemporary art, as part of an ambitious program typical of Nantes' innovative creative energies. The umbilical cord of communication between city and sea has never been cut, shaping centuries of commercial and colonial history as it has itself been shaped in turn by urbanization.

Nantes was once the ducal capital of Brittany, much favored in the fifteenth century by François II and his daughter Anne de Bretagne, although it lost out to Rennes after the union with France as a political center. During the German occupation in the Second World War the Vichy government took the decision to sheer off Nantes' economic powerhouse and its surroundings districts from the Armorican peninsula. Post-war arrangements confirmed the change of status with Nantes heading up a new *département* called Loire-Atlantique, so that technically today it is no longer even in Brittany. This controversial situation has kept the symbolic status of Nantes as a representative of that long-lost independent state of "historic Brittany" alive. Various organizations work for reunification, but economic and political issues—the relative status of Rennes, for example—make this a difficult reality to envisage.

The subject is avoided in the public presentation of the city today, which naturally concentrates on the cultural cornucopia on offer at every turn, and the multidirectional faces of its ambitions. Nantes has no identity crisis, more of a multiple-personality issue. The astonishing effervescence of ideas and artistic manifestations that is "so Nantes" has created a new focus for the Loire, which might have acquired an uncharacteristic insignificance alongside industrial decline. It is through the river that the city's expansive vision has been forged and brought such tangible rewards.

Strange fact: a contemporary casual visitor to Nantes could visit the château and cathedral, look at the famous *mascarons* (decorative stone carved faces) of the Ile Feydeau—now only an island in the sense of being surrounded by a sea of cars—and never see the estuary at all. The Erdre, which leads north towards the start of the Nantes-Brest canal twenty-two kilometers away, is more in evidence, with open sections in the city center and a beautiful Japanese garden on the Ile de Versailles a short walk upstream. From the vantage point of the Le Nid bar on the 32nd floor of the Tour Bretagne, an iconic 1970s office block, it is easy to see how far the Loire has moved from the days when it ran below the walls of the château and the *ville close*.

The original settlement was formed at the confluence of the Erdre and the Loire, with the latter a crucial instrument in the future fortunes of Nantes—from the Gallo-Romano *Portus Namnetum* trading salt and fish for wine and oil from the Mediterranean to Bishop Felix's ambitious sixth-century works to create a new channel to improve harbor access and commercial development. The vulnerability of any estuary town was apparent in 843 when a savage Viking attack saw Bishop Gothard and not a few of the inhabitants slain at mass in the cathedral. A handy base for further attacks on the city was created with a Viking camp on the Ile de Biesse in the Loire. This is now fused into part of the Ile de Nantes, but in those days the channel contained a mini archipelago of islands. From the eleventh century a series of six bridges between these linked the north and south banks, and this general form remained for the next 600 years. Initially used as pasture land—with names like Prairie au Duc or Pré de la Madeleine—the islets were gradually merged and turned to industrial use with dykes and canals to focus the flow of the Loire through specific channels, giving the best access to the port on the Quai de la Fosse. So, once an integral part of everyday life, the Loire has steadily retreated from the city center, reflecting the changing priorities of city planning as its numerous branches were gradually filled in during the nineteenth and twentieth centuries, making way for road and rail links judged more efficient for urban prosperity. Today only the Ile de Nantes remains.

The associated challenge posed for engineers from the earliest times has been the shallow channel littered by sandbanks and very prone to silting. Vauban had already commented on the problem in 1699, and in the 1780s the *Encyclopédie Méthodique* claimed that "Nantes is no longer a sea port" because of sand blocking river traffic, warning that commerce would have to move downriver to Paimboeuf if nothing was done.

Despite this drawback, Nantes rose to become one of the busiest ports in France, first as a river port relying on its *ligériennes* (of the Loire) connections, then from the fifteenth century with international trade at the heart of its success. Many foreign merchants were based in the city—

An eye on Nantes (Wendy Mewes)

Spanish wine traders, Hanseatic salt dealers—reflecting European interests, although local *armateurs* came into their own in the eighteenth century and dominated commerce with places like Guinea, the Antilles, and Guyana. The name of the Hangar des Bananes, a vast warehouse now sporting restaurants and galleries near the former naval construction site on the south bank of the Loire is an evocative hangover from this colonial trading.

Much of the city's wealth and glorious architecture came from the sickeningly lucrative eighteenth-century slave trade, with Nantes the main French port for this human traffic of "black gold," or (a more accepted euphemism) *bois d'ébène*. The horrors of this wretched practice are detailed in the city museum housed in the ducal château, an interesting transformation of medieval building into modern functionality, red leather against time-worn granite blocks, a hydraulic lift to supplement turret staircases. The slave-dealing brought incredible fortunes on the back of human misery. Fine merchants' houses along the quai de la Fosse and Ile Feydeau with their decorated façades and scrolled-iron balconies are typical examples of the lifestyle this money could buy in eighteenth-century Nantes. The "triangular trade" took cheap cargoes from the city to Africa to exchange for slaves, then moved this human commodity to the Caribbean to sell as labor on the plantations before loading up with sugar, coffee, rum, spices, and cotton to bring home for local consumption and redistribution all over Europe.

On the quai de la Fosse is a powerful, recently devised memorial to the sufferings of the slave trade, reminder of the harsh realities on which the wealth of Nantes was based. Two thousand tiny glass plaques on the riverside walkway record the names and dates of ships involved in the all too numerous expeditions, their names often at grim variance with their purpose: *Les Bons Frères* (1789), *La Félicité,* and *Le Prince Noir* (both 1775). The subterranean sections of the memorial are both a reminder of the extent of the servitude business (the French trade alone accounting for almost one and a half million displaced people) and a record of the long struggle for human rights and dignity before abolition was finally achieved in 1848. The riverside placing of the memorial is potent: the Loire has led Nantes to some dismal moral territories. A recent initiative to get street-names honoring the *armateurs* involved in slave trading changed met with only a lukewarm response from the powers that be, pointing to the Mémorial de l'Abolition de l'Esclavage as acknowledgment of a moral debt.

With the Revolution came one of the Loire's most bloody memories in which the river itself figures as an instrument of torture during Nantes' own version of the Terror. The city was Republican, holding a port that was of great worth to the English-backed counter-Revolutionaries. Following an attack on the city in June 1793, Jean-Baptiste Carrier was sent later in the same year from Paris to suppress the Vendéen uprising, and the brutality of his methods was soon in evidence as "non-Republicans" were sniffed out indiscriminately for execution. The relatively straightforward guillotine and firing squad soon gave way to "vertical deportation," or death by drowning in the Loire. Boatloads of men, women, and children were taken onto the water at night and pushed overboard, held submerged by boathooks if necessary or mutilated with swords if they sought to avoid their fate. Engravings portray savage glee in the boatmen's faces as they force their victims down to death. It is estimated that at least 4,000 people died in these grisly so-called "patriotic baptisms."

There was a lull in trade between 1790 and 1815 as the port was paralyzed by Revolutionary wars. Although new venues like North Africa and the Ile Bourbon (Reunion Island) were exploited by traders from the 1820s onwards, the nineteenth century saw a move towards industrialization: shipbuilding, sugar refineries, and the manufacture of cookies became the triple prongs of development. Nantes imported all the ingredients for the latter commodity and took to production in the 1860s. The former LU factory, with its one remaining minaret-like tower, is today a cultural center, the epitome of industrial chic in decor. Romain Lefèvre began selling English-style cookies in the market in the Bouffay district of Nantes, then had the first *petits-beurre*s (still a bestseller) made by hand. His son Louis Lefèvre-Utile started the LU enterprise in 1886, with English manufacturers Huntley & Palmer as his model, combining quality with mass-production. By 1913 the factory was producing 6,000 tons of cookies a year and had more than 500 employees on what was then the Ile de la Madeleine. The enameled containers became collectors' items featuring artists' designs and Art Nouveau decoration. In 1928 Louis complained bitterly about the filling in of the branch of the Loire that separated his factory from the château in order to create a new railway line. His pamphlet was entitled "The Loire, a program of destruction and infection for the city of Nantes."

The nineteenth century brought many foreign travelers. The arrogant decorations of the *armateurs*' houses on Île Feydeau, stone faces and symbols mirroring their colonial triumphs eloquently carved on the façades, can be seen in one of J. M. W. Turner's paintings. He presents the view from there across a branch of the Loire (no longer in existence), with boats thronging the river and the cathedral towers in the background. It now hangs in the château museum, one of a series from his visit in the 1820s on his way upriver to Orléans, while his sketchbook from that same trip is in the Tate in London. This reveals many outlines of individual structures—the Théâtre Graslin, the château, the Louis Guibert steamer on the river, and many *Nantais* city skylines.

A few years later Leitch Ritchie, a Scots journalist and author, wrote an account of his own trip, *Wandering by the Loire*, using engravings of Turner's pictures as illustration. Clearly the same old problems bedeviled the river in the 1830s:

The Loire, which has been reckoned one of the principal rivers of France, threatens to become one of the meanest, acted upon by some strange principle of destruction that is mingled with its very being.

He went on to say that if nothing major was done about the silting situation, Nantes would in effect become an inland city.

In 1839 Fortuné du Boisgobey did not think much of Nantes but found a certain fascination with *la coquette* (enticing) *Loire*, which appeared at its best just when he and his companion were about to leave the city behind, revealing "all its calm and marvellous beauty." He came to appreciate the river on a journey downstream, stopping at Paimboeuf where "a pretty tree-lined promenade looks over the river," and St-Nazaire, then nothing more than a tiny village and literally a two-horse place, according to Boisgobey. Thirty years later, Nantes, in the wake of the railway's arrival, would decide to create an "avant-port" at St-Nazaire, a sort of nautical Frankenstein that was to become as much rival as ally. Another attempt in the late nineteenth century to facilitate shipping access was the construction of the Canal de la Martinière from Paimboeuf to Le Pellerin, running parallel with the Loire to avoid the most turbulent sections of the tidal estuary.

The Loire was the starting point for the imagination of Jules Verne, author of *Twenty Thousand Leagues under the Sea* and *Around the World in Eighty Days*. He was born in Nantes in 1828 on the edge of Ile Feydeau (when it was still an island) and grew up with the sense and sound of port activity and mental images of the exotic destinations of the boats that thronged the quays. Voyages to strange landscapes, remote islands and foreign cities filled his thoughts, an internal world inspired by the advances of science combined with the colorful scenarios of his own imagination. He deserves a place as one of the precursors of science fiction.

The family acquired a holiday house at Chantenay, a western district of Nantes where the Musée Jules Verne stands today. From the lower garden he watched the traffic on the Loire and made his first forays on the water with his brother Paul. Wyss' *Swiss Family Robinson* (published in 1812) was a favorite story. His memoirs of childhood pay tribute to the overriding importance of the river in his formative years: "My childhood was steeped in the maritime movements of a great commercial city, point of arrival and departure for many long-haul voyages."

Verne recalled that he could not see any kind of ship without imagining himself setting off on board, a fantasy fueled by his first view of the sea at St-Nazaire at the age of twelve. The river entered many of his later writings. In *Le superbe Orénoque* (The Mighty Orinoco), sailors are reminded of "their beloved country of Brittany" and the Loire seeing banks of yellow sand, the jumble of *chalands* with their square sails and the expanses of flat plains like those around Pellerin and Paimboeuf.

Anyone who takes a boat from Nantes to St-Nazaire today will be conscious of those marshy expanses on both sides of the river, villages set back on firmer ground behind bands of greenery. The ground is too soft for luxurious mansions with grounds sweeping down to the fluid waterline backed by banks of reeds, pasture, or low trees bulging into the water. One of the works of art is unmissable: a house wedged lopsidedly in the silty sludge of the channel, surrounded by water when the tide is up. *La Maison dans la Loire* by Jean-Luc Concourt makes a statement about the river in its context of nature with this "unoccupied wreck," but it speaks also of survival: "It seems as isolated as we sometimes find ourselves in nature."

The art of semi-submersion (Wendy Mewes)

As the route unfolds, the contrast between the pastoral idyll of the south bank and the industrial occupation of the north becomes more marked. The red roofs of pretty Paimboeuf signal a great widening of the river and a swing in the channel brings the boat right in close to the refineries of Donges, belching out a single flame of smoky fire above the tankers drawn up outside, the smell of hot oil tainting the air as the petrol plant is passed. The potential for explosive accidents seems terrifyingly real at these close quarters, but there are other dangers. The inevitable reminder is of the wreck of the tanker *Erika* in 1999 (see p.89), which caused particular environmental damage here at the mouth of the estuary.

Passing beneath the towering height of the Pont de St-Nazaire, gateway to warmer climes marked by crossing the Loire, the journey ends in a harbor within the Second World War submarine base at St-Nazaire. Here German resistance lasted beyond the Nazi surrender and the town was the last in Europe to be liberated, on May 11, 1945. Officially at least, today the two towns' harbors share a name: Port Atlantique Nantes-St-Nazaire. Here the golden beaches of the Atlantic extend on either side and the Loire is no more.

## THE RANCE: A MIOCENE SEA, HEROIC DINAN, AND DONKEYS WITH TWISTED HEADS

"If the Rance has grace and gaiety, it also sometimes has mischievous episodes, even angry outbursts, which can be awful…"

Amand Dagnet

The Rance rises in the Méné, a range of hills in Côtes d'Armor culminating in the Col de Bel Air, at a lofty (by Breton standards) 336 meters. From this viewpoint spreads out a vast rolling tapestry of central Brittany, but the summit has lost any magical atmosphere it once had with the ugly installation of satellite antennae and a decidedly unalluring chapel. The other end of the river is much better known as it flows out after a hundred kilometers into the Channel between Dinard and St-Malo via the barrage and tidal power station. The Rance has everything one could ask of a river: radiance, drama, legend, and plenty of functionality.

The source near Collinée is marked by a well and the few remaining stones of a *lavoir* in the hamlet of Cas de la Plesse, where the trickle of water sets off across meadows, evolving into a small bucolic stream before being dammed into two lakes to serve an industrial estate as once it powered grain mills for the *commune*.

A road trip east from here via Langourla, Lanrelas, and Caulnes will crisscross the ever-growing river which takes a meandering course towards its first power play when it merges with the Néal in a V-shaped junction before the dam at Rophemel. The construction of this hydroelectric plant was started in 1929, with many workers on the dam coming on from the newly finished project of Lac de Guerlédan on the Nantes-Brest Canal. The footpath along the wooded slopes is frustratingly high up with little more than glimpses of water down the steep valley sides, but the adjacent lake formed by the Néal offers a pleasanter prospect with its little cascade by the bridge.

The Rance Valley beyond was once at the bottom of a sea linking what would be the Channel and the Atlantic in the Miocene period about fifteen million years ago. This separated the "Ile d'Armorique" (later western Brittany) from the eastern part and later mainland France. These warm, shallow (forty meters at most) waters in the depression around Tréfumel and Le Quiou harbored all kinds of marine creatures—stingrays, the huge megalodon, a prehistoric shark, and snub-nosed sea cows—and created an accumulation of shell sand, called *le falun*. This sedimentary layer has yielded a myriad of fossils, revealing the forms of life that once dominated this river valley. In the modern era the more solid masses of *falun* were quarried and the light, malleable limestone called *pierre de jauge* used in architecture for ornamentation, particularly noticeable in decorative dormer windows in local villages.

A slow, sullen stretch of the Rance passes the leisure lake of Bétineuc, which it feeds before shedding its fluvial aspect to take part in the Ille-et-Rance Canal, linking Rennes and St-Malo. The junction is just north of Évran before the Écluse de la Roche. Managed paths as part of the Green Ways network make this a busy stretch of waterway, given character by boating activity as Évran is a popular narrow boat port. The gentle canalization is not such a burden as to transform the essential character of the river and its surroundings, which retain a natural air and offer a sheltered home to fluvial wildlife.

The Rance is channeled through a series of four locks over about ten kilometers to reach the start of its historically glamorous stage at Léhon.

This little known and painfully romantic village has all the essential attributes of beautiful houses, a ruined castle, old abbey, and enticing riverside walks. It is in fact only a kilometer from Dinan and the proximity is apparent from the château hill where one of the oldest castles in Brittany lies in fragments. The earliest foundation here was destroyed by Henry II in 1168, but the lords of Dinan rebuilt soon after as a fortified outpost of the town. In 1264 it became ducal property, but like so many others suffered several violent episodes in the Wars of Succession and fell into disuse except for a minor revival in the Wars of Religion. In 1644 the ruins were given by Louis XIII to the prior and much of the stone was used to refurbish the abbey. The church is the burial place of the Beaumanoir family, probably including Jean III de Beaumanoir, hero of the Battle of the Thirty (see p.12), who died around 1366.

Just downstream is Dinan, a town where the full weight of history is felt in every stone. The old port on the Rance, with the narrow stone bridge remade in 1923 from three arches to two, is tucked under the citadel: the best bird's eye views over the river are from the "English garden" on top of the Tour Ste-Catherine, part of the ramparts which now provide a circuit around the town. The green fields visible on the opposite

Painfully romantic: Léhon (Wendy Mewes)

bank are adjacent to the Maison de la Rance, an information center about the river. Dinan is famous for the association with the medieval warrior Bertrand du Guesclin and not so well known as the birthplace of Théodore Botrel, the Breton bard born in the rue de la Mittrie in 1868. He later described the view from nearby Lanvallay "emerging from the sweet blue mists of the Rance."

A steep cobbled climb from the port leads up to the historic center where a strong buzz of modern life takes place against a gaudy array of half-timbered houses, towers and the fifteenth-century donjon turned bell tower in the rue de l'Horloge. The castle at Dinan was constructed by Jean IV, victor in the War of Succession, who was determined to assert his authority at this strategic point overlooking the Rance valley. The most atmospheric part, the Tour de Coëtquen, with its damply green tombs of medieval knights in the basement, was added a hundred years later.

During that war, Bertrand du Guesclin had a dispute with Thomas of Canterbury over dishonorable behavior during a truce at the siege of Rennes. He appealed to the English commander, the Duke of Lancaster, who was at Dinan, and a duel was agreed to settle the matter. It took place in the place des Lices—the current marketplace—where there is an equestrian statue of the victor du Guesclin, plus a less noticeable plaque. The great hero's heart is interred in the church of St-Sauveur, where the façade is adorned with eastern creatures (note the camels on the entry pillars) as tradition has it that it was founded by Rivallon le Roux on his return from the Holy Land in 1112.

The Rance continues north past Taden where the *bourg* uphill from the river has a rare fourteenth-century survival, the Manoir de la Grand'Cour, with its great vaulted upper hall. A little port on the bank here once served the Roman town of Corseul, center of the Coriosolites tribe. The water starts to widen now and soon takes a graceful bend through cliffs of schist, beloved by cormorants, before the pleasure port of Lyvet and the final lock of the canal, Le Châtelier. This is the dividing point of clear and salt water at the limit of the tidal reach. Here the Rance is finally freed from captivity and the beauty of its estuary can unfold. Beyond the bridge lie a row of *cabanes à carrelets*, fishing huts on stilts, with strange aerial like structures, originally built for the manipulation of huge three to four-meter nets also used from special boats, and raised or lowered according to the tide.

A curiosity at Mordreuc on the east bank is the regular appearance of a seal who has been befriended by the locals over many years. The quay here is a favorite spot for encounters and the restaurant there now sports the creature as its logo.

St-Suliac is an exceptionally pretty village, noted for the practice of draping fishing nets right across the façades of the houses. The settlement takes it name from an early saint. Suliac's budding monastery on the shores of the Rance was troubled by the raids of local donkeys from Riporden, who waded across the narrow strait at low tide and ate all the monks' carefully tended vegetables. No amount of fencing could thwart these determined beasts and the saint was forced to resort to extreme measures. He used his miraculous powers to root each donkey to the spot of their crimes and for a final flourish twisted all their heads to face backwards. Not long after the owners turned up looking for their lost animals and begged St Suliac to release them from their punishment, on the solemn promise of keeping them away in the future. The saint relented and granted the donkeys their freedom, but recognizing the force of the temptation, he took the precaution of causing the river to widen its banks at this very point—it now expands to two kilometers. A hideous grotto topped by an oratory stands on the headland outside the village, a vow fulfilled by sailors returning safely from Newfoundland in the nineteenth century.

St Suliac was also responsible for a little-known Breton triumph—the production of wine. He planted the first vines on the sunny hillsides of the Rance, a practice continued by monks of the Benedictine abbey of St-Laurent on Mont Garrot and extended in the area down as far as Dinan. Al Idrissi, the twelfth-century Arabian geographer who produced a detailed atlas for Roger of Sicily, describes Dinan's port as having "much grain, many vineyards and plantations of all kinds." Wine became a major product of the region in medieval times: a document of 1478 shows the Baron of Quintin purchasing "XX pipes de vin Breton du creu de Saint-Suliau." Another from 1587 refers to the sale of land in this area "planted with vines."

Louis XIV decreed in 1687 that no more vines were to be planted in Brittany—one among many deprivations—but cultivation of existing vineyards was eked out until the end of the eighteenth century. Reference to the industry remains in place names like the Anse de Vigneux at La Ville-ès-Nonais. A flourishing vineyard can be seen today on the southern slope of Mont Garrot, reviving that ancient tradition. A few hundred liters a year of Le Clos de Garo are produced by a not-for-profit association on the half-hectare plot. The grapes may thrive on the bones of Gargantua, for this is the burial site of the giant (folded in seven, as it is not a wide hill) and one of his teeth masquerading as a *menhir* can be seen not far away in a private garden. (And incidentally, some of the best cider in Brittany is produced not far from here at Pleuhiden-sur-Rance under the Val de Rance label.)

A reminder of the river's incursion route that attracted many Viking raids in the ninth and tenth centuries can be found in the Rance at St-Suliac. Below Mount Garrot, when the tide is low, the outline of a camp appears, probably originally an Iron Age site reutilized by the Danish invaders. It seems to have been in use for as much as half a century, suggesting that settlement was as likely an objective as blind greed and destructive urges.

The river fans out past St-Suliac into a series of inlets and creeks housing tidal mills that processed grain in predam days. Today it is a yachtsman's paradise, with white sails dotted all over the water on sunny weekends. A trip on the river from the dam shows off the impressive eighteenth-century piles of wealthy *armateurs* from St-Malo like the family of Magon du Bos who, not content with the Château du Bos, went on to build Montmarin, now famous for its gardens. Grim stories enliven the route here such as the unsolved mystery of a terrible crime in 1790 when the ferryman of La Passagère together with his wife and two of his children had their throats cut one night, probably at the hands of one of the smugglers active in the vicinity. On the Ile de Chevret, better known to locals as the Isle of Rats, a woman who bred the little vermin lived and died alone. The rats all died too, possibly because of the lack of fresh water on the islet.

The dam that brings the Rance's flow to an abrupt end is soon visible beyond the Pointe de Cancaval on the west bank, a wooded *éperon barré* (fortified spur) that now gives viewpoints up and down the river. The main road D266 runs across the water for 750 meters between the Pointe de la Briantais on the eastern bank and the Pointe de la Brebis in the west and houses (almost) the largest tidal power plant in the world, constructed in the early 1960s. This river's effectiveness for electricity production is based on the exceptional range between high and low tides—up to nearly fourteen meters—on this part of the northern coast of Brittany. Twenty-four turbines take advantage of this tidal power to create an annual production of 600,000,000 kWh, enough to supply the capital Rennes. There is an underground information center where the workings of the plant are vaguely visible. A sea lock opens at fixed times to allow a clutch of boats through, causing swift car traffic backups from both sides.

Beyond the dam, the Bay of St-Malo looms. On one side is Dinard, famous for its early English settlers, nineteenth-century English-style villas with their bay windows and balconies and a renowned British film festival each October. There is a statue of Alfred Hitchcock, with pigeons doing impressions of scenes from *The Birds*, on the sea front. Locals claim a house on the Pointe du Moulinet was the model for that in *Psycho*, although the director himself talked of ugly houses in North Carolina and "Californian gothic."

On the other side of the bay is the Tour Solidor, living up to its name and built in the 1370s by Jean de Montfort to overlook the entrance to the Rance estuary, the best he could do at a time when St-Malo defied his authority. The wooded hill of the former Roman settlement Alet is now the only obstacle to the splendid panorama of St-Malo's islands, walled city and multiple harbors, which all too quickly banish thoughts of the valiant efforts of the Rance.

## THE OUST: WITNESS OF HISTORY, A JOURNEY ON FOOT UPRIVER

The Oust is first recorded in the sixth century by Gregory of Tours when he describes a Frankish army sent to the Marches of Brittany to deal with Waroc, who was busy laying waste to the land between Rennes and Nantes. After crossing the Vilaine, they came to the Oust (*ad Uldam fluvium pervenerunt*) and had to bridge it to get the soldiers across. The subsequent battle was a victory for the Bretons.

I got to know the Oust in a back-to-front fashion the first time I walked the 365-kilometer Nantes-Brest Canal right across Brittany from east to west. After the flat, marshy lands of Loire-Atlantique, it was a relief to reach Redon, the historic port of Rennes and a major communications center, and then to begin a route of intoxicating, sinuous loveliness from the Barrage de la Potinais just to the north of the town where the Oust ends its utilitarian work on an eighty-four-kilometer and thirty-six-lock stretch of the canal. Even here it breaks free of constraint every so often, preserving a series of meanders sometimes of several kilometers through water meadows a little distance from the short links cut by canal engineers to hold the main course. The entire length of this mostly beautiful river is not always so desirable: the industrial plants and quarries from St-Martin up to St-Laurent have done little to enhance the silent pleasures of the walk or the purity of the water, which has also suffered in places from the high nitrate levels of intensive farming, bugbear of not a few Breton waterways.

The confluence of the Vilaine and the Oust, which sees the end of our river, is just south of Redon, famous for the square Romanesque abbey tower, its role as a staging post on the Santiago de Compostela trail and the junction of two canals, the Ille-et-Vilaine and the Nantes-Brest. The Musée de la Batellerie on quai Jean Bart tells the story of Brittany's inland waterways, a significant social history in itself as lines of communications brought new products and new ideas to rural areas.

The origin of the ninth-century abbey was an interesting test case of Nominoë's self-perception in the 830s. A local official called a *machtiern* had granted the monks, led by Conwoïon, land for their foundation, but permission was needed from the Emperor of the Franks, especially as the cathedral of Vannes was not keen on such close rivals. Louis Le Pieux seemed in no hurry to make a decision: twice Conwoïon sought a personal audience and twice he failed. In 834 Nominoë told them to go ahead: Louis' postdated ratification was forthcoming a few months later.

The old port is a reminder of the vital trading role of Redon, accessible by sea-going ships on the tide of the Vilaine. Here cargoes were unloaded and taken on to Rennes in smaller vessels. The merchants' houses with their ornate iron balconies and ground floor storage areas still line the area, which also did an important trade in salt from Guérande, as the name Passage des Saulniers and two former salt warehouses testify.

A few kilometers from the town, the junction of canal and Oust at the Barrage de la Potinais at once suggests that great things are in store for this expansive, bucolic river. Moving west, the walk soon reaches one of the most imposing spots in Brittany, as the broad River Oust passes between *les falaises*, steep cliffs of granite and schist up to fifty meters high, dotted with stark fir trees. This geological feature is known as a *cluse*, where the river has taken advantage of a fault line in the rocky strata on the edge of the Landes de Lanvaux to wear an anticlinal bed and form the gorge of the Ile aux Pies. This unusual scenery feels like a statement, a massive gateway making an impressive entrance to the heartlands of Brittany.

It is over all too soon as the Oust takes a moment to twirl aside with the Aff, leaving a long straight artificial arm of canal between locks 19 and 20 before resuming its task and the journey up to Malestroit, one of the most appealing little towns in the region. There are some significant moments in the canal's history on the way: at Rieux and Beaumont, locks 22 and 23 today, attempts were made as early as the sixteenth century to create *écluses à sas*, locks with V-shaped gates held closed by water pressure, an invention of Leonard da Vinci. This idea facilitated trade between Redon and Malestroit and fared better than similar short-lived efforts on behalf of Rennes on the turbulent Vilaine.

Many proposals for canals were made before military necessity and commercial possibility caused Napoleon to back a plan in 1804 and the Nantes-Brest Canal became a reality. The value of a secure inland route when the British Navy was active around the coast and blockading many ports was clear. The transport of goods and supplies between the naval arsenals of Nantes, Brest and Lorient was sufficient motivation for the large sums of money initially ploughed into the construction of the canal, at a time when much of the work was to be done by hand.

The Oust is not the only major river to play a part: the Blavet (Morbihan/Côtes d'Armor) and Aulne (Finistère) are also mainstays of the route: in fact only about twenty percent of the 365-kilometer length is artificial, and to imagine the canal as following a narrow, straight, tedious route would be a misconception. The sheer scale of the project, connecting numerous river valleys by crossing heights up to 184 meters, meant that it was no quick fix. Napoleon was long gone before the first boats began to move around in the 1830s and the entire route was only fully operational in 1842. The canal's heyday at the end of the century was short: it could not match the speed and efficiency of the railway which pressed at its heels from the 1860s. In the 1920s the Lac de Guerlédan with its barrage and hydroelectric station was created, submerging twelve locks and severing the canal, putting an end to through traffic. Economically the canal was a huge white elephant, without the speed or infrastructure to generate commercial profit, but goods such as building stone, wood, sand, and groceries continued to be moved around until after the

Second World War. The very last working boat, *Le Mistral*, unloaded its cargo of sand at the Port d'Oust in the *commune* of St-Congard—the stone quay is still in evidence—on December 7, 1977.

Today the two ends are busy with leisure boats, but a shorter central section remains unnavigable on each side of the lake. The towpath provides a continuous route for walkers and cyclists and much is now part of the Green Ways scheme, giving access to countryside and towns of exceptional interest like Malestroit—"the pearl of the Oust"—where the well-preserved town center offers a glorious range of stone and half-timbered houses including the Maison de la Truie qui file, an idiosyncratic example of medieval decorative sculpture, starring a hare playing the *biniou* and a pig spinning thread.

Across the river, where the Oust diverts again at a wide weir next to old mills marking the economic past of river and town, lie the ruined remains of the Chapelle de la Madeleine. Here in 1343 a treaty was signed between England and France to mark a breathing space in the Hundred Years' War. The chapel saw more violent action during 1795 when five Chouans—defenders of the faith—were trapped and killed by Republican troops. The incident was later recorded by the French artist Alexandre Bloch, who contrasts an air of religious calm and peaceful light with the dead bodies on the floor, prostrate before the eyes of their saints.

Continuing northwest, it is the little village of Monterterlot that always lingers in my mind as the epitome of the atmosphere of the Oust. The river loops round a little island and widens over a broad weir, leaving the well-tended lock a tranquil space overlooked by the church and a sacred *fontaine*, backed by the small settlement of stone houses. Pleasure boats are always moored—a sign that the waterway still lives—but the pervading sense is of tranquility, the elements in harmony, sun, earth, air, and water. Trees dominate, massing over the banks, laying out their green contrast to the grey and blue of sky and river, the combination of reflection and reality here particularly memorable.

A sweep of tree-lined bend flows on, opening up the way to new discoveries, and a few miles upstream few will forget rounding a distinctively curved purple path of local schist to catch sight of the forbidding fortress of Josselin looming over the water, rising like a sentry from the very riverbed. This is now the heart of Rohan country, a family who have loomed large in Breton history since the twelfth century, never attaining the dukedom they felt they deserved, but using marriage alliances to promote their status in various royal families of Europe, including Scotland. Their control of land was extensive—up to a fifth of the duchy in the medieval period, with holdings far from their central Brittany base, such as sixty-three parishes in Léon, north Finistère. Their implacability and sense of entitlement in the face of Montfort dominance was only equaled by that of the Penthièvres. The Rohans were great self-publicists, overweaningly proud of an ancestry they claimed stemmed from Conan Meriadec (see p.8), this an important boast to "prove" superiority over rivals like the Montforts. Rohan opposition to these rulers became even more entrenched with Duke François II's rejection of Jean de Rohan's son as a possible husband for his daughter Anne, preferring a more powerful but distant ally, Maximilian of Austria. The two mottos associated with the family give the general flavor: *A plus* and the derivative *roi ne puis, prince ne daigne, Rohan suis* (I can't be king, I won't be prince, I'm a Rohan). The Rohans were among the few noble Protestant families—with the Lavals and the Rieux—in a staunchly Catholic Brittany, and the Wars of Religion in the late sixteenth century were sometimes referred to as "les guerres de Monsieur de Rohan." Ordered to dismantle parts of the castle when the conflicts were over, Henri de Rohan ignored the instruction, and there is a story that Cardinal Richelieu himself (Commendatory Abbot of Redon, 1622–42) turned up in Josselin one day and greeted him with the words: "I have come, Your Grace, to throw a ball in your game of skittles."

The Oust at Josselin runs right below the walls of the mighty château, built originally by the rulers of Porhoët and bought by Olivier de Clisson, later Connétable of France, in 1370. It was Clisson who created the defensive nine-towered structure, of which only four remain. He died in 1407 and is buried with his wife Marguerite in the beautiful church of Our Lady of the Brambles, named after a miracle when the Virgin's statue was found in waste ground, a tale told in stained-glass windows there. A visit to the château today is highly organized and limited to a few rooms, but the north façade is an exquisite example of Renaissance art and the dominant position of the castle can be well appreciated from within the walls. Today the Rohan family still lives here. Josselin Charles Louis Jean Marie de Rohan-Chabot—fourteenth Duke of Rohan if you still believe in such things—has been a major political force in national (UMP senator) and regional politics and was head of the Conseil Régional de Bretagne

Rising from the Oust: Château de Josselin (Wendy Mewes)

from 1998 to 2004.

The Oust now passes through an area that was largely economically dependent on Rohan enterprises from feudal farms to horse breeding and charcoal to metalwork. There were studs in both Lanouée and Branguily, with horses roaming freely in the forests. Les Forges, supplied with water by a feeder channel from the Oust, was the site of a foundry constructed by the Duke de Rohan with permission from Louis XV in 1756, its main purpose being to provide weaponry for the Royal Navy.

Of many treats offered by exploration of the Oust, one of the most unusual is easy access to cheese made by Trappist monks. A mere 400 meters uphill from the towpath at Timadeuc sits the abbey founded in 1841 in a ruined manorhouse donated by the local gentry. The river was used to bring building materials for the necessary renovations, including stones from the (literally) dilapidated castle at Rohan. Farms were also part of the package and the monks have made good use of their herds of cows to produce the famous cheese, with the disappointingly prosaic name of Trappe de Timadeuc. The abbey is open for retreats, but otherwise has limited public access beyond the large shop packed with religious products and… cheese. It is one response to the statement that Brittany has no native cheese, an appalling allegation easily refuted by visiting markets all over the region.

Rohan is the final staging post on the canal in this direction, an unobtrusive sort of place making the most of its riverside location with leisure facilities. Taking the family name ("little rock"), this was the Rohans' first power base, now devoid of a castle since the activities of the Count of Northampton in 1342 left it severely damaged, and subsequent changes of fortune led to its abandonment by the Rohans—who transferred their operations to Pontivy in the fifteenth century—after the loss of Breton independence. It was a ruin in 1682 and finally sold off by the family in 1802. It is not entirely absent from the town—in 2000 two artists obligingly made up for the deficiency with a huge romantic mural of the castle near the bridge by the pretty Chapelle Notre-Dame de Bonne-Encontre (built in 1510 by Jean II de Rohan), where the towpath changes sides of the river.

Just beyond Rohan at lock 55 (Coët Prat), the Oust finally separates from the canal, its route north an elusive little ribbon winding up an intensively farmed valley past St-Caradec and St-Thélo towards the lake and barrage of Bosméléac, created in the 1830s to make use of the upper Oust in providing water for the Rigole d'Hilvern. This crazy serpentine feeder channel, more in evidence than the river from a road route, covers an incredible 63.5 kilometers in length, and was deemed necessary to supply the stepped series of locks in the Forêt de Branguily and beyond, to take an ambitious artificial section of the Nantes-Brest Canal up and over to join the Blavet valley at Pontivy. It took fourteen years to construct. When the Rigole was first filled and opened, very little water actually reached its faraway destination, leaking away into surrounding fields, and remedial work was needed to seal and secure the narrow channel. Today it is mostly dry, as modern machinery can pump the necessary watery supplements, but the Association des Canaux works to reestablish this monument to hope over experience.

Bosméléac is the last sign of the Oust's former importance and from there it gets harder to follow the stream which gradually diminishes over a further ten kilometers to the source beneath the hill of Kerchouan, not far from Corlay.

## The Queffleuth: floods, paper-making, and the associative life

This little river could feature in any advertisement for "sparkling water"—the Breton name probably means a lively stream. The clear and busy Queffleuth, historic boundary of Trégor and Léon despite often being only a few meters wide, is capable of rising quickly from a quiet trickle to flood level when swollen with rain. An old story says that a horseman was posted on the dyke at the Abbaye du Relec, ever ready to gallop off to Morlaix and warn of impending disaster when the river level began to rise. He would have been useful in the winter of 2013–14 when there were major inundations.

The Queffleuth has its source just north of the Monts d'Arrée, near Roc'h Trédudon in Plouneour-Menez. It meanders along to Le Relec, skirting the twelfth-century Cistercian abbey where it was managed by the monks to form fish ponds, irrigation channels for the vegetable gardens, and two lakes. Turning north, the river enters one of the loveliest valleys in Brittany, a route traced by the sinuous D769 main road. Here the skittish water tumbles over granite boulders in what feels like a secret celebration of the typical natural beauty of the area.

The purity of the water—the presence of otters is a sign—and its lack of iron or chalk content made this a good resource for paper making, with as many as thirty mills in operation in the seventeenth and eighteenth centuries, an important source of commerce and employment. Local lords of the manor saw an economic advantage in welcoming skilled artisans to their territory. The Moulin de Glaslan was built in 1629 on land granted by the *seigneur* of Lesquiffiou to Julien Cordier and his wife Catherine Guesnon, who had come from Normandy, in return for rent in money (21 *livres*) and kind (four reams of paper). A hundred and fifty years later, it was producing about 3,000 reams a year. In the early nineteenth century François-Marie Andrieux continued the success of Glaslan, at first employing twenty workers. In 1831 he invested in a steam-powered paper-making machine from London, and increased production twentyfold. The Andrieux were socially responsible employers, providing accommodation and even a school for their employees and encouraging enterprises to work together for economic security. In 1866 Aristide Andrieux founded a *société de secours* to provide support for struggling paper workers.

The Norman influence was important and many local families today have ancestors from this economic migration. In 1635 Julien Cordier went on to strike a deal with local lord Yves de Coatanscour to convert a mill formerly used for grinding corn at Pont-Paul (*commune* of Plourin-lès-Morlaix) to paper production. Two hundred years later this became a *moulin à teiller*, separating fibers for the cloth industry, a good example of changing industrial demands in the locality. It went on working in one form or another right up until 1958.

The territory of the Queffleuth was at the heart of the immensely important and lucrative cloth industry from the fifteenth to eighteenth centuries, and the presence of numerous *pilhaouerien,* or rag-men (see p.192), at nearby La Feuillée meant that the mills were easily supplied with copious rags that formed the essence of the paper making process. The two industries were natural partners.

Au Fils du Queffleuth et Penzé is an association devoted to the study and presentation of two local rivers. Its interests are environmental and educative, with aims of sharing knowledge and understanding, promoting responsible enjoyment of the countryside and cooperation between humans and the land, all in a spirit of pleasure and social interaction: principles much in evidence in contemporary Breton society. Under the passionate and engaging leadership of President François Bouget and Director Caroline Leroy-Deniel, they have done careful work in researching the use of the Queffleuth and establishing paths—like the five-kilometer Sentier Riboul Potic, starting from the picnic area at Le Pleen off the D769—to explore the valley of the Queffleuth. Throughout the year they offer educational and entertaining events for adults and children, with themed walks and visits to discover the natural and economic history of the area. Associations like this are an exercise in social harmony, as well as a reflection of the ubiquitous and remarkable Breton devotion to local heritage and history.

Alone, the Queffleuth is only nineteen kilometers long, but on reaching Morlaix it finds a confluence with the Jarlot just in front of where the Town Hall now stands. The medieval walled city was formerly located in the V between their valleys. Once exposed, this merging of waters is now underground and together the two form the Morlaix river, more commonly once called the Dossen, and flow out into the Bay of Morlaix and the Channel at Carantec, thirteen kilometers away.

In 1522 Morlaix was devastated by an English raid involving sixty ships that penetrated almost right up to the town, on a day when the garrison was absent at an army review and many merchants away at a major fair. The English sacked the town, burning and pillaging much of the *ville close* before carrying rich plunder back to their ships. The merchants' houses along the quays offered large quantities of wine, Morlaix being a stage on the Bordeaux trading route, and while some loaded their loot and got away promptly, a few hundred English remained in the Bois de Styvel above the river, drinking in celebration of their exploit. It seems that they were drinking too much, as they were still there when the alerted soldiers rushed back in time for wholesale slaughter on the hillside. The Fontaine aux Anglais on the quay is said to have got its name from the bloody water running down from the site of carnage.

The attack was a severe economic blow for the town, but there were two consequences still with us today. The Château du Taureau was built on a rock at the mouth of the estuary in 1544 to ensure—successfully—that no one ever attacked the town by this route again. And the town of Morlaix (much later) acquired the clever pun of its motto: *s'ils te mordent, mors-les!* (If they bite you, bite them back!)

## Chapter Eleven

# ISLAND

## ALL AROUND THE EDGE

Surrounded by water like fluid in the womb, islands have a sense of self-contained identity and the separate character of individuals. The Breton islands are part of the Iles Ponant, which run from Normandy to Charente-Maritime, island communities forming a natural unit as they share the same concerns and issues. All face the stern reality that, with the decline of older forms of economic sustenance, demonstrably closed societies are now held hostage by the demands of tourism. Strangeness and a frugal exoticism may be the draw of islands for visitors, but the practicalities of everyday life revolve around pragmatic meteorological concerns. Bréhat near Paimpol and Batz just off Roscoff are perfect day-trip destinations, minutes from the coast, small enough to walk round and balmy in climate compared to the harsher conditions in the Atlantic. All islanders exchange the precariousness of their lives for an enviable security of identity, their own community and its self-contained history the first line of self-determination, with regionalism and nationalism a good deal less significant and evident. Incomers cannot change the fundamental nature of a relatively small territory with its natural limits and lack of economic scope, and a traditional way of life, though lost, remains ingrained on the landscape.

## OUESSANT: ISLAND THE TERRIBLE, A SWIMMING COW, AND 'BYE, BYE BLACK SHEEP

"…and it's Ushant slams the door on us
Whirling like a windmill through the dirty scud to lee:…"
                              Rudyard Kipling, "Anchor Song," 1893

The first significant thing about Ouessant (Breton Enez Eusa, English Ushant) is that it is a long twenty kilometers from the mainland. A real journey is needed, from Brest or Le Conquet with a stop at Molène en route. Then there is a sense of going beyond the beyond as that small island is left behind and the boat picks up speed seemingly into a watery wilderness, remote from the tame and civilized world. Jacques Cambry in his *Voyage dans le Finistère* (1799) refers to an oral tradition that Ouessant was actually the fabled Thule of classical authors. It does not quite fit with the geographer Pytheas' description of a semipolar region six days' sail from Britain, but the island exudes enough of a sense of separation to fit Virgil's symbolic *ultima Thule*, signifying the western edge of the known world.

Paul Gruyer asserts in an essay of 1899 entitled *Ouessant, Enez Heusa, l'île de l'épouvante* (Island the Terrible) that no ship's pilot would ever pass for pleasure between Ouessant and the continent. The romance of the voyage is enhanced even today by a notion of danger on the notoriously turbulent crossing: how much more daunting it must have appeared when visitors from outside began to arrive from the mid-nineteenth century.

The Passage du Fromveur separating Ouessant and the Molène archipelago is an ill-tempered stretch of complicated water named after the Breton *froud* (current) and *meur* (great) for the cross-purposes of its winds and currents, the latter turning about with the rise and fall of each tide. This five-nautical-mile zone was the scene of numerous shipwrecks until the creation of the supervised *rail de Ouessant* to the north of the island prevented large cargo vessels from taking a perilous short cut and left the passage to small fishing boats and ferries. What the Fromveur tells us at once is that Ouessant is all about direction and perception.

The approach to port reinforces the impression of wildness: stark cliffs rise up and there is no snug, smiling harbor with a comforting line of houses and a bar or two. The port is like an afterthought, an intrusion in the face of the rude nature that dominates Ouessant. In times of severe weather the ferry has to use the harbor of the *bourg* of Lampaul, the only commercial center, four kilometers away at the opposite end of the island, set in a deep bay between two thin arms of land.

The paradox of Ouessant is that for all the imagery of isolation, the island is in some senses the most international of locations—not remote, but a place of passage. Excavations over twenty years directed by Jean-Paul Le Bihan at Mez Notariou have revealed a Bronze Age settlement from around 1500 BCE and an Iron Age village almost adjacent. Finds on the site from all over Europe attest to Ouessant's important position for travelers moving between south and north, commanding as it does the tricky entry to the Channel. The pottery paralleled in style with a site in Switzerland puts the island on the cultural map of the continent at that time.

The island itself has a history of austerity for man and a richness of nature surprising in such a treeless and weather-swept landscape. At eight by three-and-a-half kilometers and 1,550 hectares it is a sizeable terrain, split along an east-west fault line, now a lush green valley of low vegetation and reservoirs. There is no shortage of freshwater sources, as stone *lavoirs* in the scattered hamlets show. Traditionally the houses are whitewashed with blue shutters, the archetypal colors of the island, with no garish constructions by wealthy incomers to spoil the simplicity of a vernacular architecture dictated by the demands of the weather.

In no sense, however, is Ouessant dull. The *bourg* of Lampaul is rife with flowers, pink and white valerian exploding like fireworks from the high stone walls, every garden planted to burst out in brightness as early as the seasons allow. On the swaths of pasture and clifftop *landes*, a colored quilt of wild flowers has replaced the traditional patchwork of tiny walled plots of land which once covered the island, the women's domain of production. Nearly gone too are the numerous tiny windmills, wooden huts on a round granite base, which ground each family's corn. Star-shaped sheep shelters remain here and there, designed to offer relief from the multidirectional blasts of wind. On the springy surface of the moors are gorse—in places deliberately cultivated within walls for fuel and fodder—heather and yellow flowers of fresh broom which pop up despite the wind ordering their flattened foliage to stay low. Clumps of thrift, blue freckles of scilla, pink scabious, wild thyme, and honeysuckle brighten the grassy plains.

The sea has always rolled out the imaginative and everyday rhythm of this place. Local legends feature the Morganed and Morganezed, merpeople who live in the ocean and sport on the shore, enjoying unpredictable contact with humans like the arrogantly beautiful Mona Kerbili who was snatched away to an underwater kingdom. Reality, however, is about life at the behest of the elements and striking a balance between the demands of land and sea. Ouessant itself is the strong, solid hub at the center of turbulence, ringed by lighthouses protective of mariners and islanders alike. Watching the entrance to the Bay of Lampaul is the Phare de la Jument, and the Kéréon lighthouse, named in honor of a young

Ouessant: not for the faint-hearted (Wendy Mewes)

victim of the Revolution, stands sentinel over the Fromveur. On the north-eastern and highest point at sixty meters is Le Stiff, the oldest still-working example in France, ordered by Vauban in 1695 and now looking like a functional pimple beside by the elegant grace of the seventy-five-meter radar tower built in 1982.

The ragged edge of the north coast from Le Stiff to the Pointe de Pern has borne the brunt of the weather and tides, raw rock faces like eviscerated innards of the earth, the granite slowly disintegrating via fissures where the insidious moisture of the salt air has penetrated. Fantastic formations contribute to the sense of rough brute creation, hewn of gigantic movements over aeons of time, a work in progress if the elements have their brutal way, shearing off any telltale friability. Looking seaward beyond the Île de Keller with the eerie outline of its single house, there is only ocean, often merging into a misty, muzzy soft blue-gray of sky.

Past the Baie de Calgrac'h, the black-and-white-striped Phare de Creac'h (1863) dominates the view. Here is the Musée des Phares et Balises, presenting the evolving techniques of maritime communication and the great work of lighthouse construction in hazardous conditions, a summary of man's response to the challenges of sky and sea. The former guardian's house is also the base of a writer-in-residence program. Contemporary literature thrives in this environment that thrusts man into often dangerous relationship with the natural world and the self. (The island hosts a famous international Salon des Livres each August, and has a Maison des Écrivains or writers' center in the *bourg*.)

The Pointe de Pern at the western extremity defines the turbulence and relentless savagery of the sea that is the body to Ouessant's heart. The lighthouse of Le Nividic and its two redundant pylons rise above the treacherous knobs of rock and whirling breakers. The seethe of currents pushes and shoves in all directions, constantly sparring like an unruly mob bent on violence. When mist obscured the early lantern's beam, only the echo of a foghorn could give a warning beyond the narrow visibility. The ruined building on the point once housed this simple device, based on a compressed air tank and powered by horses at its inauguration in 1866. Steam was soon preferred as the free-ranging animals had proved unresponsive to urgency. Today it is often called the Maison des Tempêtes, a reference to the novel *Das Meer* (*The Sea*) by Bernhard Kellerman, who stayed on the island in 1907 and invoked in his emotive text the extraordinary change that a single moment makes to light and air on Ouessant.

The southern shores of the island offer a softer profile, facing Molène and its cluster of islets across the Fromveur. Here mica-schist predominates, headlands punctuated by the only real beaches, although the chill of the water may surprise swimmers. High on Penn Arlan, the least walked area on the island, stands a Neolithic stone circle—unusual in Brittany—near the solitary Croix de St-Pol, dating from 1704, which follows a tradition that the saint first landed near this spot. His "stone boat," complete with two indentations worn by many hours of kneeling prayers, lies beside the cross. He is said to have chased away a group of pagan priestesses who then moved to the other end of the island.

Ouessant was the first landfall for St Pol after leaving Britain to evangelize in Armorica, with the *bourg* bearing his name (Lampaul is Lan Pol, the holy place of the saint) to this day. Speculation that St Pol came with the deliberate intention of breaking up a *lieu fort* of paganism on Ouessant is not so farfetched. According to the account of Admiral Thévenard, who visited in 1771, there were remains of a large pagan temple at the Pointe de Pern. St Gildas (Gueltas in Breton), also a combatant in the fight to establish Christian supremacy, had a chapel nearby, memory of the saint being retained in the hamlet name of Locqueltas. Another paradox of Ouessant, with its reputation for paganism and also deep Catholic religiosity, was brought into focus by the missions of Michel Le Nobletz (1610) and Père Maunoir (1641 and 1642).

A more sobering indication of Ouessant's international connections is the proliferation of wreckage encircling the island: an American ship carrying cocoa, rice, and tobacco in 1739; an English brig full of salt in 1817; an Austrian ship taking coal from Swansea to Trieste in 1908; the Russian *Vostok* in 1978 with that most useful of cargoes for a treeless island—planks. These are but a few in a long list. Cargoes from the foundered ships may have found their way into many a Ouessantin household (when a load of shoes came ashore in 1990 the pragmatic islanders held a get-together to match up pairs), but there has been no lack of courageous aid for struggling sailors.

Most famous of all was the disaster of the *Castle Drummond*, a liner on its return voyage from Cape Town to Southampton in 1896 which sunk within minutes in the mist after striking *les pierres vertes*. Five of the 248 victims were buried on the island and more on Molène, which has a little museum dedicated to the disaster. Queen Victoria rewarded both islands for their valiant attempts to bring help. Molène, with its lack of fresh water, got a cistern; Ouessant finally had the church bell tower finished after a thirty-year delay for lack of funds.

Among all the disastrous foundering of ships and beleaguered attempts to rescue foreign crews, the islanders have suffered their own losses at sea mainly in service of the French Navy. A custom originating at least from the eighteenth century which developed on Ouessant was the *proëlla* (possibly from the Latin *pro illa*, in the place of), a special funerary rite for those whose remains were never recovered, using tiny wax crosses to stand as substitutes for the dead. A male relative would collect a ritual silver cross and the wax one from the church and hold a night of prayer in the victim's house. The next day the priest would fetch both crosses and then perform a funeral service in the church, finally placing the wax cross in a wooden urn, today fixed to a pillar in the choir and decorated with a sculpted cloth marked by tadpole-like tears. There it would wait, perhaps not alone, for the visit of a bishop or missionary to the island to be ceremonially placed in a small mausoleum in the cemetery designed for this purpose, to give a focus for the bereaved family. This can still be seen today, its unique north-south alignment making the small structure stand out from the traditionally appointed crowd of graves. The inscription reads: "Here we place the crosses of *proëlla* in memory of our sailors who died far from their country."

A shocking intrusion into the simple rhythms of the island came in 1898 with the decision to establish the huge Fort St-Michel, hidden like a guilty secret where the terrain begins to rise towards Cadoran. Its presense was the result of the Fashoda incident in the Sudan when French and British colonial ambitions clashed in Africa to such a pitch that coastal defense again became the concern of the government in Paris. The construction is vast, sunken into the earth and today well-barricaded against curious eyes and the danger of unexploded Second World War mines. The arrival of colonial troops at the start of the twentieth century destabilized this small island, where men were conspicuous by their absence at sea. It was an astonishing and for some a cruel awakening to the ways of the wider world. The women seemed easy prey, and a surfeit of alcohol available to bored soldiers fueled the fires.

André Savignon's novel *Filles de la pluie* examines the temptations and harsh tribulations of some young *Ouessantines* in a series of sketches. This kind of exposure was unwelcome to island society who preferred to keep their hardships private. Although the book won the Prix Goncourt in 1912, it was not well received on the island. Complaints to the military authorities about the soldiers' behavior brought little result, and the arrival of *disciplinaires*—a company of soldiers designated for their insubordination and willful behavior—in 1911 only exacerbated the situation. Revelations in the press finally opened the ears of the government and the soldiers were gradually withdrawn. With the start of the First World War a kind of peace returned to the bruised island.

Ouessant has been the domain of women for much of its history with the men away in naval service for months and years at a time. It fell to them to till the land to maintain basic production of grain and potatoes, collect seaweed for fuel and fertilizer, rear the children, and perform all domestic tasks. It was an essentially matriarchal society, with the women being the ones to choose their husbands and make a proposal, although men were in shorter supply. Hence the island saying: "hook him if you can, there are not enough to go round." They kept their maiden names even after marriage, a firm statement of individual identity. Paul Gruyder's essay outlines an arrangement of living together platonically as a trial of compatibility after which a woman could return to her own house without any compromise to her reputation if the relationship did not suit. He also describes their tall, strong physique and dark hair, matched by a robust strength of character.

It must have been hard to surprise those tough women of Ouessant, but not impossible. On May 6, 1924 the regular mail boat *l'Île de Ouessant* struck a rock, tried to reach the safety of port at Lampaul and finally sank near Youc'h Korz, the great mound in the center of the harbor mouth. All the crew were saved. One of them had released the tether of a cow on board when disaster became inevitable. This brave creature struck out for shore and provided a moment of astonishment for the women washing clothes on the shore at Porz Koret as it emerged on the beach before them.

Everyone knows the famous black Ouessant sheep. A friend in the Monts d'Arrée is proud of his small flock of these thin, hardy, scraggy creatures that can survive notoriously poor conditions. The puzzle is that almost all the sheep on the actual island are plump white specimens with smug faces, often chained in twos for grazing according to the old custom. A pair of their black brothers can be seen, appropriately enough, at the Écomusée du Niou Huella, among other relics of the past. So what happened? It is still possible to make out the wreck of the *Mykonos* from the end of the slipway at Calgrac'h at low tide. The cargo of this Greek ship which foundered in 1936 included fluffy white sheep, some of which were so delighted to get out of the hold that they made it ashore, where a quick-thinking local tucked them away in a holding. And before too long, it was bye, bye black sheep…

## ÎLE DE SEIN: WET, WET, WET AND FLAT, FLAT, FLAT

The Île de Sein is unique among the Breton islands for its combination of location in the far west, difficult access, and almost flat terrain. The mainland appears and disappears as the weather wills, looking like a country where giants must dwell in comparison to the tiny splayed strip of land on which you stand gingerly when the weather is lively.

The earliest mention of Sein is in the record of Pomponius Mela, a Roman geographer of the first century CE who told of

> …an important oracle, said to consist of nine virgin priestesses. They can conjure up tides and winds with their spells, take on the form of any animal they please and heal that which others regard as beyond all help.

This reference, together with geography and setting, has contributed to the archetypal, primitive profile of Sein, a barbarous land of amoral men whose behavior is characterized by their reputation as wreckers, luring boats onto their perilous shores. Its harsh location prevents any idyllic image of an island paradise untouched by the corruption of the mainland. Bad land, bad men is an easier analogy.

Certainly men from the Admiralty seeking to take possession of goods from shipwrecks were not welcomed with open arms here any more than in other coastal communities. In 1740 Pierre de l'Abbaye called the *Sénans* "people who are never satisfied and contemptuous of commands" after he was hit on the knee by a stone thrown by a woman, an incident recounted by Karine Salomé in *Les îles bretonnes*.

The island was on the short end of a comparison with the fine human beings of Ouessant in a refined eighteenth-century rant by the Paris-based man of letters Billardon de Sauvigny. Elie Fréron (1718–76), who had grown up in Quimper and is best-known for his ill-tempered snit with Voltaire, felt more than qualified to mount a stingingly spirited response to the fanciful inaccuracies of his literary rival. He inversed the argument to represent the *Ouessantins* as mediocre specimens of mankind and the *Sénans* glorious heroes of hardship, simple men of exceptional heart and courage.

The island shimmers in the sunlight on a clear day, easily visible from the Pointe du Raz across the notoriously tempestuous Raz de Sein. Even in calm spring weather the swell heaves the ferry boat up and down and side to side, dashing brief floods over the lower outside deck. When the mist is down, land looms up late, the church dominant on a slight eminence above the port. Reality intrudes too crudely for Sein to be pretty or charming. It really is almost flat, with no point rising more than eight meters above sea level, considerably less at the time of the highest tides. This vulnerability and the crucial role of the defensive banks of pebbles are everywhere apparent as a short stroll takes in everything there is to see.

It is a place rather for the imagination. Past the monument to the war dead emphatically placed away from the village on a little point with only the sea for backdrop lies the Chapelle St-Corentin, a small building low-set in a miniscule fold of land, fitting its landscape so much better than the ostentatiously big and modern structure in the village. Beyond the chapel is the western shore and then a vast expanse of wave and sharp black rock like a shoal of shark fins and just as dangerous. Far on the horizon in the haze is the height of the Armen lighthouse, that hostage to fortune in a gale. Here you look out to nowhere, a fittingly imprecise location for the Iles of the Blessed where the good dead end up, for the seemingly endless horizon must house such another world.

The occupation of Sein and its harsh land has been a matter of un-certainty and fluctuation. A document of 1604 describes the island as *in-occupée* and although fishermen were in evidence later, it was deserted again in 1664. Records show 350 inhabitants in 1720 rising to 726 by 1876.

The humble chapel of St-Corentin (Wendy Mewes)

The first cholera epidemic hit in 1849, and again from December 1885 to January 1886. There were twenty-four deaths, burials taking place in a cemetery which has now disappeared, and from this time the famous black costume was adopted by the women, the *jibilinnen* headdress replacing the *capenn*.

Charles Le Goffic's (1863-1932) graphic account of the storm of December 1896 that almost swept the island from existence portrays an anthropomorphism of the lighthouses, symbols of protection, safety, and existence itself. The lighthouse of Sein was badly damaged and for a time without light, a horrifying hiatus of illumination during the worst of the cruel dark pounding of the island, when all looked to the light as an assurance of security and survival.

> Finally it shone out once more, to sighs of relief all around. This high flare on the sea, so joyful, so clear, this was safety, a sign that the final word had not been said after all, that one could hope once more, that life went on.

On this occasion the seawall broke and flooded parts of the island. Inhabitants had to be evacuated, more than twenty houses were destroyed, and the lighthouse damaged. Even the recoil left a destructive layer of salt over the land. Fresh food was not to be had and the island was cut off for sixteen days before the tug *Le Haleur* managed to put in with supplies of biscuits to be distributed scrupulously among the hungry islanders.

At the end of the nineteenth century population figures were swollen (840 in 1895 and about 1,000 in 1901) by the regular arrival of *Pampolais* fishermen (in fact mostly from Loguivy-de-la-Mer) who lodged with their families in basements and attics of houses along the quay that now bears their name. They were after the langoustines and lobsters of the Raz de Sein. The population rose to its height in the 1930s to a maximum of 1,330 in 1936. Post-war numbers declined gradually, with fishermen following the scallop harvest first to the Rade de Brest, then moving on to the Bay of St-Brieuc when stocks failed.

The 1960s saw notable falls of inhabitants—835 in 1968; 607 in 1975; 348 in 1990 as the traditional way of life declined. Today the permanent population is under 300, although tourism fills the island during the season and family homecomings may boost numbers in winter.

Women's roles on the islands have developed from weather witches to land laborers. The task was left to them as their menfolk were off at sea, an occupation deemed more worthy of male endeavor. Crops of potatoes, beans, and barley were cultivated in tiny patches, some as small as ten square meters, tucked inside the protective dry-stone walling that still riddles the land in places. Despite the availability of seaweed fertilizer, grain crops did not fare well and rye was abandoned, with bread eventually brought in from the mainland.

The Île de Sein is today most famous for the fact that in 1940 all its able-bodied men sailed to England in response to General de Gaulle's appeal to fight for French freedom. There is an extensive section on the Second World War in the island's museum. Pierre Jakez Hélias' imaginative response envisages their womenfolk, longing to contribute their own effort, lying awake fantasizing about using the island itself as a raft to ferry them to the English shore. Suddenly they feel the earth shake beneath them as Sein tears itself free from the clutch of the sea and the little island rolls on the swell, ready to be rowed away. The women pull on their oars throughout the night, desperate to join the men abroad, but when the light of morning breaks, they find themselves exactly where they began.

Sein's relationship with the Church has been a complex one. The island came into the possession of the Abbey of Landévennec and St Corentin himself is said to have come to evangelize the island originally. His tiny chapel (restored in 1972) contained a statue of the saint holding a cross. Mariners prayed for a good wind before their hazardous journeys, turning the cross in the appropriate direction with the words, "Bon vent, saint Corentin, je vous en prie" (I beg you to grant me a favorable wind). There was a pragmatic sense of reciprocity: if the saint failed to perform, his statue was turned around and draped in seaweed as a punishment until the desired wind materialized. This semipagan practice reflects the double-edged faith of the islanders.

Increased population figures in the late nineteenth century were used to justify the need for a new church, so much the fashion elsewhere in Brittany. When the money was forthcoming and building material arrived, women carried the stones in baskets on their heads from port to site, just as they carried other loads on a daily basis. The structure could not be accused of blending into its landscape, but two large standing stones, perhaps once the focus of another kind of religious ritual, remained untouched in what was to be the churchyard, and stand today in incongruous proximity, testament to the coexistence of faiths.

It was sometimes impossible to find a priest prepared to settle in such an inhospitable environment. When the great missionary Michel Le Nobletz came in 1614, there had been none for more than twenty years. He encouraged an islander, François Guilcher (known as Le Su), to continue religious practices on Sein, reciting prayers in church and organizing processions on religious days. Guilcher took up the task with diligence: when Nobletz's successor, Père Maunoir, arrived in 1641, he was impressed by religious order on the island. Despite his lack of education and training and the initial scorn of mainland clerics, Guilcher eventually became an official priest, ordained at St-Pol-de-Léon.

This quietly extraordinary life was the seed for a later work by the popular novelist Henri Queffélec (1910–92) who was born in Brest and became famous for his maritime settings. In 1944 he published *Un recteur de l'île de Sein*, with Thomas Gourvennec the eponymous character. Five years later Jean Delannoy made a film, *Dieu a besoin des hommes*, based on the book. Strangely enough Queffélec denied in a contemporary interview that his book was based on specific traditions or events on Sein, although he later modified this claim. Certainly the parallels are striking.

A recent court case has brought the question of tough conditions on the island into the public spotlight. In 2013 a family court in Montpellier heard that a mother wanted to move to Sein with her three young children, making it impossible for their father to see them. His lawyer presented a case for refusal arguing that Sein was an isolated place, without electricity and running water, in danger of violent storms and isolation from the mainland. The judge accepted that it was "a relatively hostile environment for children" and ruled against the mother. Not surprisingly there has been an angry reaction from the island's mayor, and the row rumbles on.

## Île de Groix: "qui voit Groix, voit sa croix," the Sea Wolf and his land of many colors

The little harbor of Port Tudy tucked into a line of low cliffs offers a welcoming embrace on arrival from Lorient at the Île de Groix. The island is about eight by three kilometers, covering an area of 1,700 hectares and making it the second largest of the Breton islands after Belle-Île. Most famous for its geology, it was also the home of poet Yann-Ber Calloc'h (Jean-Pierre Hyacinthe Calloc'h), whose short life (1888–1917) ties together so many strands of Bretonism—the sea, Celticism, faith in God—yet speaks with a distinctive individual voice through his articles, letters, and primarily his poetry. He took the bardic name Bleimor, or Sea Wolf, and retained a deep attachment to his native island through the severe tribulations of his brief flowering:

> *Me énézenn e sau, du é kreiz er mor glaz*
> My island stands out darkly in the midst of a green sea

> *O mem broig ha Hroé, a pen don pell dohout,*
> *Klanu on, ha e halon heb éhan e hivroud*

> O my little land of Groix,
> When I am far from you
> I am sick and my heart never ceases to complain

My first visit to Groix was in search of Calloch's roots, but I took along a Breton-speaking geologist friend, an essential extra for an interpretation of the wonders of the southern coastline. The island is famous for its blue-green rocks and red garnets, in unique profusion here. Tectonic plate movement more than 450 million years ago caused the transformation of sedimentary elements into the metamorphic schists and mica-schists that bear the memory in their excessively folded structure today.

The weather was not inspiring on that day for an inspection of multicolors. A local took pity and gave us a lift through the driving rain to Locmaria, where we began to slip and slide our way along one beach after another towards the lighthouse at the Pointe des Chats. The garnet is worth the trouble, the most extraordinary phenomenon, studding the layers of dark blue glaucophane like bloody polka dots.

Once the rain stopped it was easier to appreciate the well-cultivated open countryside of the interior, everything shining with that fresh green only May can offer, the presence of tall, deciduous trees in gardens of the *bourg* a marked contrast with the exposed western islands. The village is gathered around the church with its unusual tuna fish weathervane, a reflection of former economic wealth. After a well-deserved stop at the

Cinquante restaurant with its troglodyte-style toilets displaying the local geological wealth, we went off in search of a poet.

Groix was always engrained in the heart of Yann-Ber Calloc'h, who was born on the island in 1888. His fisherman father drowned when the poet was fourteen and already in the seminary of Ste-Anne in Vannes. He had determined from a young age to become a priest, having a devout faith allied to his sense of the melancholic Celtic soul inheritance. At the age of sixteen he was already writing about this innate *tristesse du Celte*:

I am young, not yet twenty
The sun blazes its rays around me
I walk in the perfumed wind of flowers
And yet I am always melancholic.
So why? God knows why. When he created the Breton
He sealed sadness in his heart forever.

All his inspiration derived from the twin instincts of love of God and his homeland. His first writings were in French but he soon changed to the *Vannetais* strain of Breton. He was an early contributor to the contemporary blossoming of bilingual and Breton-only periodicals like *Le Pays Breton* (where he argued against Charles Le Goffic's support for a statue of Madame de Sévigné to be erected in Vitré), *Le Clocher Breton, Ar Bobl,* and *Dihunamb (Réveillons-nous)*, a Breton review founded by Loeic Herrieu which first appeared in Lorient in 1905. In a host of articles he rehearsed his views on the merits of regionalism and the impracticality of separatism; the issue of June 1911 features "Contre le séparatisme." Calloc'h was a natural member of the URB (Union Régionaliste Bretonne), which had well-defined cultural aims (to the exclusion of politics), then the splinter group FRB (Fédération Régionaliste de Bretagne), which argued for decentralization and respect for Brittany's ancestral traditions. He was also passionately committed to the notion of Celticism within a wider framework.

A genetic twist robbed the young poet of the religious vocation he had assumed would bring fulfillment to his life. One of his sisters died at the age of twenty-three of a nervous disorder and his brother demonstrated similar symptoms. It was a firm policy of the Catholic Church to refuse ordination to anyone from a family with this type of illness, so he had to accept the devastating blow of his unacceptability as a potential priest. His other option was a teaching role and, needing to provide money for his afflicted family, he began conscientiously, at Reims and then for three years in Paris. City life was not congenial to the quiet, poetic Breton who was nevertheless capable of harsh words about a corrupt aristocracy in his letters to friends. He remained devout and studious, researching the history of Groix and reading widely in his spare time. He had the hypersensitivity of the Breton saints, a simple soul of pure heart and faith, much given to melancholy and tears. The forced separation from Brittany was keenly felt: "my mood goes up and down like the tides—I understand how many Bretons fail to thrive here."

Returning to Groix as often as possible, he would go out with friends on the tuna-fishing boat, *L'Aquilon*. The captain Eugène Even recalled him trying to find old Breton words to enrich the contemporary vocabulary, playing religious airs on the flute and being lost in deep meditation faced with the immensity of the ocean.

Calloc'h was called up for military service—the Army being unmoved by family medical history—and found himself in Vitré, where he engaged in teaching literacy and providing a means of communication for fellow-Bretons.

His devotion to the cause of the Breton language reverberates through his writings and letters. He wrote to Achille Colin in 1915 urging a post-war petition to the government for the teaching of Breton language and history in all schools. Realist enough not to anticipate success, he still knew the importance of "making a noise," and believed fervently that the immediate post-war period would be a window of opportunity while the Breton contribution to the slaughter was remembered and while issues of incorporating distinctive cultures such as Alsace-Lorraine were on the political table. He warned that if the Breton language was lost, Brittany would become just another *banale* (commonplace) region of France within twenty-five years. But if the language was saved, administrative, economic, and religious autonomy could follow. He recognized that the teaching of Breton in schools was the key, engaging the will of future generations.

Calloc'h volunteered for the auxiliary services when war broke out. He became a sublieutenant and proved himself courageous and calm in the shocking conditions of the trenches. He died of head wounds at Urvillers on Easter Tuesday 1916, remembered by his comrades as a good Breton, a good soldier, and a good Christian. For all the melancholic religious bravery of his poetry, a more rounded character is indicated by the books found in his bag at the end: H. G. Wells' *The History of Mr Polly*, *Chants des Bretons du Morbihan* (in Breton), a detective story, plays by Aeschylus, Réné Bazin's *Gingolph l'abandonné*, the Bible, and a work on the ancient Celts.

From the very first cliff-top viewpoint on the winding coastal path from the port, you can look down on a beach whose sand is distinctively red from garnet dust. It is a pretty route through tunnels of greenery with glimpses of sea and the continent beyond. The rectangular harbor of Port Lay, proud of its honor of being one of the smallest ports in Europe, is renowned for an international festival of films about islands, founded in 2001 by the journalist Jean-Luc Blain. Before the dam of the freshwater reservoir at Kerlivio, an inland turn leads to a stark memorial rising high above the bright gorse of the *landes* near Yann-Ber Calloc'h's family home in the hamlet of Clavezic. The Sea Wolf's statue is raised up to gaze across the sea towards the continent, to Larmor Plage and unlovely Lorient.

"I am the great watchman" (Wendy Mewes)

It is placed to echo a line from "The Watchman's Prayer," written in the trenches a few months before the poet's death:

I am the great watchman standing alert above the trench
I know who I am and what I am doing:
The spirit of the West, its land, its daughters and its flowers -
This night I guard all the beauty of the world.

It was these words that prompted René Bazin, the French academician and prolific author, to make contact with Calloc'h after receiving the poem in an envelope during the war with nothing other than the author's name, rank, and company. They exchanged letters and had a brief meeting, but shortly afterwards Calloc'h was dead and it was Bazin who determined to bring his work to a wider audience. An article appeared in *L'Écho de Paris* on May 6, 1917 and Calloc'h's posthumous fame was assured.

Hearing the words of his most famous poem read aloud, the resonant rise and fall of Breton, the home language on the home soil brings a sudden tears to the eye, as rain began to fall.

*Me zo ganet é kreiz er mor*
*Ter lèu ér méz*
*Un tiig gwenn duhont em-es,*
*Er benal 'gresk etal en nor*
*Hag el lann e hol en anvez.*
*Me zo ganet é kreiz er mor,*
*E bro Arvor.*

I was born in the midst of the sea
Three leagues of ocean
I had a little white house there
Broom flourished by the door
And the moor was all around,
I was born in the midst of the sea
In the land of Armor.

At home again in the cemetery on Groix he has a special memorial stone next to that of his family. The heavy, complex Celtic decoration seems much less appropriate than that unadorned statue on the moor. In the main square, a cretin has defaced the war memorial where his name is one of a list with the family name Calloc'h, changing his initials JPH into JAH as if to distort his identity and contribution.

He had left a manuscript of poems in Breton with his friend Pierre Mocaër to be published in the event of his death. Bazin's article paved the way for their reception and the acknowledgement of the Sea Wolf as a great poet of his time, place, and native language.

When we left the island the sun gave us an ironic farewell, dazzling off the convex beach of Les Grands Sables, unique in Europe and shifting infinitesimally with time. There was a rumble of aircraft engines and soon cameras were clicking wildly as all ferry passengers rushed to the rail on the lee side to capture the parachutists gliding like aliens from the sky. Before we reached dock at Lorient the Marines were whizzing past us in speedboats to complete their training exercise. The thought of war is never far away.

## BELLE-ÎLE: HAMLET EATEN BY A CROCODILE

Belle-Île has it too easy. It is Brittany's poster island, the name an indication of the soft climate, lush vegetation, and varied landscape from towering cliffs to gentle beaches and river valleys. There is something of the film set even in the most dramatic scenery on the southern coast, around the Aiguilles (Needles) of Port Coton, so-called for the cottonball effect of thick sea foam hurled with such force that it remains fixed on their points during violent storms. The secondary port of Sauzon with its colored houses offers one of the most photographed images of relaxed harbor life, and there can be few more impressive arrivals than under the domineering gaze of La Citadelle, Vauban's star-shaped fort presiding over the sea entrance to the capital, Le Palais.

But it is another fort that steals the show for quirks. On the weather-tossed peninsula of the Pointe des Poulains, the northwest tip of the island, lies a lighthouse and, half-dipped into the landscape nearby, an eighteenth-century fort, the abandoned defensive work that caught the eye and soon after the heart of Sarah Bernhardt. The great actress fell in love with the "wild, grandiose beauty" of Belle-Île in general and the fort above all.

The first time I saw Belle-Ile, I felt it was a haven, a paradise, a refuge. I discovered a fort there on the windiest edge, a particularly inaccessible spot, also particularly uninhabitable and uncomfortable. And this enchanted me.

This was in 1894 when Bernhardt, aged fifty, was at the height of a stage career that had played out from the Parisian stage across continents, and Brittany was a prime target for seekers of romantic exoticism. Her long-term fascination with the windy promontory and island life reflects a passion felt by many incomers that went far beyond the holiday home syndrome. After purchasing the fort two years later, "La Divine" was to spend most summers there until her death in 1923. The nearby Villa Lysiane, built for her daughter, is now an exhibition center. The amputation of a leg in 1915 was no hindrance to these excursions. If she was set down at the point, the boatman would carry Sarah ashore and up the steep steps she had made in the rock to her fortress home.

Home of the Divine (Wendy Mewes)

The arrival of the actress and that celebrity essential, the entourage, was a moment of entertainment for the population, seeing famous personalities like King Edward VII and many musicians, artists, and actors take the air of the island. They called her with affection "la bonne dame de Penhoët" (the name of the manor house bought to accommodate family and friends and destroyed by the Germans during the Second World War). She was supportive of local life, using her wealth to help fishermen in a time of crisis, giving money for the church in nearby Sauzon, and funding among other things a cooperative bakery venture on the island.

The fort was adapted from military functionality to a space of surprising intimacy, serving the demands and foibles of Bernhardt's pleasure-loving nature and instinct for staging relaxation. Rooms in the converted fort have been created from photographs to show her style in clothes and possessions, recapturing the atmosphere of the notorious house parties. Ever a lover of exoticism, she traveled to the island with a veritable menagerie, including a monkey, a boa constrictor, a crocodile, and various dogs, the most unfortunate of which—named Hamlet—was eaten by the reptile. The ultimate fate of the latter was to get stuffed.

# *Afterword*

Brittany today is a land of promise, confident in the quality of its unique offering to the outside world. Resilience is a Breton trait and it has been necessary in recent years of economic challenge, but the palpable quality of life and a well-balanced society derive from this inner strength, from a commitment to family ties and strong personal values. Being at home is what a Breton likes best.

It is to be hoped that new enterprise and development find the necessary support from central government, or better still that greater political and financial powers are devolved to the region. Battles remain to be fought for the security of the Breton language but signing the European Charter for Regional or Minority Languages will be a good start. Diwan schools still flourish and there are plenty of well-subscribed courses for adults wishing to learn. The degree of success of these initiatives will have a profound effect on the future of Breton culture.

Social organization remains strongly based on the family unit and attachment to the land of birth—notable numbers of expatriate Bretons return home from France or abroad later in life or even at the very end, to be buried in family plots on Breton soil. A recent poll here revealed that to eighty-six percent of respondents "being Breton" was very important, and this pride in their native land is further emphasized by the fact that sixty-three percent believed it was possible to become Breton through a love of Brittany rather than parentage or birthplace. I count myself as such a Breton of the heart.

At a popular level, associations (non-profit groups) continue to be set up by enthusiastic individuals, many designed to study, conserve, celebrate, and promulgate aspects of Breton culture and history. These contribute hugely to social life, with regular meetings and frequent fêtes. The huge festivals are not the best places to demonstrate that Bretons know well how to enjoy themselves. For that, any simple village *fest-noz* or Pardon confirms that music, dancing, and *crêpes* are never far away from ordinary people in any part of the country at any time of year. For many this is the natural rhythm of life to this day.

What is certain is that Breton culture will remain fertile. The association Dastum ("collect") continues its crucial work in mining the oral and musical resources of the past, foundations from which the next generations can learn and develop their own ideas. Through such work the past in Brittany has come to service the future, providing roots from which new shoots are continuously sprouting.

New directions and new connections have proved the vitality and passion of Breton song, dance and music, an openness of spirit that augurs well for the future. The Ramoneurs de Menhirs (*menhir* sweeps!) are a punk band whose members have formed a very popular association with Louise Ebrel (b. 1932), doyenne of the traditional *kann ha diskan*. It is an unexpected partnership enthusiastically embracing the possible—a distinctive feature of contemporary Breton culture. This speaks the truth for the joyful spirit of a Brittany that is not only alive but kicking.

# Further Reading

*Armen,* in-depth cultural review, six issues a year

Batt, Michael, Galliou, Patrick, *The Bretons.* Oxford: Blackwell, 1996

Cadiou, Georges, *EMSAV - dictionnaire critique, historique et biographique.* Spézet: Coop Breizh, 2013

Cornette, Joël, *Histoire de la Bretagne et des Bretons* (2 vols). Paris: Éditions du Seuil, 2005

Croix, Alain, *La Bretagne: entre histoire et identité.* Paris: Découvertes Gallimard, 2008

Gibson, Jacqueline and Gwyn Griffiths, *The Turn of the Ermine: an Anthology of Breton Literature.* London: Francis Boutle, 2006

Giot, Pierre-Roland, *Préhistoire de la Bretagne.* Rennes: Éditions Ouest-France, 1979

Giot, Pierre-Roland, *Prehistory in Brittany: Menhirs and Dolmens.* Châteaulin: Éditions Jos le Doare, 1995

Giraudon, Daniel, *Dictons, proverbes et autre expressions populaires de Bretagne.* Barembach: Presses du Donon, 2012

Guilcher, Jean-Michel, *La tradition populaire de danse en Basse-Bretagne.* Spézet: Coop Breizh, 1995

Guillou, Anne, *Pour en finir avec le matriarcat Breton: essai sur la condition féminine.* Morlaix: Skol Vreizh, 2007

Hue, André and Ewen Southby-Tailyour, *The Next Moon: The Extraordinary True Story of a British Agent Behind Enemy Lines.* London: Penguin, 2009

*Le celtisme et l'interceltisme aujourd'hui: actes du colloque de Lorient.* Rennes: TIR, 2010

Le Coadic, Ronan, *L'identité bretonne.* Rennes: Presses Universitaires de Rennes, 1998

Mewes, Wendy, *Discovering the History of Brittany.* Plounéour-Menez: Red Dog Books, 2006

Mewes, Wendy, *Legends of Brittany.* Plounéour-Menez: Red Dog Books, 2012

Richards, Brook, *Secret Flotillas, Clandestine Sea Operations to Brittany 1940-44.* Vol.1. Barnsley: Pen and Sword, 2012

Salomé, Karine, *Les îles bretonnes: une image en construction (1750-1914).* Rennes: Presses Universitaires de Rennes, 2003

White, Kenneth, *House of Tides: Letters from Brittany and Other Lands of the West.* Edinburgh: Polygon, 2000

# Index of Literary & Historical Figures

Alain Fergent 6
Alain the Great 11
Alain Barbetorte 11, 61
Ankou 2, 48, 199, 200
Anne de Bretagne 12, 13, 63, 64, 68, 83, 87, 96,156, 161, 224-225, 232, 249
Abernot, Denez 126
Arretche, Louis 163
Arthur, King 23, 25, 81, 216, 217

Balzac, Honoré de 14, 64, 68, 69, 70, 71, 213
Bécassine 17
Bernhardt, Sarah 273-275
Bigot, Joseph 179
Boisgobey, Fortuné du 34, 44, 49, 116, 172, 237
Blackburn, Henry 36, 38, 45, 145
*Bonnets rouges* 14, 134, 135-137, 139, 160, 190
Borderie, Arthur de la 17, 22, 61, 80, 81, 83
Botrel, Théodore 87, 103, 104, 105, 108, 142, 223, 242
Boudin, Eugène 114

Cadic, François 199
Cadoudal, Georges 157, 168
Calloc'h, Jean-Pierre 268-273
Cambry, Jacques 35, 137, 194, 222, 256
Camp, Maxime du 78, 209
Carrier, Jean-Baptiste 234
Cartier, Jacques 96
Celts/Celtic 4, 22, 30, 37, 91, 110, 132, 148, 152, 174, 181, 185, 200, 228, 229, 268, 269
Charles VIII, King of France 13, 56, 63, 156, 161, 212
Charles the Bald 9, 11, 59, 61
Charles de Blois 12, 156
Chateaubriand, François-René de 66, 73-80, 211, 219
Chaucer, Geoffrey 117, 118
Childebert 59, 133
Chouans 14, 68, 69, 70, 72, 167, 168, 248
Chrétien de Troyes 217
Colas, Yannick 143
Conan II, Duke of Brittany 11, 156
Conan IV, Duke of Brittany 12, 61
Conan Meriadec 8, 80, 249
Conomor 9, 132, 133
Conwoïon 246
Coriosolites 7, 269

Dahut (Ahès) 89, 90, 91
Dallam, Thomas 51
Davin, François 220
Davis, Edward William Lewis 35, 137, 145, 203, 206-207
De Gaulle, Général 128, 130, 266
Déceneux, Christophe 219
Doré, Roland 49, 50, 226
Drouet, Juliette 71
Druids 22, 30, 34, 36, 210, 228-229
Du Guesclin, Bertrand 63, 83, 159, 242
Du Laurens de la Barre, Ernest 141
Duguay-Trouin, René 97-99, 226
Duparc, Bishop 54, 180

Ebrel, Louise 278
Éon de l'Étoile 220-221
Erispoë, King of Brittany 11, 52, 61
Eugénie, Empress 170-171

Flaubert, Gustave 34, 78, 176, 212
Fleury, Guillaume 102
François I, King of France 13, 157, 212
François II, Duke of Brittany 12, 63, 64, 65, 68, 232, 249
Franks 9, 58, 59, 81, 132, 133, 156, 245, 246
Fréminville, Chévalier de 228-229

Gargantua 25, 141
Geoffrey of Monmouth 8, 216
Geoffrey Plantagenet 12, 62
Gillard, Abbé 215
Glenmor 81, 150, 152
Goadec, Soeurs 149
Gracq, Julien 267
Gradlon, King 89, 90, 177, 229
Grall, Xavier 151, 182-183, 185, 189
Gregory of Tours 58, 245
Gruyer, Paul 256, 262
Guéguen, Jacques 127
Guéhenno, Jean 212
Guilcher, François 267
Guilcher, Jean-Michel 150
Guillemot, Pierre 167, 168
Guillotin, Abbé 220

Hélias, Pierre Jakez 25, 181-183, 266
Hemon, Roparz 17, 21
Henri IV, King of France 134, 158, 218
Henry II, King of England 11, 12, 57, 61, 68, 227, 241
Henry VIII, King of England 64, 87
Hitchcock, Alfred 245
Hollande, François 22, 139
Hugo, Victor 14, 66, 68, 71, 72, 213

Jacob, Max 51, 112, 114, 122, 179, 180, 181
Jean III, Duke of Brittany 12
Jean IV, Duke of Brittany 12, 63
Jean de Montfort 12, 63, 156, 245
John, King of England 62

Judicaël 59, 215
Julius Caesar 22, 211
Katell Gollet 49, 146
Kellerman, Bernhard 259

La Fontenelle, Guy Eder de 114, 119
La Villemarqué, Théodore Hersart de 20, 80, 91
Lainé, Célestin 17, 191
Lancelot 216, 217, 220
Laval, Guy de 218, 220
Le Balp, Sébastien 135-136, 137
Le Borgne, Olivier 129
Le Braz, Anatole 20, 39, 173, 185, 186, 199, 201, 224, 226, 229
Le Cor, Pierre 102
Le Febvre, Yves 189-190
Le Flanchec, Daniel 112, 113
Le Goffic, Charles 197, 264, 269
Le Guillou, Philippe 225
Le Guyader, Fréderic 39
Le Men, Yvon 153
Le Roy, Florian 123
Loti, Pierre 102, 103, 104, 105
Louis XI 63
Louis XII 13, 64
Louis XIV 75, 99, 109, 134, 135, 161, 227, 243
Louis Le Pieux 9, 59, 133, 246
Luzel, François-Marie 20, 86, 92, 224

Maillols, Georges 163
Malraux, André 32
Marc'h/Mark, King 110, 132
Marchal, Morvan 17
Mari Morgan 92
Marion du Faouët 132
Maunoir, Père 260, 267
Méheut, Mathurin 119, 123-127
Mérimée, Prosper 214
Merlin 216, 217, 218, 219, 220, 221
Miliau 52, 54
Miln, James 36

Mordrel, Olivier 17, 180-181, 191
Morel, Michel 44
Morvan 59, 132, 151
Morvan, Frères 149
Musse, Blanchard de la 218

Napoleon Bonaparte 15, 122, 168, 169, 170, 247
Napoleon III 80, 170-171, 195
Nemours, Aurélie 164
Nominoë 6, 9, 11, 59, 61, 80, 81, 83, 133, 151, 156, 246

Ogès, Louis 197
Orain, Adolphe 21
Osismes 7, 132

Pencalet, Josephine 113
Pepin the Short 59
Perrot, Abbé 18, 191
Philippe VI, King of France 12
Philippe-Auguste, King of France 12, 62
Picasso, Pablo 115, 179
Pierre de Dreux 12, 62
Portzmoguer, Hervé de 87
Prigent, Denez 126

Queffélec, Henri 267

Renan, Ernest 42, 172-176
Richards, Brook 129
Richelieu, Cardinal de 227, 249
Riedones 7, 155, 211
Rivallon 57, 74
Rohan family 8, 64, 166, 248, 251
Ropars, Loeiz 148-150
Rouërie, Marquis de la 66, 67, 73, 80

Salomon, King of Brittany 52
Sarkozy, Nicolas 1
Saint-Pol-Roux 19, 25
Savignon, André 261
Sébillot, Paul 92, 198

Sévigné, Madame de 83, 136, 146, 160, 269
Shakespeare, William 52
Sibiril, Ernest 127-130
Souvestre, Émile 33, 91, 116, 131, 141, 192, 196, 229
St Brieuc 8, 203
St Conval 226
St Corentin 8, 89, 177, 264, 266
St Cornely 34
St Guénolé 89, 90, 229
St Hervé 203
St Pol 8, 259-260
St Samson 8, 59
St Suliac 243
St Thégonnec 203
St Tugdual 8, 114, 172
St Yves 53, 172-173, 176
Ste Anne 53
Stendahl 155
Stivell, Alan 20, 23, 152-153, 182
Surcouf, Robert 94, 99

Tanguy, Yves 115
Tench, Watkin 117-118
Tosser, Lili 193
Trellu René 200
Troyes, Chrétien de 217
Tri Yann 89
Troadec, Christian 139-140
Trollope, Augustus 6, 7, 16, 23, 37, 38, 86, 141
Turner, J. M. W. 236

Vauban, Sébastien Le Prestre de 109, 251
Velly, Sébastien 112, 113
Verne, Jules 237-238
Vikings 6, 11, 41, 61, 156, 233
Villéon, Emmanuel de la 66
Vivianne 216, 218

Wace 217

Waroc 58, 245
Washington, George 66
Weisburger, Leo 21
White, Kenneth 25, 26
William of Normandy 11, 57, 156
Wood, George 129-130
Wood, Kit 114, 115, 179

Young, Arthur 162

# Index of Places & Landmarks

Abbaye du Relec 188, 252
Abbaye de Timadeuc 251
America 1, 66, 77, 227
An Eured Vein 31, 202
Angers 55, 61
Armorica 8, 25, 58, 91, 123, 185, 209, 216, 232
Aulne, river 6, 131, 226, 247
Auray 63, 167

Baie de Quiberon 29
Baie des Trépassés 2, 91
Bains-sur-Oust 61, 80, 81
Ballon 55, 61, 81
Barnenez 31-32
Basse-Bretagne 6, 7, 17, 88, 145,146, 148, 174, 200, 201, 202
Batz, Île de 255
Belle-Île 223-224
Berrien 186
Binic 100, 101
Blavet, river 166, 247, 252
Bosméléac 251-252
Botmeur 193, 195
Brasparts 189, 193, 194, 226
Bréhat, Île de 100, 255
Brennilis 27, 185, 187, 193, 199, 202
Brest 15, 18, 19, 86, 87, 99, 102, 129, 177, 178, 247, 256, 267
Brière 55, 213
Brocéliande 211, 215, 216-219
Broons 63
Bro-Waroc 58

Camaret 19, 195
Canada 96
Cancale 5
Cap Fréhel 5
Cap Sizun 110

Carantec 127-130, 254
Carhaix 27, 132-140, 144, 149, 151, 152, 182, 194, 206
Carnac 26, 29, 30-36
Carnoët 53
Chaire des Druides 31
Chapelle de Ste-Anne 57
Château de Comper 216
Château de Kerjean 45
Château du Taureau 254
Châteaulin 137, 138
Châteauneuf-du-Faou 145
Coatloc'h, Forêt de 221-225
Collinée 7, 239
Combourg 62, 73-80, 216, 219
Commana 28, 47, 197, 201, 204
Concarneau 5, 112, 148, 179
Cordon des Druides 31
Cornouaille 5, 11, 21, 58, 145, 174
Cornwall 7, 9, 20, 23, 129, 132
Corseul 7, 242
Côtes d'Armor 3, 5, 8, 25, 44, 48, 53, 123, 132, 185, 201, 239
Couesnon, river 55, 56, 57, 62
Cragou, Landes du 185, 203, 207
Cranou, Forêt du 225-230
Crozon peninsula 30, 31, 110, 193

Dinan 62, 63, 73, 156, 211, 241, 242, 243
Dinard 239, 245
Dol-de-Bretagne 8, 56, 57, 58, 63, 73, 74, 210, 211, 216, 219
Donges 89, 239
Douarnenez 5, 8, 91, 110-116, 179
Duault 206

Elorn, river 6
England 11, 15, 45, 57, 58, 63, 77, 87,

117, 168, 181, 195, 248, 266
Er Lannic 30
Erdeven 30
Ergué-Gaberic 51
Erquy 101

Finistère 3, 5, 25, 89, 124, 131, 137, 143, 149, 185, 221, 225
Fort La Latte 5
Fougères 62, 63, 65-72, 73, 174, 210, 211, 213, 214
Fougères, Forêt de 31, 71, 209-214
France 9, 11, 55, 56, 57, 62, 68, 81, 87, 109, 142, 157, 161, 168, 178, 187, 204, 209, 213, 232, 248, 258, 277

Gavrinis 29
Giants of Kerzerho 30
Goënidou 189
Gourin 132, 143, 152
Groix, Île de 89, 267-273
Guémené-sur-Scorff 146
Guérande 63, 64, 75, 123, 213, 246
Guimiliau 45, 48, 49, 50, 51, 52
Gulf of Morbihan 29, 30, 31, 94, 193

Haute-Bretagne 6, 13, 21, 22, 92, 142, 147, 165
Huelgoat 25, 141, 144, 186, 191, 206

Iceland 100, 107
Île aux Pies 247
Île d'Arz 93
Île Tristan 114
Ille-et-Vilaine 3, 28, 62, 80, 246
Ireland 8, 18, 20, 23, 91, 199

Jengland 55, 61
Josselin 12, 168, 248

Kergloff 135
Kerity (Paimpol) 100, 104

Kerity (Pays Bigouden) 117, 118

La Bataille 61, 81
La Feuillée 189, 192, 194, 195, 253
La Martyre 52
Lac de Guerlédan 240, 247
Lac St-Michel 27, 185, 187
Lagatjar 31
Lamballe 174
Lampaul-Guimiliau 45, 51
Landerneau 45, 177, 231
Langonnet 59, 132, 151-2, 194
Lanildut 127
Lannédern 47, 49
Le Cloître St-Thégonnec 203, 204, 206, 207
Le Faou 225, 226, 227
Le Faouët 132
Le Guilvinec 5
Léhon 240-241
Léon 5, 6, 14, 21, 45, 58, 87, 143, 144, 146, 174, 190, 192, 197, 252
Les Quatre Salines 57
Locmariaquer 29, 30, 31
Locquirec 25, 193
Locronan 110, 115
Loire, river 7, 55, 61, 89, 231-239
Loire-Atlantique 3, 20, 232, 245
Loqueffret 192, 195, 196, 206
Lorient 15, 18, 19, 20, 23, 166, 170, 247, 269, 273
Lostmarc'h 31
Loudeac 145

Maël-Carhaix 123, 132, 145, 151
Maison Cornec 39-41
Malestroit 247, 248
Manoir de Bodilis 43
Manoir de Fornebello 42
Manoir du Carpont 42
Marches of Brittany 9, 55, 58, 59, 62, 63, 81, 156, 210, 216, 219, 245
Men Marz 31

Menez Dregan 31
Menez Hom 110
Menhir de Kerloas 29
Mer d'Iroise 1
Molène 1, 256, 259, 260
Mont Dol 57, 219
Mont Garrot 243, 244
Mont-St-Michel 55, 56, 57, 61, 216, 219
Mont-St-Michel-de-Brasparts 31, 185, 188
Montagnes Noires 110, 132, 145, 186, 192
Montertelot 248
Monteneuf 30
Monts d'Arrée 6, 28, 31, 39, 185-191, 192, 195, 197, 198-203, 204, 207, 225, 252
Morbihan 3, 6, 7, 14, 128, 132, 137, 167, 168, 174
Mordreuc 243
Morlaix 12, 45, 129, 134, 136, 139, 144, 231, 252, 254
Mougou Bihan 28, 29, 189
Nantes 3, 5, 7, 8, 9, 11, 19, 20, 55, 58, 59, 80, 89, 158, 162, 164, 215, 231-239, 247
Nantes-Brest Canal 6, 137, 166, 232, 240, 245, 246, 247, 252
Normandy 6, 55, 62, 69, 157, 214, 217, 253, 255

Odet, river 6, 176
Ouessant, Île d' 1, 31, 88, 92, 255-262
Oust, river 6, 245-252

Paimboeuf 237, 238, 239
Paimpol 86, 100-108
Paimpont, Forêt de 215-221
Paris 1, 6, 14, 15, 17, 20, 62, 66, 99, 114, 139, 142, 151, 152, 166, 169, 173, 179, 218, 235, 261, 270
Parlement de Bretagne 155, 158

Paule 152
Pays Bigouden 116, 135, 137, 146, 181, 182
Pellerin 237, 238
Penmarc'h 31, 114, 116-123, 124
Pestivien 43
Phare de Creac'h 259
Phare d'Eckmühl 121-122
Pierres Plates 29
Pleyben 51, 145, 193
Ploërmel 12, 144
Plogoff 1
Plomelin 144
Plouarzel 141
Ploubazlanec 105
Plougonven 50
Plouguerneau 121, 127
Plouneour-Menez 189, 197, 204, 252
Poher 59, 131-140, 145, 147, 151
Pointe de Corsen 1
Pointe de la Torche 122
Pointe du Raz 1, 91, 121, 263
Pont l'Abbé 116, 118, 120, 137, 182
Pontivy 166-171, 251, 252
Pors Even 102
Portsall 88
Pouldreuzic 182
Poullaouen 134, 148, 150, 205

Queffleuth, river 188, 252-254
Quiberon 14, 168
Quimper 8, 54, 89, 115, 118, 124, 148, 176-181, 191, 195, 199, 231

Rade de Brest 86, 226
Rance, river 6, 239-245
Redon 59, 142, 158, 231, 245-6
Rennes 5, 7, 8, 9, 19, 21, 25, 38, 55, 57, 58, 59, 63, 73, 79, 80, 81, 135, 138, 142, 143, 148, 155-166, 211, 215, 232, 242, 245
Rigole d'Hilvern 252
Roche aux Fées 28

Roc'h Trédudon 185, 252
Roc'h Trévézel 185, 200
Roc'h St-Barnabas 185
Roc'h Ruz 186
Rohan 251
Roscoff 5, 100, 123, 186, 255
Rostrenen 145
Roz-sur-Couesnon 57
Rumengol 225, 227-229

Scaër 221, 222
Scissy, Forêt de 55
Scrignac 191
Scotland 18, 23, 57, 181, 199
Sein, Île de 1, 2, 88, 91, 262-267
Sélune, river 62
Spain 23, 87, 101
Spézet 135, 137
St-Aubin-du-Cormier 55, 62, 63, 64, 65
St-Brieuc 6, 8, 92, 100, 172
St-Broladre 57
St-Cast-Le-Guildo 88
St-Guénolé 117, 118, 19, 124
St-Just 26, 36
St-Malo 5, 8, 19, 68, 73, 75, 76, 88, 94-100, 174, 211, 239, 244, 245
St-Marcel 128
St-Nazaire 18, 89, 168, 231, 237, 238
St-Pierre 117
St-Pol-de-Léon 267
St-Rivoal 39, 206
St-Suliac 243, 244
St-Thégonnec 45, 47, 49, 51, 52, 150
St-Urnel 123
St-Uzec 31
Ste-Anne-la-Palud 110

Taden 242
Telgrunc 144
Tours 55
Treffrin 149
Trégor 5, 6, 21, 174, 189, 197, 252

Tréguier 8, 16, 42, 172-176
Tréhorenteuc 215
Trézien 1
Tuchenn Gador 185
Tumulus de Kercado 34
Tumulus de St-Michel 34
Ty Meur 134, 136

Vallée des Saints 53
Vannes 5, 6, 8, 13, 21, 58, 59, 161, 168, 170, 246, 269
Vendée 14, 69, 235
Vilaine, river 6, 157, 231, 245, 246, 247
Vitré 62, 63, 80, 83, 269, 270

Wales 8, 18, 20, 23

Yeun Elez 185, 200, 201
Yorkshire 11, 57
Ys 89-90, 229